Kohl, Herbert R.

Growing with your
children

DATE DUE

Growing with Your Children

Books by Herbert Kohl:

THE AGE OF COMPLEXITY

THE LANGUAGE AND EDUCATION OF THE DEAF

36 CHILDREN

THE OPEN CLASSROOM

MATH, WRITING AND GAMES

GOLDEN BOY AS ANTHONY COOL

READING, HOW TO

HALF THE HOUSE

ON TEACHING

GROWING WITH YOUR CHILDREN

Books for children:

THE VIEW FROM THE OAK (with Judith Kohl)

Growing with Your Children

HERBERT KOHL

Little, Brown and Company
Boston–Toronto

FIRST EDITION
T11/78

LIBRARY OF CONGRESS CATALOGING IN PUBLICATION DATA

Kohl, Herbert R.
Growing with your children

Includes index.
1. Children—Management. 2. Parent and child.
I. Title.
HQ769.H5576 649'.1 78-16683
ISBN 0-316-50135-2

Designed by Susan Windheim
Published simultaneously in Canada
by Little, Brown & Company (Canada) Limited

PRINTED IN THE UNITED STATES OF AMERICA

To Susan and Robert Lescher

Contents

Preface

This book is about becoming a parent. It is about the major decisions we have to make as parents that affect our children's lives; about such issues as discipline and the development of intellectual, physical, and emotional strength; about respect, pride, fairness, and justice; and fundamentally about the joys of being a parent despite all the problems. My oldest child is eleven and therefore I feel confident writing about only the first eleven years of parenthood. I have been lucky enough over the last eighteen years to have been a teacher as well as a parent and to have spent time with other people's children as well as my own. This book is a distillation of what I've learned and experienced, an attempt to share what seems to help children grow strong, loving, and happy.

There are many people I want to thank for making this book possible. First, there is my family and then, of course, all of my students and their parents. I also want to thank Eve and Gale Bach, Susan and Arnold Perkins, Cynthia and Jim Brown, and all the other friends whose children have grown up with our children and with whom Judy and I have shared the joys and anxieties of having children in troubled times.

Toni Burbank and Bill Phillips, my editors and friends, helped me with their concern and criticisms and patience to stay with the work at times when I was tired and not sure that the work would be of value to other parents. Marcie McGaugh, Betsy Barker, Lorna Cordy, and Judith Tannenbaum have read, criticized, and typed all the drafts of this manuscript and as parents themselves helped me to understand more about what it is to become a parent.

Growing with Your Children

1

Being a Parent and Being a Child: A Personal Introduction

When Judy was pregnant with Antonia, our first child, I spent a lot of time imagining how I would act as a parent. There were hours of fantasizing holding, feeding, and changing a baby, of worrying about colic and croup. I remember reading and forgetting Gesell and Spock a dozen times, thinking about asking my parents and grandparents about bringing up infants and then shying away because I didn't want to treat my children the way I'd been treated as a child. Beyond these practical anxieties over how to care for an infant, I found myself confronted with problems of values: What would I do about discipline? Would my children respect me? What limits should they be given and what should they be expected to learn? Would they get as angry at me as I sometimes did at my parents — and would they be justified?

I was concerned about the kind of adult they would become and agonized over how to enable them to be compassionate and concerned with justice while at the same time being competitive enough to survive. As these speculations evolved it became clear that these moral and social problems weren't that much different from those faced by my parents and grandparents, though their worlds were different from mine. Though I had more choices open to me, they too worried about the roles respect, discipline, strength, justice, and love would play in their children's lives. The more I thought of myself as a parent the more I remembered my parents and grandparents and the choices they made about how to raise children. And I began sorting out what they did that was nurturing and what they did that tore me down and made me resent them. Coming to terms with their actions and values has been and continues to be helpful to me in learning how to be a decent and nurturing parent.

I grew up in a two-family house in a working and lower-middle-class neighborhood in the Bronx. My grandmother and grandfather and two uncles lived upstairs. I lived downstairs with my brother, sister, and parents. The smell of wet sand, two-by-fours, sacks of nails, bags of plaster, and cement reached my bedroom from the garage beneath which the Herbert Construction Company truck was parked every night. Everyone in the family worked for Herbert, which made me feel awkward. My parents told me that when I was four I used to go around saying, "Me Herbert Construction." I'm not sure that it was an assertion so much as a question.

I remember my grandfather pacing in front of the house at 5:30 in the morning, muttering to himself about the stupidity of the world, waiting for Rogers, the truck driver, who wasn't due until 6:30 but would be cursed for being late whenever he arrived. There was no being early or being on time in Pop's world. Everything and everybody was always too late.

He came to the United States some time around 1905 — no one was quite sure of the exact date. Before that he spent a year in Whitechapel in London. He remembered every detail of his stay in that ghetto, and over fifty years later, in 1959, on my return from a trip to England he described that part of London with amazing accuracy. In fact, as he got older he remembered the details of his life in Poland and the passage to New York with increasing clarity while his sense of the present faded. Just before he died he told me that he remembered every detail of the mill in Bialystok and of Hamburg and the boat to Liverpool but couldn't remember what had happened last week.

Pop's passage to the United States was not motivated by any desire to seek a new life in the land of golden opportunity. He was drafted into the Tsar's army, as were many other poor young men. The fact that he was Jewish and poor meant to the Tsar's officers that he was doubly expendable. He was put in a crew whose role was to haul cannon from Moscow to Vladivostok. When he learned from other soldiers how far Vladivostok was from Moscow, much less from Bialystok, he managed to escape and find protection in the Jewish underground. It isn't clear how he managed to get away, but the facts seemed too harsh to detail for grandchildren like me who were well on their way to joining the American middle class.

All I can piece together is that he was hidden from city to city, given train fare and lodging with Jews or sympathetic Christians until he reached Hamburg, where other exiles from Polish Russia, some of whom were relatives, received and helped him until he could earn passage to Liverpool. From Liverpool he went to Whitechapel in London, where he repeated the process until he somehow managed to earn steerage fare to New York, where he met my grandmother, who had lived no more than twenty miles from him in Poland.

My grandmother earned her way to New York on the underground railway too. She took other people's infants from Warsaw to Hamburg, pretending at least a half-dozen times to be a mother. She's told me how she managed to slip off trains with the babies before reaching the station and connect with people who would protect them until they caught the next train.

A few years ago a friend of mine told me about his great-grandmother's escaping to Canada through the underground railroad from Georgia. His African great-grandmother's experience was no different from that of my grandmother. And her pride and strength were just what I have known from both of my grandparents.

I remember my grandfather as tough, somewhat wild, yet very gentle with me, the oldest son of his oldest son. He smelled of the construction jobs he worked at twelve hours a day. He was a framer — a rough carpenter — who built walls and partitions for over fifty years. He received a gold card to commemorate fifty years as a member of the carpenters' union. The union itself couldn't have been much older than that at the time he received the card. Unions and the Workman's Circle were a central part of his life. He was socialist as a matter of nature rather than intellectual conviction. He shared what he had and expected his fellow workers to do the same. This often led to trouble. He would give away everything he had to friends in trouble and then have to work even harder to support his own family. However, his generosity was frequently and necessarily tempered by my grandmother's shrewd understanding of American culture and fierce determination to see that her children made it on American terms. It is almost no exaggeration to say that my grandparents lived a continent apart in the same apartment. Pop never came to the United States, and to emphasize this refused to learn how to read or write English and never signed his name in over fifty years in this country. My grandmother went to night school briefly to learn to read and write and did manage to learn to sign her name. However, before her lessons progressed much, my grandfather invaded the class and forced my grandmother to withdraw. He was convinced that the teacher, a man, was trying to seduce his wife. Mom barely restrained Pop from beating up the teacher and reluctantly gave up her dream of educating herself.

Pop was strict and possessive when it came to his wife and children. He believed that life was a struggle and you had to be prepared for difficulties and protect your family. It was as if he believed that the Cossacks might descend at any moment and that one always had to be ready. His conception of the United States was both political and personal. This was not a land of opportunity for him so much as a place to work with less oppression.

He was also full of fun, a trickster in many ways. Neither work nor politics made him grim. There was in him a love of living and an ability to put aside all his problems and play when he was with his family. The ability to work for justice and still live with a joy that flowed to others was his most special characteristic.

Pop worked in construction as he had worked as a peasant in Europe, and was proud of his labor and his class. He was a misfit in the United States because though he knew how to work he didn't know how to compete. He was too trusting and generous to be a successful businessman, and he left it to his wife and children to learn how to make it.

Recently I asked my father what kind of a father Pop was. My father began negatively — Pop never tried to be a pal or companion to his children. He left their education to the schools, though he insisted his children do their homework. Since he couldn't read English, he couldn't help with their homework, which he didn't think was his job anyway. All he had to do was see that they spent time seeming to do their assignments.

He never took his children to museums or movies or shows. Whenever he wasn't working he was resting or at the Workman's Circle, or out partying with *landsmen,* men who had also escaped from eastern Europe. He liked to go to the Russian baths, to drink a bit and play cards, to fool around. I have a photograph of Pop and his cronies dressed up as cowboys looking wild and funny. It seems that one Friday night they stumbled into a photography store and had their pictures taken in costumes.

Every day after work Pop would come home, wash the smell of construction off, have a few shots of Canadian Club, and settle down at the kitchen table and wait for dinner. He would joke around a bit, sometimes fall asleep — he wasn't to be bothered with taking care of children. He was physically exhausted from working from 6:30 A.M. to 5:30 P.M. — something he did until he was well over seventy. After we got a TV he spent evenings watching wrestling — screaming and cursing, scaring me until I realized that wrestling was an act and that Pop's response was theatre too.

Pop defined certain duties for himself as a father. He had to support the family, no matter how hard he had to work. He didn't want my grandmother to work, though early in their marriage she had taken in piecework. He also assumed the role of upholder of respect in the family. If any of his children cursed, threatened, or talked back to my grandmother, he could become irrational and violent. There was no negotiating or bargaining with the children or investigating the facts. My grandmother was always right. In his way he instilled respect in his children for himself and for my grandmother and taught something I see in my own parents — loyalty to another human being and the strength to share hard times with someone else.

From a contemporary perspective a lot of my grandfather's manner can be seen as sexist and uncompassionate toward children. However, that is a way of misunderstanding and putting him down. He did not look upon women as unequal, as weak or helpless or dumb. He didn't even look at women as a group. Central to his view of the world were the notions of family and *landsmen,* tempered by a bitter awareness that simple survival was never guaranteed. One had to work and had to nurture the family. There also were responsibilities to *landsmen* — to relatives and countrymen, to Jews from one's hometown and to family left in Europe. There was more to be done than could be done by one person, and men and women had to assume responsibilities — he worked as hard as possible so my grandmother would have time to nurture the children. My grandmother regretted not being able to finish school and not having time to grow and learn about the world. She regretted having to flee Europe (though she was far from romantic about the pogroms that forced her to leave) and having to work so hard taking care of five children and numerous relatives. She didn't resent my grandfather so much as the social forces that made life such an unpredictable struggle. I remember her fierce pride in the way she maintained and controlled our house. She held things together, guided and supported her children's education even though she couldn't read or write English. There were times when she was severe and demanding, when she forced my grandfather to say "no" or to drive a hard bargain with his *landsmen.* But with her grandchildren she was always kind and indulgent — she let us know in many ways that our lives were to be the fruits of her struggles.

Both my grandparents did what they felt had to be done to survive. They did not expect of life the gift of personal fulfillment. They never had time or the security to think about fundamental changes in the conditions of their lives beyond their struggles to establish unions. They always felt that living with greater ease and developing one's self were gifts they would provide for their grandchildren through their work and love, and through the opportunities they gave their children. They were aware that it would take two generations of work to produce one generation who would have the time and security to grow without struggling for necessities. That was why grandchildren were so special for them. We were to be the first free children. And they weren't wrong in the case of my family. The fruit of their and my parents' labor was the leisure it afforded me to go to college, travel, and choose what to be, both professionally and as a person. When I was younger, I resented their inability to understand me. Now I often feel foolish for not understanding the gift they offered me. Perhaps part of that resentment came from my bewilderment at the freedom I had — the burden of being able to choose where to live, whom to become or to love, what to work at, and choose with no guidelines or tradition since my parents' and grandparents' worlds were not the same as mine.

Work, the job, was the main bond between my grandfather and his sons, just as the house and the market were the main bonds between my grandmother and her two daughters, who lived across the street from us. The men and women spent a lot of time in separated worlds, and, as a child, not surprisingly it was the men's world I identified with and the women's world I spied on. One of the first toys I remember being excited by was a miniature toolbox, which I carried around while pretending to be my grandfather.

My father described to me the experience of working with his father during the summers. He remembers first how hard Pop worked. It was profoundly affecting. Though Pop came home tired every day, it was another thing to see him work, carrying lumber all day, throwing up partitions, walking up and down the half-built frames of buildings carrying tools and lumber, keeping at it for nine and ten hours with only short breaks. My father worked alongside his father and told me that it was one of his most profound, difficult, and yet joyous experiences. He came to understand his own father, to know what he did with his time and the world he lived in most. He learned to work himself and came to understand and share the knowledge generated by years of intuitive building accumulated by my grandfather's generation. Later, when my father graduated from Cooper Union as a civil engineer and, along with my grandfather, formed Herbert Construction Company, he was able to combine that intuitive knowledge with some of the more technical knowledge he picked up in college. Working with my grandfather also taught him respect for the work of the elders, which I too learned forty years later when I worked several summers with my grandfather.

The qualities my grandfather embodied — respect for family, loyalty and generosity towards *landsmen,* a hatred of bossism, a need to work to exhaustion, and a teacher's concern with passing these values on to his own children — are things I value too. As a parent I am not libertarian — there are values, both personal and collective, that I want my children to respect. I realize now that many of these I learned by watching my grandfather. And from my grandmother I'm sure I acquired that love of a home full of people that makes me center so much of my life and work about the house I live in. Often I catch myself in the middle of a meeting around our kitchen table and remember my aunts, my mother, and my grandmother in the kitchen at Grand Avenue in the Bronx.

My mother and father tried to be different kinds of parents from my grandparents. Choices were opening up to their generation, and when I was born in 1937 my parents already had a sense that the old ways had their limits. Physical punishment was out except for outrageous behavior or when adults simply lost their tempers. Children were seen as more delicate, needing care and attention, perhaps a little pushing. The emphasis was psychological — see that the child was happy and give him or her enough attention and training to succeed in school. Perhaps the nervousness about academic success was unique to Jews, but I doubt it, for I've seen the same feelings in Black, Chicano, and Puerto Rican communities I've worked in.

My mother was somewhat of a stranger in my grandmother's house. All the other adults around spoke Yiddish; my mother didn't. The Cohens (that was my father's name before it was changed to Kohl) were all in construction; my mother's family were cab and truck drivers, printers, and artists. The Cohens worked for themselves and were moving into the middle class. My mother's family was less ambitious and more aesthetic. My mother's sisters were lovely, fairly low-pressure people who seemed more concerned with people than with success — I enjoyed being with them, since to me as a child they seemed to enjoy themselves more than the Cohens did and to demand less from me. Certainly their lives weren't easy. Two of my aunts suffered the consequences of marrying out of Judaism when doing so wasn't common; none of the family ever became wealthy. Still, they had and have a flair for life, a curiosity about things in the world that seems to have been put aside by my father's family in the pursuit of economic success.

Both sides of the family came together on formal occasions and were polite to each other. I grew up with two worlds and as a child had to sort them out. What of the Cohens' was valuable? What of the Jacobses'? Like most children I didn't imitate the adults around me so much as watch them and sort out what was worth learning and what I should reject.

My mother was right in the middle of these two different families. She once told me that her mother, my Grandmother Rose, who died when I was six, was a militant feminist, a friend to everyone in need, and a negligent parent. Evidently she had a passion for social issues, enormous compassion, and an inability to keep her own house in order. My aunts' niceness and concern for people obviously was influenced by her. However, my mother reacted to her mother's looseness and, from the time she was fourteen, ran the house and raised her three younger sisters. She taught herself how to manage money, to work and maintain a home. In these ways she was the equal of my Grandmother Cohen. She met my father when she was chief buyer for a restaurant firm and he came to her office about a construction job he was doing with his father. She was making more money than he was at the time. However, for all her drive and orderliness there was something of my Grandmother Rose in my mother — she could be soft and irrationally generous, overindulgent, incapable of saying "no." I have a feeling that she spent a good part of her early life proving herself to the Cohens, and a good part of her later life trying to figure what was the right way to behave in the middle class. She seemed scared and inconsistent to me when I was a teenager, as if she wondered continually how she got to be where she was. The most relaxed I've seen her was when she was with her sisters, unwinding, laughing, being silly, and paying no attention to money or success.

If my mother was hesitant and confused sometimes within the family, she wasn't when it came to fighting for her children's place in the world beyond the family. There she and my father acted in unison. For example, the attitude of my mother and father toward the school as an institution was very different from that of their parents. They were literate in English, could and did help their children with schoolwork, and developed working relationships with their children's teachers. One of my earliest memories is of having trouble learning how to read in the first grade. When my mother saw that her son was behind in reading during the first half of the first grade, she just about fainted. When my father came home from work, he read the report card and brooded about it all evening. The next morning he took off from work and went to school with me. His not working was so unprecedented that I realized for the first time that reading was serious business.

I remember sitting in an office with my teacher on one side of me and my father on the other. The teacher held up words I was supposed to know. For "BOY" I said "girl," for "THE" I said "to." My mind was heavy and slow; I had to go to the toilet. My father looked alternately angry and humiliated. He left me at school. By the time I got home he had been to Barnes and Noble and bought all of their beginning reading workbooks. He also bought some magazines and set me to work cutting out words, then doing some worksheets. My mother made sure I did them when I came home from school. I very quickly learned to read. In fact I was afraid *not* to learn.

My grandfather also made occasional trips to school for his children, the results of which would be a beating instead of an avalanche of books and worksheets. But the value he placed on education was no different.

There were no limits to what my father would do to further his children's learning. He would buy chemistry sets, get resource books. When I was about ten he even bought a set of the *Encyclopaedia Britannica* because it was the best encyclopedia on the market. It made no difference that it was too complex for me to read until I was in high school and needed it less.

I knew how much was sacrificed for my education — my parents talked about it, my aunts and uncles told me how grateful I should be. It made me quite nervous — the obligation to perform well because others were making sacrifices to insure my successes. There were times when I felt so driven to perform academically that there seemed to be no time to learn anything. Only perfection would satisfy my father — there were no rewards for B's or even for A's, since they were expected. Anything less than A indicated a need to improve.

The sacrifices my parents felt they made for their children also became justification for planning their futures. Not surprisingly, I was to become a doctor. It wasn't until I was thirty that my father told me that he had always wanted to be a doctor, but that the need to work to help his father support the family made it impossible. I was to embody in my life what he had wanted to be. We fought foolishly for years over my total lack of interest in medicine, and I am not sure that he still doesn't believe we would both be better off if I had just given in.

My father struggled and worked, not to remake the world, but to make a small part of it livable for his family. At one time I resented his obsession with work, but now it seems that there was nothing else he could have done but quit and become resigned to poverty. All of his life he worked as hard as my grandfather and now, at sixty-seven, still runs from one construction job to another from 6:30 in the morning to 6:00 at night. He is not a laborer but does everything else — estimates the cost of work, supervises construction, gets new jobs, does quality control on the work of his men, and generally runs a successful middle-size construction company.

As a child I noticed how work drained him. He came home

at night exhausted, went to bed early, lived and ate and drank construction. Often during the evening we tiptoed around him after dinner. If something was wrong at home — if one of us fought with my mother or stole something or had a fight — my mother did her best to deal with it herself. She didn't like to bother him with home problems since he worked so hard and came home so tired. Often, if she needed his help, she told him of the problem, and we all waited for his response, which was unpredictable and determined by the magnitude of the burdens he brought home from work. If it was a good day, he could be kind and firm and reasonable, protecting my mother just as his father had protected my grandmother, reasoning with my brother or sister or myself, listening to us and letting the problem be talked away. More often he responded to the problem by brooding, refusing to talk but just sitting in the middle of the living room looking pained. We children suffered from the grief we caused him after a hard day's work. On occasion, if something serious had happened and he lost his temper, one of us would be physically threatened, but this happened very rarely. Psychological tension and silence were the most characteristic modes of response. This behavior made me jumpy, so I tried to conceal as many of my transgressions as possible or keep them between my mother and myself. Because of the continual possibility of a brooding response, I confined personal talks between my father and myself to aspects of my life that I knew beforehand he would approve of. It got to the point that for several years I communicated with him through my mother. I couldn't bear the thought of hurting him and causing so much pain and frustration and at the same time couldn't relinquish my life. And I had choices — I could have become just about anything I wanted, could choose my college and major. The choices facing me at the time were much greater than those that had faced my parents.

Weekends were very different from weekdays when I was growing up. That was when my father consciously gave time to my brother, sister, and me. He tried to be our pal and companion, both out of a desire to spend time with us and because he understood that Dr. Spock said that it was a healthy and important thing for fathers to do. Whether Spock had written any such thing or not was irrelevant. The feeling in the late forties and early fifties was that men had to become friends with their children, something that would never have occurred to my grandfather. It was a way of integrating men into the everyday functioning of the family and, from the perspective of an older generation, seemed a pretty radical thing to do.

On Saturdays and Sundays my father and mother would take us to a museum or the Gilbert Hall of Science or the aquarium. Occasionally we would go swimming or to a ball game or a movie. Some of these times my father enjoyed himself. I know for me trips to places he liked, such as the Gilbert Hall of Science, were wonderful, and a sense of companionship and apprenticeship developed. He could take me some places and explain what was there. I liked his explaining things to me as much as being at the places.

Other experiences were more complex. Our family visits to the Metropolitan Museum of Art never provided unmixed pleasure. We stayed away from rooms with paintings of crucifixes; my parents didn't know very much about painting or sculpture, and often I felt that they didn't like them but felt it was necessary to give their children high culture despite their tastes. They wanted us to be better than they were, Americans for whom the specters of poverty and pogroms didn't exist.

The desire to have children who were "better" proved a very mixed blessing in my case at least. I didn't become any better but did become different, and it has taken years for us to come close again.

Being a pal of young people was a hard role for my father to sustain. He was much more comfortable being an authority, an older and wiser counselor to his children. This was his role when he took my brother and me to places where he felt at ease, especially to his office or one of his jobs. There it was somewhat analogous to the way he developed closeness to his own father. We did not work alongside him, however. At most we played while the men on the job (including my grandfather) worked. We ran errands, and when I got older and worked summers, I brought beer and sandwiches and knocked down walls with a sledgehammer. There was no need for me to work or contribute to the family budget. It was made clear to me that our family had enough and that physical labor was not to be my fate. Still, I learned so much by understanding my father's and grandfather's work. I saw them transform buildings, build new stores and banks — I got a sense of how my father planned and developed a job and how my uncle and grandfather transformed the plans into reality. I saw them improvise, come up with solutions to construction problems caused by architectural plans that ignored the actual structures of buildings to be renovated. I was jealous of the central role work played in my father's life and at the same time understood how he could love building, and I admired him for it.

Work seems to me to be a crucial medium of communication between the generations. My brother and I were taken into a man's world where we were honored guests and, more important, where as children we could see how work made sense. It was impossible for me as a child not to admire people who could build and change things, who used tools, understood how to make walls, install doors, move windows, build cabinets.

It was more difficult for my sister to develop that bond with my father. There were no women on the job, and it was inappropriate for her to visit jobs. All the women who worked for Herbert Construction Company worked in the office. Initially my mother was bookkeeper, paymaster, secretary, clerk, receptionist. The office was in our house just as the company supply depot was in our garage. As the company grew, my mother gave up her role and devoted herself to taking care of her children and educating herself. Evelyn, a secretary/bookkeeper, was hired to do all those things previously done by my mother and soon became indispensable to the company. She was the cement in the office — she held things together, knew where everything was, knew whom my father and uncle wanted to talk to on the phone and whom to put off. She knew all the workmen and job superintendents and contributed to making the whole operation feel like a family affair. It was to Evelyn that Roz, my sister, was introduced. Sex roles were clearly defined in the company, and when she was in college Roz worked in the office typing and answering phones — the female equivalent of my knocking down walls and buying beer.

My brother, Ted, after graduating from college, joined the company and eventually became a partner. That route was simply not available to a female, and I think it made it very difficult for Roz to get close to the men in the family. The sexual biases in work go deep into determining family relations.

But even among the male family members, the direct expression of tender feelings and compassion was difficult. My father and I have always experienced a certain awkwardness in expressing our affection for each other. One incident stands out in my mind. It happened on the day I came home from camp when I was eleven or twelve. That summer was the first time I had been away from home, and it was a good independent time. I walked into the house nervously. My brother and sister made welcome-home banners; my parents had made a cake. Everything was warm and welcoming, but to me it all seemed smothering and small — that summer I had learned about sexuality, had my first girlfriend, played ball, and learned to swim. I came home feeling big and independent and the homecoming made me feel small and dependent. I burst into tears and couldn't control my feelings of sadness and powerlessness. My mother and brother and sister tried to console me, but nothing worked. My father suggested we take a drive. I remember driving down the West Side Highway pouring out my feelings in between sobs. It was a matter of my independence, an understanding that my parents made love to make me and my brother and sister, a fear of what I had learned over the summer and an urge to try it out. I was struggling with whether to grow up or not. My father kept his eyes on the road, trying to decide how to respond. He was kind yet tough, listened, then tried to assure me that everything was all right. He was struggling with how to express his understanding and support, how to reassure me in the kindest possible way.

Somehow he couldn't bring himself to talk about anything that was on my mind. Nevertheless, he was there to accompany me through the storm, divert me if possible so I could get back to normal. We drove to the Gilbert Hall of Science and he told me to pick out a microscope or chemistry set — I don't remember which. After hesitating, somehow I put my feelings aside and turned my attention to the objects, selected one, and returned home to the welcoming party, which I was able to manage. It was through that gift that he found a way to express his affection and reaffirm the bond between us as father and son, though I didn't understand it at the time and resented him for replacing feelings with a thing. I have tried to be more direct with my children and not shy away from expressing affection. However, I had to learn how to do that both as a teacher and a parent, and it has taken time.

I became a father myself in the most traditional and cliché way. About 1 of the morning that Antonia was born, Judy's labor pains began. We rushed over to Doctors Hospital in Manhattan. I was terrified and excited — wanted to embrace Judy and was afraid to touch her. Fortunately the cab ride to the hospital took only a few minutes.

As soon as we entered the hospital we were separated. Judy was whisked away by a nurse, and I sat and filled out forms and fumbled with my Social Security number and home phone number. Nothing stayed in my mind.

The obstetrician came out to talk to me after a while. It was the first time we had met, and I can't remember his face. He informed me that Judy would be in labor for at least three or four hours and walked me to the elevator. He said to come back at 5 or 6 in the morning. I had intended to wait at the hospital but let myself be directed downstairs and made my way to the nearest bar.

I found myself buying drinks for strangers who, once they heard my wife was in labor, became philosophical and full of advice and jokes, many implying that a father could never tell if a child was his, others suggesting that children were nothing more than financial burdens. Occasionally, someone hinted that with all the grief there was some joy. Especially if it were a boy, they told me. I listened and felt sick — Judy was somewhere else almost with a child, our child, and I was sitting around drinking in the cynical goodwill of bitter people. I left the bar and walked and walked until dawn and returned to the hospital just as Judy was being wheeled from the delivery room. She looked tired — no, rested — and beautiful. We had a girl. I squeezed her hand, then the nurses pushed me aside and told me she needed to sleep. I sat down in the waiting room, relieved and tired myself. One of the other waiting fathers asked me what it was. "A boy," I blurted out and then collapsed into confused silence, afraid I'd cursed our child with my previously unarticulated desire to have my firstborn be a male. At that moment the birth of a child seemed like something that happened behind closed doors to someone else despite yourself. There was no joy in the first minutes of being a father. I resolved to be with Judy for our next child, to be part of the event for my own sake as well as to help Judy and know our child from the beginning of life.

There were many other ways I stumbled into a traditional fatherly role despite my desire to share the responsibilities and joys of nurturing Tonia with Judy. It was comfortable to play at being a father and avoid most of the little but exhausting attentions infants require. I let feeding, changing, burping, walking, and comforting Tonia become woman's work. The baby frightened me. I hadn't been around infants for twenty years and had to force myself to relieve Judy when she was fatigued. Otherwise I enjoyed Tonia when she was laughing, playing, sleeping, or being shown off to relatives and friends.

I don't care much for infants and yet love being and working with elementary school children. Teaching is one of the great joys in my life, yet for the most part I was reserved and nervous around my own child for the first five or six months.

I watched Judy care for Tonia and assumed initially that she liked infants better than I did, or at least that some psychological or instinctual mechanism was at work that enabled her to give so much to such a passive and unformed being. As it turned out, Judy didn't care for infants any more than I did. We both loved the signs of growth and independence in our children and never wanted them to stay as babies. She did the nurturing because Tonia needed to be nurtured and I seemed shy, somewhat reluctant and scared. It simply had to be done.

With Erica, our second child, whose birth I experienced alongside Judy, I was less scared and able to be more useful. By the time Joshua was born, I no longer was afraid of infants, knew the feel of them, understood their strengths, and intuited some of their needs. It was possible to learn how to share caring for him as an infant.

Over the past eleven years, as my children have grown, I've had to grow too and respond to needs they articulated and problems that arose in our lives together. Many of the conditions we face as a family are different from those faced by my parents and grandparents. Judy's from the Midwest and isn't Jewish. We don't live in a culturally homogeneous world as my family did, and we don't live near relatives. Antonia was born in New York City and we moved to California when she was five months old. Joshua and Erica are native Californians.

Most of our friends have been as mobile as we and are as cut off from traditional family life. We are involved in creating our own social and family lives rather than fitting into our parents' worlds. We have greater freedom than our parents and grandparents did in deciding where and how to live, in choosing life-styles and experimenting with values. That freedom, however, has been a mixed blessing — we have lost the organic connection with tradition and the certainty about what was the right and the wrong way to bring up children that my grandparents had. There are times when we try out values and ways of behaving and other times when we simply don't know what to do with our children. Sometimes we become too permissive, other times too strict. We spend a lot of time and energy trying to discover, invent, reinvent, or possibly create a centered and nurturing family existence that also embodies the social values we believe in and try to live.

This search for value has another dimension too. Judy and I both graduated from college. We have been involved in the civil rights movement and the antiwar movements. We don't have the same uncritical faith in the values of competition and acceptance of authority that my parents had. We want a more caring and authentic life for ourselves and our children than the lives we have seen our parents lead. And we don't trust in professionals and experts the way our parents did, or believe there is one best way to raise children or some simple formula for conflict-free child-raising. That's probably because we went to college with many people who became experts and professional and see them facing the same problems with their children as we face with ours. For my parents, professionals were a class apart, not friends whose lives one shared.

The social disparity between generations, however, doesn't mean that there is nothing we can learn from each other. In thinking about myself as a parent I've found values in my parents' and grandparents' lives that I reject and others that seem essential for a compassionate and decent life. There are also things I believe in that I hope my children will value. The questions of what to keep of past values and how to transmit values to one's own children are central issues parents have to face.

There are many aspects of life with children where values are constantly at issue and there is no objective "best" way to act as a parent. The way you act depends upon what you care about, what you believe in, what control you have over your own life, and how you have come to terms with your parents', grandparents', and other older adults' ways of raising children.

Consider discipline, for example. The proper way to discipline children is not a scientific question but rather a question of how you believe people should treat each other. In deciding upon how to discipline one's own children (and I've never known a child who doesn't get out of hand sometimes) there are certain questions that one has to answer for oneself. For example, who has authority? Is there any behavior that needs to be controlled? If so, what should the goal of control be for the child? The adult? Who has a right to tell someone else to do something? Should anyone control another's behavior? Should the goal of discipline be obedience or the development of self-discipline?

Related to discipline and equally dependent upon personal decisions about values is the problem of strength and violence. Are there times when violence is necessary? Is it possible to prevent or avoid violence? Are violence and strength the same? What kinds of physical, intellectual, and emotional strengths should be valued and how can they be developed?

Going along with discipline and strength is another problem we all face — respect. Can respect be legislated or earned? How does it develop and what is the meaning of mutual respect between parents and children? And why should respect be important?

Fairness is as important in our lives with children as is respect. However, what is fair? What is our share of the world and what should belong to our children? Can a sense of justice be developed and lived in a complex and often cruel world? Can our children be expected to be just if we don't act justly ourselves?

And lastly, what of joy — of the things we value and take pleasure from? What are ways in which we can enjoy things with our children as well as take pleasure in what they enjoy doing that we can't be part of?

These five themes, *discipline, strength, respect, fairness,* and *joy,* are the major ones I've had to come to terms with as a parent and teacher, and as an adult trying to understand and learn from my own parents and grandparents. They make up the themes of the five chapters of this book. I've found that the parents of my students as well as many of my friends are facing the same questions, and on the assumption that many other people are also struggling with values as they are learning to be decent parents, I've tried to share what I've learned as a parent and a teacher in this book. This is not a book on how to be a perfect parent, since I don't think it's possible or desirable. Nor is it about how to avoid all conflict with your children, since conflict is often necessary for growth. It is practical and personal, about my life and family, and about what I have learned from working with young children. It is an attempt to share problems and solutions, stories, specific suggestions, and general speculations about being a parent in difficult times. It is about the frustrations of being a parent but, more than that, it is an affirmation of the joys of having and being with children and the values of family life despite the problems.

2

Discipline and Self-Discipline

Giving Up the Strap

My grandparents, specifically my father's parents, with whom I grew up, didn't have problems dealing with discipline. They were clear about how they wanted their children to behave and clear that my grandfather had responsibility for punishing misbehavior. My father and his brothers and sisters knew what was expected of them and knew they would be hit if they were caught doing something wrong. Physical punishment was not looked on by my grandparents and their friends as horrible or damaging. If anything, it was looked upon as healthy preparation for life, especially for boys. Pop worked with his hands, and lived in a pretty tough world. Men and boys were supposed to know how to fight and how to take physical punishment. Spanking was merely an extension of street fighting, an ordinary fact of life, nothing to be concerned about.

It was more difficult to spank girls than boys, but they were not immune from physical punishment, especially if they were disrespectful toward their parents.

My grandparents' attitude toward physical punishment didn't imply cruelty or lack of love. They were fair people and never hit their children arbitrarily or with the intent of injuring them. My father didn't like being hit and resolved not to hit his children, but he accepted that mode as natural for his parents. I know many people who grew up in similar situations, whose parents used physical punishment in a fair way, simply as a settling of accounts for things done. These people didn't like being hit and don't hit their own children. But they don't feel damaged from being spanked, nor do they feel that their parents rejected them. In fact, they wish they could find some nonphysical equivalent of spanking so that when something bad is done they could punish their children and make an end of the affair instead of talking or brooding about the act and dragging it out for days.

This is not meant to romanticize spanking, nor to deny the reality and magnitude of child abuse in our society. There are people who hit and hurt their children out of their own bitterness and despair; who resent the existence of children in their lives; who hate themselves and see in their children their own misery. What has to be pointed out, though, is that not everyone who spanks a child means to damage the child, and that not every case of an adult hitting a child is child abuse. Many people like my grandparents believed that physical punishment was a necessary burden that they had to assume in order to help their children grow to be successful and respectful adults. For them, children had to learn to be respectful and obedient. The idea of a child having choices or being the equal of adults was not part of their experience. Children were not to be reasoned with so much as taught what was right.

My parents saw things differently. I believe that they didn't have such a clear vision of the right way to behave that my grandparents acquired growing up in a small town in eastern Europe. My parents were mobile, from a working-class community but not fully part of it. My father was a college graduate and my mother had a responsible and well-paying job. They were moving into the middle class, and though they weren't sure what that entailed in terms of their behavior, they knew it meant giving up the roughness and physicalness of working-class life. In terms of their children it meant giving up the strap. They wanted to be progressive parents and hoped their children would be even more successful than they were. This meant substituting words for physical punishment, encouraging intellectual development, and treating their children more as equals, as friends almost. I'm not sure how clearly my parents thought out the differences between their generation and their parents' generation. I know they looked around for new models of behavior and tried to treat their children differently from the way they had been treated as children. They read Spock and Gesell and tried to be as reasonable and verbal with their children as possible.

However, giving up the strap caused unexpected problems. When adults give up using their physical superiority over children, they also free the child to talk back, argue, and debate. Giving up the strap has the unexpected effect of giving children power that adults have to deal with. My parents faced this problem continually. For example, my father tried to be close to me in a way that his father couldn't be with him. He gave up the strap with no real guidance as to how to replace it, nor with any articulated set of limits he wanted observed. I remember doing things that upset my mother. She could tell my father about them. Sometimes he would look pained, go in the living room, and sit brooding. I fantasized he didn't love me. He wouldn't talk to me, and I was never sure exactly what he was angry at or how angry he was. It took years for me to understand that that brooding silence which I took as rejection represented an internal struggle on his part. He wouldn't hit me, wasn't sure how angry he was or what to do about the anger.

Sometimes he came home and instead of brooding he would call a family meeting to talk over a problem my mother had with one of us. The meeting always ended inconclusively. I accused my mother of being unfair, she defended herself, accused me or perhaps my brother. My father, exhausted from work, tried to mediate the opposing views and usually succeeded in having everyone apologize. Only nothing was really resolved by those attempts to develop a family democracy. I often went to bed unpunished and guilty — there were times when I actually wished my father would simply hit me and make an end to my guilt.

Occasionally my parents tried to use a completely different strategy to control our behavior when we were bad. They threatened to deprive us of things we liked. However, these threats always caused my parents conflict and were often not enforced. For example, they would threaten to send me to bed without dinner yet felt I needed nourishment; would threaten not to take me to the museum on Sunday yet believed that as middle-class parents they owed me the trip. They wanted to give their children every opportunity they missed as children and at the same time have their children obey their wishes. It was a neurotic system they were trapped in — they felt compelled to indulge their children while at the same time controlling them and turning them into well-behaved, nonphysical, middle-class children. I remember a certain scared look that came into my mother's eyes when we did anything wrong. She didn't know how to handle the situation, didn't know how to punish us without damaging us, and usually retreated from the situation in despair.

Discovering Limits

All these attempts to set and enforce limits of acceptable children's behavior forced my parents to articulate what they wanted from their children. This often led to unexpected problems, since my parents didn't always agree on what was to be expected of us. I've seen the same problem arise in families of friends of mine who also moved rapidly from working-class families into a professional middle-class world.

Moving into the middle class in our culture is more than simply having more money. Usually it involves moving away from a neighborhood and a culture one grew up in. This is as true for people who grew up in a Black or Chicano or Italian or Polish community as for people who grew up in a Jewish working-class community as I did. It also means being free of traditional patterns of rearing and disciplining children. However, this freedom is usually mixed with anxiety over how to function in ways that won't be embarrassing in one's new world.

Moving into the middle class isn't, however, the only way traditional child-rearing patterns are broken. For some people, simply moving to a new community where there are no relatives or old friends forces them to define their values at the same time that it frees them to experiment with different ways of approaching their roles as parents.

As people become free to set limits based on the way they feel children should behave rather than on traditional ideas, differences often develop within a family. One parent turns out to be more lenient than another; one cares more about what the neighbors say than the other does. As these differences emerge, people discover that they don't respect each other's limits, leaving the children torn between two emerging sets of values.

This confusion occurs over little things as well as big ones. For example, a child asks for a toy. One parent says no, the other yes. Or one parent says they cannot afford it and the other brings it home as a surprise.

One parent sets a time for the children to go to bed, the other parent ignores it; one says the children must stay home after school and study, the other lets them go out and play; one says there are to be no sweets between meals, the other brings home gifts of gum and candy.

This makes it difficult for children to know how to behave. Children are not born with an innate sense of the limits of health, sanity, and safety. On the physical level, they explore the environment without a prior knowledge of what is dangerous and have to be protected from heights, fire, electricity, and so on. On an economic level, they don't know what their parents can afford or understand the social, racial, or class circumstances they have been born into. Nor do they know what makes their parents angry or pleased. They have to explore and one way to do that is to push everything until limits are set for them. It is normal for children to be unreasonable and sometimes seem outrageous in their behavior. They push things to see how adults will respond to their behavior; this gives them a sense of what adult limits are and what they need to do in order to survive in a world of other people.

I remember testing my parents and I see my children testing me in the same way. However, my parents weren't sure where to set limits and, in breaking away from the traditional and strict standards of my grandparents, often acted inconsistently. They sometimes took a hard line on bedtimes, on the family having dinner together, on when we had to come in at night. Other times they let us do as we chose. They were what has mistakenly been called permissive or Spock parents, afraid of damaging their children psychically and more concerned with being liked than with being obeyed. I can hardly label as permissiveness their tentative attempts to relate to children in a more open and egalitarian way than their parents did. It was more that they realized that obedience and physical toughness weren't qualities that would make their children successes. They understood that moving into the middle class or the professions would come through self-discipline, the ability to make decisions and function in new situations as well as get along with strange people and be facile with words. The world they saw for their children was not as insular and closed as my grandparents' immigrant world. Spock, openness, letting us make decisions, loosening up on limits, giving up the strap all converged on their notions of what a successful American was like. However, my parents were uneasy with their roles as parents and I often felt confused by their inconsistency and inability to take a clear stand on what I should do. I almost wished for stricter parents. At least our battles would be clearer and a problem would have some resolution. As it was my parents would never let anything end. For example, if they disliked a friend of mine they wouldn't prevent me from seeing him but would hint about, try to manipulate my time so we couldn't play together, and at the same time tell me that I was free to choose my friends. In growing up I thought that inconsistency about limits was characteristic of just my parents. As I've talked with friends recently it's become clear that many people of my parents' generation were confused and scared about how to set limits in their children's lives. Their own lives were changing so quickly, especially during the economic boom after the Second World War, that they didn't know what would be functional in the world they were moving into. The displacements caused by the war and its consequences were so great, it's no wonder they were unsure about the best way to bring up their children.

A number of people in my generation have reacted to their parents' inconsistency by giving up limits altogether. They didn't return to the strict and often arbitrary ways of several generations ago but chose the libertarian alternative instead. I remember being at a potluck dinner with a number of these people a few years ago. The adults were sitting around in one room planning a cooperative publishing venture. A number of children were playing outside. However, a boy and girl decided to bug the adults. First they came running through the room screaming, "expressing themselves and developing their creativity," as one of the adults informed me. Then they planted themselves in the middle of the room and began to fight, "working out their needs," someone else informed me. Finally, they moved off in a corner and began to toss around some of the food that was left over from the potluck. I didn't wait for a rationale, but went over to the children, feeling my grandfather in me. I felt like spanking them, even though I don't believe in hitting children or anyone I don't have to. Instead, I grabbed them by the arms and walked them outside. As soon as we got to the lawn the boy began to cry uncontrollably. It scared me — had I crushed him or damaged him? Maybe he should have been allowed to do what he wanted, no matter how disruptive it was.

His sister tried to comfort him but looked as if she were about to cry too. In desperation I shook him and asked what was the matter. It poured out — they wouldn't pay attention to him, no matter what he did. He told me about feeling neglected and abandoned. He wanted to be stopped, to know what adults thought was worth doing and what was stupid. His parents, who did love him, in a reaction against their parents' inconsistency and the pain it caused, let him alone without knowing that it made him feel neglected and unprotected.

I've seen similar things any number of times. Children ask for attention, protection, and love in complicated ways. Sometimes they do it by deliberately doing something dangerous while an adult they care about is near. They are asking to be rescued in order to establish for themselves that they are not on their own, that there is some protection from things out of their control.

I have never found the libertarian alternative attractive. I believe that there are certain values that children should accept as long as they live in the family, and as adults we have an obligation to try to teach these values. Basically they are concerned with mutual respect, with people listening to each other, and not taking advantage of strength or age to push other people around or destroy their possessions. They are also concerned with equity, with the idea that everybody in a family is entitled to a fair share of the resources available. Of course this isn't simply confined to the family. The same notions apply to the community one lives in and to finding a sensible place for oneself within the community of all people on earth.

I've always been troubled by the problem of what responsibilities we have when other people are being hurt, if we adhere to a strict interpretation of libertarian ideas. When do we have a responsibility to intervene in the affairs of other people? Should we stand by when a child is being brutalized by other children or adults? or when an adult is similarly treated? or a nation? What is our responsibility beyond what we owe to ourself? This is a problem that libertarianism avoids for the most part, and yet it is one I find impossible to avoid as a teacher and parent. I want to intervene in the lives of others as little as possible and yet not be a passive witness to pain being involuntarily inflicted on others. I agree with my grandparents and other older people in the neighborhood I grew up in who believed that it was their responsibility to prevent any child from bullying other children. They believed that bullying was wrong and that there was a neighborhood, not merely a family, responsibility to deal with it. However, their sense of neighborhood responsibility often became unreasonable itself. There were times when young people were prevented from playing on the streets because two or three older people wanted quiet that day. We weren't asked to please be quiet. We were made to be quiet and resented it since we were not bullies and went out of our way to be considerate of the other people using the streets. The line between having a responsibility to intervene in other people's activities and intervening to control them for your purposes is delicate. For that reason I've always tried to take a position of the least intervention possible when dealing with anyone else's life.

On the one hand, the libertarian mode has never been comfortable for me, and yet on the other, returning to the strict ways of my grandparents or living with the hesitancy and confusion of my parents doesn't make sense either. First as a teacher and then as a parent, I've had to face the problem of when to set limits on children's behavior and how to enforce those limits. The resolution that I've come to has to do with my feeling about the goal of discipline in a child's life. For me the goal of discipline and control is to empower children, to enable them to come to terms with reality and deal with the world as strong self-motivated individuals. The goal of discipline is to provide the framework through which a child can develop self-discipline and personal strength. Because of this resolution, the only principles I've been able to develop are (1) to look for the *fewest* limits on behavior consistent with personal development and group survival, and (2) to choose ones that I believe should have functioned in my life as a child and that in some version now hold for me as an adult. Three sensible limits on behavior have emerged in my experience that fit these principles.

Some Minimal Limits

Limit 1: Don't be violent or tolerate violence except in self-defense. People should not kill or hurt other people. This is a principle of self-defense, of protecting oneself from violence and working to stop violence when it occurs. With respect to children, it means not tolerating bullying; breaking up fights between unequal and unwilling partners (sometimes a fist-fight between willing peers is a healthy action); stopping people from torturing each other psychologically. This involves direct "no" saying, separating people, making judgments about who is hurting whom, and acting on this judgment. It does not involve punishing anyone, however, or making moral judgments about their character or rejecting people or hating them. This will become clearer through some examples.

Occasionally my children fight with each other. Usually the fighting is not serious. Tonia and Erica will push Josh around, or Josh and Erica will make fun of Tonia, or Josh and Tonia will pick on Erica — any permutation and combination seems possible. The problem usually dissipates by itself — one of the children leaves the room, a friend comes over, something funny or unexpected happens, and they forget what they were fighting about. However, there are times when things seem to get serious, and the children don't know how to get out of the situation. The tone of a serious fight is unmistakable. If I'm around and hear that sound, I simply move in and separate the children, either by telling them to go to different parts of the house, telling a joke to distract them, offering them a snack if they seem hungry, or by taking one of them away by force as a last resort. Usually if I'm not tired or irritated over something else, I can do it without getting angry or upset myself. Once the fight is defused, that is the end of it — no moralizing from me, no punishment — a simple and unambiguous enforcement of that limit on violence. When the incident is over, it is over, no psychological residues left behind to clutter up our lives.

Sometimes things are more complicated. There were two children in my class last year who always hung around together. They had a tendency to pick out another child in the class and torment him or her. They made fun of their victim, stole or wrecked his or her books and work, wouldn't let up until the child was in tears.

The violence they initiated was harder to deal with because it extended over a period of time. It was not a matter of stopping a particular act so much as isolating those boys from each other or changing their attitudes. There was, of course, the immediate problem of protecting the victims of their harassment or providing them with enough strength to defend themselves.

I noticed that the boys were unable to function on their own. If one of them was absent, the other wandered around aimlessly, almost melancholy, the whole day. Neither of them approached other children on his own. Together they were brutal, but not toward each other. On the contrary, they were gentle, supportive, and funny together. Perhaps their brutality toward the rest of the world was a way of protecting their friendship.

My problem was to find a way to get them to stop being violent while not destroying what was valuable to their friendship. I confronted them directly with the fact that violence wasn't acceptable in the class and that I would separate them if they continued to bug other children. Then I made it as clear as possible that I did not want to separate them, told them that they had a fine and deep friendship that I respected and admired. The point I tried to make as strongly as possible was that enforcing the limit on violence was boring and unpleasant for me as well as for them. I did not want to do it, but would in the service of keeping our class congenial and cohesive. Then I suggested that part of the problem was that they didn't know how to invite other people to play with them and suggested that they didn't need to be violent in order to get other children to play with them.

It took several weeks for the problem to be solved. The day I spoke to the boys they left all the other children alone. The next morning they began by teasing and pinching one of the girls. I immediately separated them for a half-hour, since I knew that it would be impossible to spend any longer than that watching them and keeping them apart. I enforced the limit with minimum hostility and without making unenforceable threats or imposing unrealistic restrictions. After a half-hour they got together again and played and worked for the rest of the day without problems. They tested me a few times and found me consistent and not hostile. They didn't feel they were hated or that their friendship was devalued. After a while it was a bore for them to be separated, so they stopped bothering other children. This had unexpected consequences. As the other children realized they would not be hurt or annoyed, they approached the boys and invited them to play. The problem of the boys' isolation was solved by the other children.

The crucial thing about enforcing limits is that the enforcement itself does not provide someone with pleasure. When an adult (or child, for that matter) enjoys being an enforcer, the issue is no longer protection or nurturance of the individual or group, but one of control and power. The enforcement of a limit does not imply a moral judgment of the character of the person who violates it. It is simply a matter of stopping destructive activity which all of us occasionally engage in through thoughtlessness, frustration, or the desire to control others.

Limit 2: Don't interfere with other people's activities if they are not oppressive. There is a second limit that is as necessary as the limit on violence — people cannot arbitrarily interfere with the activities of others. This simple principle functions in many ways. Just the other day I unthinkingly barged into my daughters' bedroom without knocking. They were outraged. I had interrupted a private game, one that was not an adult's business. They yelled at me, told me that they didn't bother me when I was writing, that they knocked when Judy's and my bedroom door was closed, that if they had to respect my privacy, I had to respect theirs. They were right; there was nothing to do but apologize, close the door, knock on it, and begin all again. Because they were right, it was crucial to have them experience the power *they* had to enforce the limit on me.

Many adults, especially men, seem incapable of allowing children the power to say that an adult is wrong. In situations like school or therapy, the young person is virtually powerless to question the adult. At home it is often no better. Saying an adult is wrong is considered an offense per se, regardless of the truth of the statement. Yet for limits to be respected and discipline to exist as a matter of course, limits must be applied consistently and equitably to all people in the group. This implies that children as well as adults can raise questions about the rules and their applications.

Of course there is always the possibility of abusing this right. Adults often get stricter when they are tired or preoccupied with personal matters. Children test the limits of adult power and will often question limits they've previously agreed upon. Perhaps the most sensible thing we can do within the family is find a way to come together and admit our excesses with some humor and reaffirm the central notion that the only reason the limits exist is so that we can live well together.

As adults we do initially have the power within the family. It is into our world that our children are born. What is crucial is how we use and share the power we have. At times we have to put limits on ourselves in order to empower our children. For example, the limit on interfering with other people's activities need not be reciprocal. The degree to which an adult accepts the same rules that apply to children is a personal and touchy matter. For example, I believe in interfering with children's activities only when something dangerous or painful is happening or about to happen. Yet there are also issues of manners and public behavior where interference seems the most sensible thing to do. If one of my children is spitting food out on the table or taking food from someone else's plate or talking so loudly that no one else at the dinner table can talk, I feel impelled to interfere. There is nothing dangerous happening, but there is a breach of community, a breaking down of a potentially pleasant group ritual. Family dinners and social conversation are important events for me and I defend them. Of course if I talk loudly (which often happens) my children should have a right to point that out to me. Interestingly, I can enforce my interference by sending the children away from the table or denying them dessert. They, however, have no means or power to enforce their right to have me quiet down unless I agree. It requires a conscious act for adults to give children power by setting up standards of behavior that apply to all and accepting the children's right to share in enforcing them.

The limit on interfering with others' activities except when danger or the coherence of social activities is at stake has many repercussions in daily life and sometimes things get a bit sticky when one gives up the prerogative of ordering children around and is committed to children's rights to make major decisions for themselves. For example, my daughter Antonia brings homework from school every day. Often she forgets about it until the next morning, five minutes before it is time to go to school. Then she panics, tries to do everything in a second, messes up, gets angry at herself, and finally goes off with the work partly done or forgotten altogether. Her teacher does not put pressure on the class to do the homework — it is optional. Tonia puts the pressure on herself.

I often am tempted to set a time aside and force Tonia to sit down and do her homework. It seems as if there would be less overall anxiety. Once I tried, but she was busy with a friend during the time. I reminded Tonia of the homework and suggested that her friend go home. Tonia refused to consider homework, and if I had persisted in trying to control her behavior, we would have had a monumental power struggle. I backed up and told her that we'd talk about homework when she was through playing. That way we both saved face.

Afterward I reminded her of morning homework anxiety. She agreed it was terrible, did about half of that day's work, and then wandered off again. The next morning there was anxiety over half-done homework. However, it occurred to me that my experience of her being so anxious must be causing me more discomfort than the anxiety was causing her. I was the one who urgently wanted the work done; obviously she didn't care that much. The sensible thing, which I disciplined myself to do, was to live with my discomfort and let her live with her anxiety, which I was only intensifying.

Getting me off her back seemed to help. She decided that she wanted to complete her homework and that it was easier to do it the night before rather than to panic in the morning. Most days, she did the work, and the anxiety in the situation subsided. By my respecting Tonia's right to choose her activities and live with the consequences of her choices, a battle was avoided, as was the resentment that usually results when one person controls another.

There are many ways in which adults are accustomed to interfering with and controlling children's activities to assert their own power. Think of the following statements that many adults make without much thought:

"Clean up your room."

"Don't make so much noise."

"You can't bring your friend over."

"You can't go to your friend's house now."

"You've played enough."

"Put those comic books away; they're bad for your eyes."

"Don't slouch in that chair."

Now try to imagine your child saying the same things to you. I once told Erica to clean up her room, and she looked at me and said, "You clean up yours." I have a tendency to leave clothes and books and magazines all over the floor, so she knew what she was talking about.

The business of cleaning up one's room is worth pursuing a bit. First of all, one person's mess isn't necessarily another's. There are some people who are obsessed by cleanliness and order and get nervous in the presence of clutter. I do my work in a room stuffed with books and records and tools and toys and games. I know where everything is, though the system of organization is idiosyncratic. Books I'm currently using are piled on one table. There are game boards and pieces laid out on another table, seemingly in disarray because I experiment with new games and don't know what parts might turn out to be useful.

Many people who visit the study joke about my tolerance for living with disorder. That's because my type of order is neither familiar nor comfortable to them. The same holds for many adults when they approach the order that children impose on their physical environments. Yet a distinction has to be made between mess and a personal ordering of the world.

My daughters share a room. At its most pristine, everything is put away in drawers and boxes. However, this pure state is unnatural — the girls like to play with their toys, read their comics, make things. Usually the girls are in the midst of some elaborate fantasy game involving dolls, stuffed animals, buildings, or caves made out of cardboard cartons, cars, string. The game is spread throughout the room and often goes on for days. To someone unfamiliar with Tonia and Erica's play the room can seem to be a hopeless and unlivable mess, when in fact it isn't.

However, there are times when the room does become a hopeless and unlivable mess (which also happens with my study when I'm depressed or overwhelmed or too fatigued to replace things). Usually the mess is a result of three overlapping games, friends sleeping over, or a wild day. One of the signs that the mess has reached that stage is that the girls stop playing in their room and begin to move into other spaces in the house. One can notice a spread factor to the mess. Josh's room, my study, the living room — all become targets. At that point it is not merely a matter of the girls and the way they choose to order their lives. The disorder affects all of our lives, and it is important for us to reorder things. The same thing is true when my study is a mess. I hang around other people's places and often bug them. We fall into a semiparalytic inertia before getting around to dealing with the problem and begin to interfere with each other's activities. When we catch ourselves at that point, Judy and I have to initiate a cleanup, though these days the girls are beginning to resent their own mess and initiate cleanups themselves.

When I nudge the girls about cleaning up, things can get nasty. Facing an unlivable mess, they feel unable to deal with things, put one or two things on a shelf, and give up. At that point they need help, and it is foolish to deny help in order to force people to clean up their own disorder. In a sense, the mess is ours — it affects all of our lives. With a little help the children can make their space livable again — and as a bonus I can call on them to help me out of my mess as well. As long as we respect the mutual limits on interfering with each others' behavior and are able to come together to solve problems, no hostility need develop over maintaining discipline.

Another case where many adults interfere in their children's lives is the selection of friends. Few adults would tolerate their children telling them who their friends should be or how they are being led astray by other adults. Yet parents often reserve for themselves the right to prohibit certain friendships and encourage others for their children. I feel that impulse occasionally and want to push away from my children certain children who I feel are manipulative. Yet part of me knows that prohibiting an association is one way of making it more attractive. Moreover, it is none of my business — my children have to be free to choose their friends and enemies. The only role I can play is to let them know my feelings and to support them in whatever they go through. Learning to be with people and sorting out honesty and affection from sham and exploitation aren't easy, and children need support as they begin to deal on their own with others. This doesn't mean being silent about one's opinions. There are some people who try to addict others, who try to make life on the streets attractive, who in one way or another intend to harm others. Often children don't know what they're getting into and as parents we have to tell them what we think, feel, and have experienced. In desperate situations we might have to violate our own limits and prohibit our children from being with some people. But these exceptions have to be few and in extreme circumstances, when issues like hard drugs or serious violence are at stake. In fact, if we honor minimal limits except in a few situations of extreme danger, it is usually clear to our children that we acted out of love and a need to protect them and not out of a personal need to control their lives. Put simply, if we criticized all of our children's friends, our children would have no reason to believe us those few times when a dangerous issue arose.

It is also important to remember that all activity is not symmetrical with respect to children and adults. Infants cannot be left home all by themselves; three-year-old children can't navigate traffic by themselves, even if they want to try. Just a few days ago, my daughter Erica, who is six and a half, went off with a friend on a long and wild bike trip through heavy traffic and up and down hills with any number of blind turns. I found out about it only after she and her friend triumphantly returned home. There is no question that Judy and I would not have let her do it. She described being followed on one street by a bus and being scared. I shuddered — was more grateful that she got home safely than angry because she went in the first place.

There are any number of ways in which very young children can unwittingly do violence to themselves. There are electric sockets, open windows, medicine bottles, knives, cars. It is not sensible to refrain from interfering with children's behavior if they are about to hurt themselves. Once again, judgment is necessary in order to know when to interfere to protect a child. It is a very delicate matter. There is a fine line between interfering with a child's activities in order to protect and interfering in order to control.

Limit 3: Don't destroy things to show you are in control. There is a third limit on people's behavior that makes for a nurturing personal and collective life — no person has the right to confiscate arbitrarily or destroy what belongs to another person or group. This may seem hardly worth saying, yet in our society many adults act as if children have no right to own anything or to have control over the products of their work. Parents assume the right to prevent their children from playing with their toys or, as a punishment, to take back what they have given.

The same attitude can be seen in the way adults often deal with children's art work or their collections of stones or bottle tops or marbles. A few paintings are considered cute; a large pile of them is unnecessary clutter. No matter that a child may treasure what he or she produces or collects. So long as it is not considered of value in the world of adults, it is treated by adults as if it had no value.

My children draw and paint a lot. They write books of their own. The amount of paper they use sometimes seems overwhelming, and it would be easy to throw out a lot of their work, especially since they probably forget most of what they've done. However, I write too and never throw out a page of my work, whether it be random notes, sentences, a sketch for a story, a random thought. The work that doesn't seem to have immediate application or is too embarrassing to show to anyone is filed away. Every few years I go through this collection and retype some of the material and keep the rest in a "miscellaneous" folder.

I decided to do the same thing with my children's work. Each has a large folder to hold their work. Every few months we go through them, and they decide what to keep and what to throw away. Tonia is very much like me in that she can't seem to give up any of her material. Erica picks a few pieces she likes and disposes of the rest without anxiety. Josh forgets his work, and each time he looks through his folder it is an act of discovery. He likes series — a set of pirate drawings or fish drawings. Individual pieces seem of less value, and often he weeds out my favorites among his work. Each of the children relates to his or her own work differently. They are free to keep, destroy, or give away what they choose.

Giving away things is a problem in our culture, where possessions are often taken to be a sign of personal value. Children are much more generous with their possessions than are adults, and so adults often try to train them to place value on things according to their dollar value. This can be seen when children trade possessions with each other. An expensive doll might be traded for a comic book or an old worn-out stuffed animal; a set of skates for a cap gun; a Barbie doll for two pieces of bubble gum. Often these trades are nullified by parents who know the "real" value of things and worry about their children being cheated. The right to nullify a trade, however, is just another indication of the way adults deny children the right of ownership.

The situation can become complex when it is clear that one child is exploiting another's ignorance. For example, I know of a case where some older children tried to get younger children to trade their bicycles for candy or cap guns. The older children then tried to sell the bikes. It was a clear case of exploitation. In a situation like that, adults have to intervene both to protect the younger children from exploitation and to protect themselves from being badgered into buying a new bike after a perfectly good one has been swindled away. No matter how the adult ends the transactions, I feel that it is crucial to explain as directly as possible to all parties involved that the younger children were being cheated. The exchange of candy for a bike was not an act of mutual respect, but a cynical seduction of the younger children by the older ones. However, this is an extreme example, and most exchanges among friends are entered into by mutual agreement and considered fair trades from the children's perspective.

In most cases, to place a money value on things and insist upon getting equal money value in a trade is one way of preparing children to take their place in the marketplace. It is a way of denying value that is based on affection and sensibility and replacing it by an external assessment of numerical worth.

The conflict between preparing children to survive in the "real" world and trying to help them develop humane and sensitive ways of living is embodied in this simple matter of children exchanging gifts. I believe that the only way this paradox can be dealt with is by talking with children about the difference between cheating someone and genuine exchange. I've found that my children have quickly understood gross examples of cheating and have forced me to broaden my view of what fair exchange means. For children it is not a matter of dollar-for-dollar so much as affection-for-affection. Trading something you hate for something someone else loves is considered unfair exchange.

Except with certain valuable and reusable items like bikes, children should own what they own — this tautology has to be pointed out, since gifts to children are often partially given. When you give something to a child, it is crucial to remember the gifts you receive. Those that can be redeemed by the givers are more curses than gifts. They tie the recipient to the giver. The object becomes a medium of control and not a token of regard.

Gifts create problems between adults as well as children because of the attitude that a gift is only to be used the way the giver intends. A number of friends of mine have been involved in ugly divorce settlements where one of the issues was the return of gifts of jewelry and bonds. In one case, when the man and woman were together, the man felt free to be lavish and generous with gifts, to buy his way to affection and control of his wife. When the relationship was over, he felt the gifts should be returned. I imagine his reasoning was that he owned his wife and therefore also owned what she owned. Therefore, a present to her was a present to himself. We had a number of arguments over the matter. It seems to me that a gift is just that, a physical token of concern or affection that is simply and unambiguously given. It is not an investment from which one expects a return and which can be redeemed at choice.

I, for one, don't want my children to spend their lives in quest of objects, and I hope they will treasure the generous gestures more than the possessive attitude. In my life I have had to learn to give without strings, to devalue objects — my children have less learning to do so long as I don't interfere with their generosity.

My father often talks about my grandfather being generous, almost to a fault. Yet from Pop's perspective, giving things to friends and sharing was not a matter of having admirable generosity. It simply was what one did with people one grew up with, worked with, and cared about. Generosity is a virtue only in an ungenerous society. Otherwise it is simply what one expects when people are valued more than objects.

One way to deal with the problem of possessions and gifts is to have some important things belong to everybody. There are many things that are too expensive or rare to be owned by individuals or whose use is too general to be controlled by a particular person. We have to learn how to deal with collective ownership of some things in order to give all people access to the limited resources available. I noticed in my class that each time a new book or game was introduced, there was a fight over who was to have first access. Some children at the beginning of the year would grab a new book, hide it somewhere, and sneak it home. The same was true over hot wheels or magnets or prisms. The hardest thing to do was to get the children to share, to help each other, look at a book together, read to each other, to feel relaxed enough by the collective atmosphere in the room to realize that everything there was available to all of them. Some children came expecting to be deprived, some came prepared to hoard, very few came with an impulse to share things. The structure of our society was embodied within that small group of children.

I noticed the same scramble for resources at home. If there was ice cream, my children would fight over who got the first cone, as if there weren't enough to go around. The children argued over each other's things, refused to let their possessions out of their hands. What was needed was a sense of "ours" as opposed to an exclusive obsession with "mine." For the last few years our children have been getting presents that are for all of them as well as a few things that are personal. I have become more open about letting my children share my study as long as they left the table with my manuscript alone. They have responded, as have I, by worrying less about what is theirs and what is someone else's. I have let go of my sense of possessiveness, and they have done the same but with greater ease. I have found that the only way that the collective, humane values I believe in can be acquired by my children is for me to live these values, observe the same limits as my children, loosen up my dependence upon objects, attend to the human values things represent, trust my children as they make decisions, remain open to discover my own inconsistencies, and make an effort to change myself.

Enforcing Minimal Limits

It is one thing to acknowledge certain behavioral limits and another to enforce those limits without using physical coercion. It is hard to walk the line between being too indulgent and being too restrictive. Some of us have to learn when and how to say "no," while others of us have to learn not to say "no" too much.

For some people, saying "no" to a child raises the fear of being rejected by the child. I have a friend who lives alone with her son. She needs and treasures his companionship and is also probably afraid that he'll reject her just as his father did. For several years she has indulged him terribly at the same time she has become increasingly distressed at the way he never seemed happy and kept on asking for more. Recently she decided that she had to say "no" to some of his more outrageous demands. He insisted that she stay home every night, that he come on dates with her, that she buy him everything he saw, even though they were living on a small budget. One night she decided to call a baby-sitter and go to a party. She needed to be out by herself, free of their relationship. She needed to assert that there were limits to how much she could be possessed by her child. She told me that before the baby-sitter came she and her son had a terrible time. She had fears of his rejecting her the next day and she experienced almost uncontrollable anxiety. He accused her of not loving him, tried to make her call the baby-sitter and ask him not to come. She refused, and the baby-sitter, who was also a friend, said that the first few moments with the boy were awkward but that then they got along fine. His mother, despite her fears, didn't spend the evening agonizing over her son. She felt confident that she had done a sensible thing and didn't start worrying again until the next morning. However, her son woke up more curious about what she did and eager to share what he did with her than angry or rejecting.

This may be an extreme case, but for people who are unaccustomed to saying "no" to their children, the first time they do and stick by it can be full of anxiety. I remember the times I have said "no" to my children, to refuse them toys or sugar-coated cereal or the right to have six friends over and stay up all night when the next day is a school day. Something in me clutches, I forget that children are strong and resilient, that their love and affection isn't dependent upon their getting their own way all the time. That fear of being rejected by my children as well as an uncertainty about whether I'm depriving them of something important for their growth never fully disappears. It's part of my own insecurity — in my experience "no" said directly and fairly is taken as just that by children. What I have to do is protect myself from saying "no" in a too hostile way, from adopting an aggressive tone rather than being direct, firm but supportive. "No" in the service of minimal limits is an act of love and support.

Let me give a few examples. I heard Fritz Redl, the author of *The Aggressive Child,* pose this discipline problem. Say you are a swimming instructor at a camp. There is one boy in the water who is jumping on everyone, pushing little children under the water, jumping on people from behind, and generally being a hazard as well as a nuisance. What do you do?

One response, the extreme libertarian one, would be to turn your back and say that it's the children's responsibility to take care of the problem themselves. If you're not willing to accept the possibility of someone drowning, however, you have to get the boy out of the water. The problem is how to do it in such a way that the boy will be able eventually to go back into the water and enjoy it with the others; the aim is not to make him hate you or himself, or drive him to get even with the other children. What is crucial here might be called the quality of the "no." Once you got him out of the water you could say, "You miserable person, you can't go in the water, you're to stay here because you don't know how to behave. You're getting what you deserve!" There's another way to deal with getting him out of the water, however: the way Redl and other people who've worked with defiant youngsters have found more effective. That would be to say something like "I'm taking you out of the water so you can get back in. You're ruining everyone's experience by doing dangerous things so no one's enjoying the water; you're out now so that other people can enjoy, and you can go back in when you're ready to enjoy swimming with the others. And by the way, I don't enjoy your being out, because then I can't get my feet wet either." This way of dealing with the problem doesn't involve making a judgment on the boy's character or invoke the idea that he is being punished. The limit is being enforced for the sake of swimming and enjoying it. It is not a personal matter and the boy is free to return to the water whenever he's ready to function in some respectful way within the group.

Here's another example of how one might deal with a difficult problem of limits. Suppose a child takes paints and smears them all over the wall, and then smashes the paint jars, scattering glass around the floor. There are a number of ways to respond. First, of course, is to get the child out of the room and clean up the glass. Then one can take a hands-off attitude, rationalizing the child's action by saying something like "He (or she) needed to do it to work out some other problem," or "It was just another form of my child's artistic exploration." With such a response there is a fairly high probability that there will be more broken glass, smeared paint, or worse when paint and glass become boring. I've known children who've graduated from breaking glass to setting fires while their parents rationalize their behavior as having moved from one psychological stage to another — from infantile glass smashing to adolescent pyromania, I guess.

Of course, there are circumstances where no response might be effective. If a child had been accustomed to controlling adults with tantrums, the way to bring mutual consideration about is to refuse to respond angrily to a tantrum or to mildly defiant behavior, and wait out the child's screams or remove him or her from the situation if it's dangerous. It is usually possible to begin talking after the storm subsides.

There is a commoner way to respond in the situation. That is to turn on the child, accuse him or her of being unworthy of using paints, of swearing that was the last time there'll be painting in the house, and in some way making the child pay so that the adult's anger gets worked out through controlling the child. What is conveyed by this overreaction is that the child is unworthy and that painting as an activity will be prohibited forever. The child feels this because of the magnitude of the adult's response. I've found myself trapped by my anger into threatening wider prohibitions than I actually intend to enforce, saying things like "You'll never go to another movie" or "This is the last time you'll stay up late and watch TV," when I knew there'd be more movies and late TV nights.

A healthier way of dealing with the spilled paint and broken glass would incorporate some of the basic facts in the situation. First of all, the adults wanted the child to paint, or there wouldn't be paints in the first place. Second, because the child couldn't handle painting that particular time doesn't mean that he or she would never want to paint or could never handle the setup. What has to be conveyed is that the adult wants the child to be able to paint, but it can't happen if the jars are broken and the paint tossed around the room, that the limit exists to encourage and not to prevent painting.

It makes sense simply to insist that the child help clean up and perhaps promise to paint with the paints next time and not smash things, and leave it at that. If the next time the same thing happens, a few days without paint might be in order. What is important is that the enforcement is clear, not morally degrading, not a matter of asserting power for the pleasure or sense of revenge it gives the adult, but only to enable the child to function without violence.

For some people such unambiguous "no" saying is very

difficult; it smacks too much of an authoritarianism they reject. Still, they acknowledge the need to limit some forms of behavior and adopt a tactic of indirect psychological manipulation, which I believe generates at least as much resentment as physical punishment does. The tactic consists of responding quietly to some outrageous behavior with a question such as "You don't really want to do that, do you?" or "You don't really mean that, do you?" I remember being at a friend's house. We were just about to sit down for dinner. There were a number of children playing in the room. The host went up to the children and said, "You don't want to play anymore, do you?" One of the children looked up at him and said, "Yes," and the game went on. So he repeated the question, this time more hostilely, and he got the same answer. The third time I wasn't sure what would happen, because the boy and the man stood firm. His daughter rescued the situation by saying to the boy, "That's his way of bossing us around. He means we have to have dinner now whether we like it or not." The child understands her father but described his behavior with a scorn that really hurt him. Afterward we talked about how a simple "no" makes it clear what is intended and who is setting the limits. It avoids the problem of having your child seeing you as a hypocrite and developing devious ways to deal with your indirectness.

Not everyone has trouble saying "no." It's probably true that more people have to struggle with their own impulses to control children's behavior than have no problem letting children do whatever they want. Little things like how children dress or sit at dinner or wear their hair can become occasions for power struggles. Many parents have images of how their children should look and behave, and they try to force these images on their children. One Sunday I was sitting in a park reading the newspaper. I was only peripherally tuned into the parents and children around me, but the word *don't* kept slipping into my consciousness. I put the paper down and started copying down all sentences containing negatives. Here's a partial list:

"Don't dirty your pants."
"Don't talk back to me."
"Don't put your hand in that dirty water."
"Don't suck your thumb."
"Don't keep your hands in your pockets."
"Don't get that ice cream on your clothes."
"Don't embarrass me in front of all these people."
"Don't cry; it doesn't really hurt."
"Don't pick your nose."

There's no point in going on with the list. Sometimes it is very hard for adults to resist bombarding children with prohibitions, even silly ones. I remember one dinner I told Erica to stop using so much ketchup. She and Josh and Judy and Tonia glanced at my hamburger, drowning in ketchup, and burst out laughing. I had to join in. That instance actually taught me a technique to use in order to uncover my own occasional excessive use of "no's." It could be called the turning-the-tables method of self-criticism — and consists of getting into the habit of turning statements you make to your children into statements they could make to you: "Don't make so much noise with your soup"; "Don't sneeze without covering your mouth"; "Sit up straight"; "You're using too much ketchup"; "Don't drink so fast." All the statements can apply equally to adults and children, but it is usually deemed inappropriate for children to criticize the habits and manners of adults. Think about your own manners, about how you eat or sit in a chair or interrupt people when they are talking. How would you feel about yourself as a child? Are you softer on yourself than on your children? I've caught myself doing silly, asymmetrical things at the dinner table, like reading a newspaper and telling Tonia that comics aren't allowed at the table, or interrupting one of my children to say something to Judy and then criticizing them for interrupting me.

This doesn't imply that there won't be times when children behave outrageously and have to be nagged about basic simple manners. Certainly there is some behavior that is minimally necessary for people to eat at a table together or live in the same house, and there are times when as adults we do behave sensibly and our children don't. At those times we have to remind children what the minimal standards are. Josh, for example, went through a period of dropping food and singing and generally disrupting dinner. It took a few weeks of persistent nagging and occasionally sending him away from the table to get him to behave sensibly. However, the reason he chose to behave with some manners was, as he expressed it, because "it's no fun being in my room when you're all talking and liking to be together at dinner."

There are times when my children have actually turned the tables on me, and those are more difficult to deal with. Tonia and Erica have been told in school, on TV, and by Judy and me that smoking is dangerous to health. They believe it and want me to be healthy. When they see me sneaking an occasional cigarette, they grab it and put it out. The first time they did it I got angry with them — what right did they have to tell me how to live! They were equally angry and confronted me with the old adult saying, "We're doing it for your own good, Herb" — and they were. I couldn't be angry. Now every time I sneak a cigarette, I feel guilty and look for them out of the corner of my eye, just like a naughty child.

Adults have to face times when their children oppose and confront them for good reasons. At those moments children discover whether the grownups are rational and consistent or just a bunch of hypocrites who like to control others but can't bear sensible criticism. It is important to remember times when your children confronted you and to try to understand whether they were right or not. A way to develop a symmetric and just relationship with your children is to allow them the same freedom to criticize you and help you curb your excesses as you assume with their behavior. When all parties can enforce limits it becomes in everybody's interest to have minimal limits in order to keep the group as harmonious as possible.

Still, there are these minimal limits, and it isn't always easy to behave responsibly and consistently. For example, bedtime for a child can be hell if the adult is exhausted, troubled, alone. There is a bedtime ritual in our house including wash-up, story time, tuck-in. If I'm exhausted and troubled on a particular night and Judy is out at a meeting or class, the rituals can seem endless and a pain. I want the kids off my back, magically asleep, or away from me and quiet. The temptation is to slack — to let the kids stay up and play as long as they are quiet. The next day, especially if it's a school day, we all have to pay. Other times, I'll just lose my temper and scream the kids to bed. But these are exceptions. I have to have self-discipline as a parent in order to make even minimal limits workable. It would not be enough simply to send the children off to bed at the moment I choose. There has to be a passage, some kindness and attention at the end of the day. Forcing oneself to be consistent is necessary, and after a while one can develop ways to make ritual tasks pleasant or tolerable.

The situation here is similar to what occurs when children are expected to do chores around the house and they make simple work sound like monumental oppressive labor. Dishwashing, a rather simple task, can in this context seem to be a difficult and unpleasant chore. I've known children who see themselves engaged in warfare with dirty dishes and who expend three or four times the energy necessary to clean the dishes. They also want to be treated like heroes and martyrs when they're done. However, it's possible to turn on the children's favorite music, or to sing or tell stories and de-emphasize the chore to make it a simple necessary part of living together.

The same holds for bedtime rituals. Read your children books you like, tell silly stories, play games. People who are new at taking care of households and playing nurturing roles with children have to learn how to make these aspects of life as pleasurable as possible. Of course, it's easier to say this than to be able to do it. One can want to deal with everyday rituals casually and act consistently and pleasantly toward one's children and still not be able to do so. There are a number of ways to help ourselves become the kind of parents we would like to be. One is to think of how we would like to have been treated as children and to try to act that way. Another is to be as patient with ourselves as we aspire to be with our children and to remember that in loving situations no single mistake or even a small number of them can destroy that love.

Limits and Self-Discipline

Limits should not exist in and for themselves. They do not dictate what should be done so much as provide a series of hedges against self-destruction. Within this basic structure it is possible to encourage and nurture self-discipline, which is what enables people to take control of their lives and live harmoniously with others.

Self-discipline is crucial for both parents and children. It implies a sense of self, of knowing that one can initiate actions, can learn new things and tackle problems. It also implies that if one is weak or ignorant or scared it is possible through personal action to overcome these conditions. Self-discipline underlies the whole development of personal strength.

One can see the beginnings of self-discipline in the efforts infants make to walk and talk and grab things, in their drive to do things for themselves. On an adult level self-discipline makes it possible for one to carry a project through from beginning to end, to bear pain while working through a difficult personal or social relationship, to plunge into a new situation and teach oneself how to cope with the conditions it presents. It is what makes it possible for people to resist being ordered about arbitrarily and to be able to create new forms of living.

Self-discipline can be undermined in children by too rigid limitations on their behavior and by no limitations on behavior. If children are continually bossed around, told what to do and how to do it, there is no space to experiment or feel responsibility for actions. Often a well-disciplined child falls apart when the authority disappears. There is no strength underlying the obedience. On a group level this can be seen in what might be called the "substitute-teacher syndrome." Classes that have had strict disciplinarian teachers go wild in the presence of a substitute teacher. There is no internalized discipline in the group nor usually any self-directed activity by the students. When the source of authority is absent and when the students know there will be no subsequent repercussions, they behave in ways that, on reflection, would repel them.

Similar problems develop when no limits exist. Children

get trapped in their own mistakes, become fearful or unmanageable. Their lives sometimes run away from them. It is exhausting to try to find a place to work, to protect your work, to find other people unpredictable because they never respond to or make demands on you.

It seems to me that self-discipline is most likely to develop when there are limits on violence, on interfering with others' activity, and on destroying personal or collective property. Beyond these limits on behavior there are also other aspects of self-discipline that provide the ground for the development of personal strength.

Being Alone

One of the main components of self-discipline is the ability to be alone and get to know oneself. For many people, however, being alone is no different from being lonely. When there is no work to be done or no person to gossip with, there is always TV or the radio to make one feel the presence of others. There is no time for the self unless it is forced, unless one seizes some solitary time for reflection and meditation. I suspect that the current popularity of Transcendental Meditation is an indication of the need people have in our society to be shown how to take a little quiet, internal time.

Young children do not usually have that much difficulty being alone. Babies seem to enjoy lying back and looking and listening. Two- and three-year-olds enjoy piling blocks or rolling balls over and over. I've often come upon young children lost in thought and fantasy, speaking softly to themselves and acting out some private world.

With my own children I've found that after they've had

friends sleep over or after we've had a siege of people staying at our house, they go off by themselves. If Judy or I try to interrupt their solitary play or reveries, they get extremely annoyed — they act as if some part of their being is violated.

Yet many parents and, later in life, teachers do violate their children's privacy and destroy their ability to be alone. There are a number of ways this happens. One is to turn every random act of exploration by a young child into a testing situation. I remember visiting an old friend's house. He had a three-year-old daughter who he felt was the smartest and most special child in the world. He showed her off to me, applauded as she made a house out of blocks, as she sorted shapes and named colors. She was very precocious and pleased with herself. After a while her father and I turned away from her and began to talk about old times. I kept my eyes on her, however. She lost all attention in her objects and started agitating to get our attention. After a while her father became annoyed and yelled at her. She cried, he melted, paid some attention to her, then turned away to talk to me, and the whole procedure began again. Finally, out of frustration he turned the TV on in the next room and placed her in front of it. The frenetic and seductive sounds of cartoons lured her into a passive silence.

A few days later, the father apologized for his daughter's behavior. He complained that though she was so smart and wonderful whenever he or his wife was around, his daughter didn't seem able to do anything by herself. Yet he set the situation up by turning her private explorations of the world into public performances. The child no longer felt free to explore the world — she wanted to do everything correctly in order to please her parents. When her parents weren't around to applaud her performance, she seemed at a loss.

Much of learning involves making mistakes and messing

around. Many parents forget this. This is especially true of parents who are so anxious for their children to be successful adults that they cannot see the child for the adult they project him or her to be.

There is no "correct" way to build with blocks, draw a picture, crawl across a room, play with dolls or balls or soldiers or stuffed animals. There is no correct way to develop a fantasy or make up a game. Parents have to drive their adult ideas of what's correct out of their heads in order to let their children grow and develop internal strength.

Growing up, I felt the effect of my parents' urgent concern that I do things correctly and be successful. The more I felt that there was a correct way to do things, the less able I was to explore things in my own way. This was true whether it came to Erector sets, puzzles, chemistry sets, or games. It took me a long time to understand that games and toys were merely cultural inventions, and they could be turned inside out and upside down, that invention and exploration were more rewarding than getting things right.

There are other ways parents can undermine their children's ability to be alone and to develop their own ways of dealing with the world. One of these is to demand too much love and attention from your child; to reverse the usual order of things and constantly demand proof that your child is not rejecting you.

Many insecure people worry that they are not worthy of being parents. They believe that their children will find them out and therefore are always attuned to signs of potential rejection. One act that is easily misinterpreted in such a situation is a demand for privacy. "My child wants to be alone, he (or she) doesn't love me anymore" is a terrible hurt cry one hears from lonely adults who feel rejected and out of control of their own lives.

Yet sometimes we have to learn how to turn our backs on our children, free them of our stares and our judgments, and let them go about their own explorations and experiments. My son Josh loves music, loves to sing and dance. However, there are times when he can only do it for himself. If Judy or I walk into a room where he is singing or dancing, he freezes; if we praise him, he gets angry. The music is his — we corrupt it with our praise.

I've found the same thing to be true of all the rest of us. If I walk in when Judy is playing the piano or Tonia is carrying on some fantasy, the activity stops. The same is true for me — I can only dance for myself. As soon as someone else is around, my feet become cast iron. It is not that we are shy or need to overcome something — rather there are times when deep recesses of one's self are explored and developed. These are times when we learn to relate to ourselves and our private matters.

The ability to be alone implies the ability in a certain part of your life to be free of the judgments and categories imposed upon you by others, and therefore the ability to explore and invent and create; to see and organize things in new ways; to discover strengths and insights that are beyond culture and moral judgment. To be alone in the sense that I am trying to convey is to stay young and fresh in part of your being, and to value and preserve that unique and unpredictable part of yourself that is private.

Being Patient and Encouraging Mistakes

There is another aspect of self-discipline that is important for children and adults: the ability to be patient, to slow time down, to plan and practice and not have everything delivered here and now. Patience also involves the willingness to make mistakes, to take an imperfect idea, plan, sketch, or essay and work on it until it becomes what one wishes.

Too many children in our culture get the idea that they have to get things right the first time or they are no good. This attitude is reinforced in school through constant testing and grading of work, but it predates school for most children. There are many parents who can't stand to see their children make mistakes. This is particularly true for fathers with respect to their sons. Girls can mess up, fail at childhood tasks, and still be tolerated and loved by their fathers so long as they remain pretty and attentive to adults. With sons it's different — the weight of future success falls on the son's shoulders, although this attitude has changed somewhat in middle-class circles where the feminist movement has had some effect.

If a child feels that it is always necessary to be perfect, the smartest response is to attempt little, limit the imagination, and become expert at doing many small, mechanical tasks well. This attitude has its rewards, not only at home, but when one reaches school. The "good" student is the mechanical child who does as instructed and repeats many small tasks without the intrusion of fantasy or imagination. This behavior often passes as patience, whereas it is actually submission, which is the opposite of patience.

Patience is the ability to work at something, to come back to things one doesn't understand, to let ideas and images and thoughts grow in one's mind, and then to express them imperfectly. It is the ability to work on these imperfect forms and shape them. It involves, above all, the absence of a fear of failure.

I've noticed that my children used to worry a lot about

messing up a drawing or a building or a sculpture. They would become angry at themselves and tear up the paper or tear down the building. I couldn't understand that attitude — quitting rather than doing something over — until Erica inadvertently explained to me what it was all about. At one moment of frustration she picked up one of my books and said, "You don't make any mess-ups — look how perfect your book is." She believed that the finished product sprung whole from my mind. She believed that cars were made with no mistakes, that things in the adult world somehow emerged in their final form without flaws, without effort, and without improvisation. And why shouldn't she believe that adult creation was flawless and complete? She never saw people working, only the products of labor and invention. In our society few children grow up in the midst of adult work. Most children grow up in residential communities, go to schools or child care centers. They are not situated so they can experience adult mess-ups firsthand. Moreover, adults don't like to expose their mess-ups to their children any more than they like to expose them to their bosses.

When Erica showed me my book, which she thought emerged so perfectly, I saw how unreal production in the adult world was to her and to Tonia and Josh. On my desk was another book I was working on. The pages were all written in longhand. There were cross-outs and mess-ups on every page. In some cases, pages were cut up and stapled together in a different order. My children looked at the manuscript in astonishment. How could that mess ever become a book? The word *become* was the key. The final work went through many stages before anyone ever saw it, much less published it.

Josh asked me then if I liked to make mess-ups. I tried to explain that it wasn't "like" or "not like." Books and all complicated works grow and get better because people have the patience to look at their mess-ups and work on them.

I then tried to show my children how other things are made, how a painting emerges from sketches and ideas; how the car they see on the street has to be designed and tested; how buildings get planned and often changed as they are built. From that time Tonia, Erica, and Josh seem to be more able to work at things, to correct and start over again when necessary, to understand the meaning of patience and process — that is, to understand that work develops and that it is possible to return to the same thing many times as your ideas change and your skill develops.

There are a number of ways to help your child develop patience. The most obvious is for you to be patient yourself. Let him or her play while you stop looking for gifts and talents. Let the child's abilities emerge. Try not to judge your child or to judge yourself by what your child does.

Another thing you can do is take your child to work with you, not once but many times. Show her or him what you do, and what other people do also. Talk about the long-term projects you have as well as the short-term ones. Don't try to make everything look perfect and conflict-free. Your child will learn more by being let in on the process and seeing the patience, persistence, and approximations you go through in order to complete some work.

Also, the way you deal with mistakes — yours and your child's — is crucial. If you panic or feel inferior when confronted with things you've done wrong, or if you put down your child's mistakes, he or she will close up and attempt less. If, on the other hand, you act insincerely and praise what is obviously a mess-up, your child will see the lie and might learn that serious work is not worth the effort.

Commenting on a mistake without overlaying those comments with moral judgments or implying praise or rejection is difficult. A method of developing this ability is to look at the things you mess up in your life and try to face them without praising or rejecting yourself. If you can come to look upon your mistakes as the material out of which you can build a creative life, you probably will be able to look upon your child's mistakes in the same way.

Learning to Observe

Closely related to the development of patience is the ability to deal with unfamiliar experiences and to learn from other people. Children are constantly encountering new situations in the physical world and in the world of people. They have to develop ways of dealing with things and skills and people that are new. When a child becomes fearful of unexpected occurrences or feels constantly menaced, he or she finds it difficult to learn how to master a skill or understand a person. Yet it is not uncommon to find adults who are fearful or closed, who spend their lives protecting themselves and are incapable of observing things without involving their egos. Such self-conscious people tend to focus all their attention in a new situation on the role they are playing and the impression they are making. The questions they ask in unfamiliar situations are: How do they feel about me? How can I develop power in this situation? How do I look to them? Who is it best to get close to? How can I see me through their eyes? Questions too often unasked in these self-conscious encounters are: Who are they? What can be learned from observing them? What is new and different here and what is familiar? What can I learn from listening?

These latter questions lead away from the self to a more heightened view of events and people. They lead to learning and growth, to the discovery of things that don't directly relate to one's feeling or position. The ability to step back from one's ego, to observe something in order to understand it, is a very important component of being able to relate to the world without feeling a need to control it. It can also sometimes provide useful information that can help one work out social and personal problems. For example, recently a friend came over to talk. She was obviously upset, and after a few minutes her problem came out. Her five-year-old son had come home from kindergarten in tears complaining that nobody wanted to be his friend. Laura was particularly sensitive to the problem of making new friends, since she and her son had moved twice in the last fourteen months and she had had to reestablish herself each time. She tried to console her son, do everything she could to support him, but the situation seemed to get worse and worse. Just that morning she had practically had to drag him to school and it hurt her to see him so unhappy. As it turned out, the situation wasn't any better in the neighborhood — her son felt equally isolated and friendless. I have known David since he was two and he seemed to me charming, intelligent, and attractive. He was at ease with adults, easy to play with. He wasn't shy or overly aggressive. If anything, he seemed too adult. I mentioned to Laura my feelings about David's sociability with adults. She had noticed the same thing and explained that it might be because he had been with adults so much during the past year when they were trying to get settled. All of her friends liked David and spent a lot of time with him. As she talked it occurred to me that David might be having trouble with his peers for precisely the same reason that he got along so well with adults. When he was with adults we all played the game he brought out, followed his leads in conversation, and were delighted by the attention he paid to us. However, this behavior when projected into the world of children might look very selfish. My intuition was that David tried to do with his friends what he did successfully with adults and was rejected by children his own age for reasons he didn't understand.

I asked Laura to describe what happened when another child came over to her house to play with David. She described a particularly unpleasant time that had occurred the week before. Another boy, Paul, came over with his favorite racing cars and wanted to play with them. David, on the other hand, wanted to play with his squigglies and rubber monsters and Paul gave in for a while. However, after half an hour Paul took out his cars and said it was car time. David refused to go along and said that it was his house and therefore they had to play with monsters. Neither of them budged, and after a while Paul asked Laura to take him home.

David, who had so much experience with getting adults to play his games, didn't have much experience in learning to join in someone else's game. As it turned out, this problem with Paul wasn't unique. David thought that a friend was someone who played the games you wanted to play when you wanted to play them. Laura had a difficult problem to deal with. David was a fine healthy child who had moved around a lot in his short life. He had to learn a new way to reach out to people his own age without giving up the considerable charm and intelligence he had already developed. It was important to avoid turning difficulty with approaching other children into a problem that created self-doubts and could have serious psychological ramifications.

I suggested that Laura forget about what had happened in the past and consider that she had a learning problem to deal with that wasn't much different from helping David learn how to ride a bike or eat in a restaurant or dunk his head under the water. In all of these cases and many others, children have to do things they initially find unpleasant, like falling, being somewhat quiet, or getting their eyes and ears wet. In order to achieve more power, children have to learn to discipline themselves and give up certain indulgences. Fortunately in the cases I mentioned, the personal rewards of learning outweigh the inconveniences one has to suffer or the indulgences one has to give up. The same is true with making friends. Considered in this light, one is dealing with a challenge in the present and not a psychological problem of undoing past failures.

I've found in my teaching and in working with parents that it is very often helpful to disregard the past failures of children. If one hasn't learned how to read it is better to simply start from scratch than to take the attitude that the child has been a failure; if a child doesn't know how to make friends, it's better to try to help him learn than to delve into past sorrow. In Laura's case I suggested a simple way of beginning that would help David understand how children who did have a lot of friends functioned in school. That evening Laura agreed to ask David to tell her who the different groups of friends were in his class. And I also suggested that she ask him how these children agreed upon what games to play.

The next day Laura called. David had told her all about the other children and had even told her who he would like to have as a friend. He also said that he didn't have the slightest idea of how the children decided on their games but that he would watch them at school.

David watched the other children in his class at the suggestion of his mother. He told her that the children who were friends fought a lot over what game to play and then they usually agreed to spend time playing each other's games. He said they sometimes decided to give up the games each of them wanted to play and play a third game that they both liked. In fact, he told his mother he had watched Paul play with a friend and had seen them almost have the same fight that he had had with Paul. However, Paul's friend played Paul's game, too, and they ended up feeling good about their friendship. And, David added, he was going to do the same thing next time he played with someone.

Laura told me that David did try and was beginning to make friends. She also added something I hadn't thought of. She said that by suggesting he observe the other children it became possible for him to think his way through the problem by himself and it made him feel stronger and pleased with himself. If she had just told him what he had discovered for himself it wouldn't have been so enriching for his sense of self.

Learning to observe and then act for oneself is an important aspect of the development of self-discipline and there is probably no better way to learn how to observe and analyze unfamiliar experiences than to watch natural phenomena—stars, animals, trees, plants, the weather, the soil. Even in a city one can develop this discipline by having and caring for house plants and pets. Our children love to watch seedlings grow, to feed and observe goldfish and algae eaters, to watch insects, to fish off the dock in Berkeley or visit a plant nursery. The slowness with which things grow and change slows down the observer. It's important for children to learn that some changes can't be grasped in a moment and that a great deal can be learned by looking at the same plant a minute a day, or by glancing at the moon every night. There's a bonus to simply observing natural phenomena with your children too. A closeness can grow in that silent sharing that no words or toys could possibly create.

It's important to understand that children like to look at the world for its own sake as well as to master it or understand its relationship to them. Infants and young children love to look, to repeat things, to pick things up and drop them down, to look at and touch animals, to play with water or simply watch it flow. I find that there are a number of components to the way children relate to the world. There is the manipulative component, which involves the child in learning how things in the world can be used. There is the personal component, which involves the child's trying to figure out what things or people will or can do to affect the child's life. And there is the contemplative component — the disinterested observing of the world, the wonder one sees in many children's faces when they see something new or beautiful. There is this experience that does not refer directly to the self, does not involve any immediate mastery of a skill, any push and pull with the world or people. It is a fragile ability because in our society little value is put on acts that do not lead to specific results. Curiosity, exploration, and observation are supposed to have a point if they are to be of value. Otherwise one is wasting time. I learned during the last years of my grandfather's life how deeply this attitude of needing to fill time up with goal-directed activity, of using one's time as a commodity is ingrained in us. He retired as a framer when he was about seventy-seven and spent almost all of his time looking out of the window of his apartment. He sat at the open window watching children play, greeting people, taking in whatever passed his way. I wanted to get him involved in projects, was vaguely annoyed by his doing nothing. One day after I had been bugging him with suggestions about reading books or building bookcases for the house, he told me that he *was* doing something, that he was tired of having to make or build something for someone. He simply wanted to look at the world, he liked to watch children playing, young people talking or running around. He enjoyed seeing the world — he didn't want anything from it or want to do anything to it.

It has taken many years for me to slow down enough to observe the world in that simple way, to watch other people move and work and play without trying to discover what was in it for me. School made me neurotic about grades, and since college I have made great effort to teach myself to be free of worry about being graded or evaluated. By observing, feeling the rhythm of things, one learns unexpectedly — understands without having to quantify or articulate. In a funny way the pure and simple observing I'm trying to describe is learning freed of compulsion, freed of any need to make something of what one has seen or understood.

Recently, a friend told me of an interesting teaching technique some craftspeople use. They work in the open, surrounded by children and adults going about their business. When children stop to observe them, they don't say anything, make no attempt to instruct. What they do is slow down the rhythm of their work, making it easier to observe. Some children observe and then go on to other aspects of life. Some observe and try to imitate what they saw. They can become apprentices. But learning the new skill never becomes a matter for instruction. Rather it is a combination of observation and exploration with the tools of the craft that leads one to develop the skill.

That combination of observation and exploration is characteristic of much learning that takes place with young children. So is the selectivity — different children choose to explore different aspects of what they observe.

Unfortunately, many parents become impatient with their children's spending time observing. Yet think about children sneaking out of bed to watch the adults at play, or about the length of time a child can watch the ocean or an animal at the zoo or the rain or snow coming down. Observing, losing oneself in thought or in the sights and sounds of the world, leads to respect for things in the world, and a heightened capacity for love and joy.

Helping children learn to observe and listen to others is often a lot easier than learning to observe and listen to our own children. It's hard to listen, for example, when what is said threatens our security and confidence as parents. If a child claims he or she is unhappy at school, this is often taken to mean the child is failing. Immediately a parent sees his or her child as a failure, wonders if remedial class is necessary, is concerned about not providing a rich home setting, and so on. I can just hear the child complaining: "But you haven't listened to me." The child was unhappy, perhaps being treated badly, and it was not an issue of success or failure. Possibly the teacher was brutal or indifferent. Parents have to learn to see the world through eyes other than their own, to see the world without constantly relating it to their ego. To develop even a modest understanding of your child you have to make an effort to see the world as he or she experiences it away from you and your concerns. You have to imagine the world your child lives in and the life he or she leads independent of your own. If you can also respect that life, it is likely that mutual respect will result.

There is another way of not seeing or listening to your child. If you're blinded by the perfection you see in your child, all the pain and confusion your child experiences, as well as all the strategies he or she may develop to manipulate adults, may be filtered out of your perceptions. I know a case of a thirteen-year-old girl whose father and mother saw her as perfect, a genius. They both worked and were involved in many political and social events and so, despite their feelings about their daughter, they didn't see very much of her. As a consequence, she became a master at manipulating them into giving her attention. Her parents were very critical of the institutions in our society, such as schools, hospitals, universities. If their daughter complained about a teacher, they would be on the teacher's back. It was pathetically in her interest to complain about teachers she liked because then her parents would jump to her defense and pay some attention to her. Because they perceived her as perfect, they couldn't see what she was doing.

During the first years of desegregation this girl, as well as a small number of other lonely white junior high school students (male and female), hit on an ingenious way to get more attention than they ever had before. All they had to do was complain that the Black students were harassing them. The parents immediately called up images of rape and violence done to their perfect but neglected children. They became vocal about trying to introduce strict discipline in the schools. After a while some of these youngsters felt guilty about what they were doing and admitted that they made up these stories of harassment. These admissions forced some of the parents to look at what they were demanding of their children and how psychic neglect can result from expecting too much.

Of course it is hard to be objective about your own children. You always want too much or feel so protective that it is difficult to see them as others see them or as they see themselves. I had a taste of how difficult this could be when Antonia was a student of mine in the first grade. I had been afraid to teach my own child, was anxious about the prejudices I might have in Tonia's favor and about my overreaction against showing favor, which she could interpret as rejection. She started the school year in another class and was very unhappy. Some of her discontent might have come from what happened to her in that class, but it sure didn't help to have Daddy teaching next door.

After a month of school Tonia was so unhappy where she was that despite my anxieties she was transferred into my class. The day before she began class we had a talk about the problems of having her father as a teacher. There was no reason to believe there would be problems, but my anxieties led me to posit them. Tonia told me that in class she just wanted to be like every other student and even promised not to call me "Daddy" in the class since it might make the other children jealous.

The first week was fine. Tonia spent all her time getting to know the other students and figuring out the daily routines. At the end of the week some of the students noticed that Tonia never called me "Daddy." I didn't anticipate their response, which was to tell Tonia that it wasn't right not to call her daddy "Daddy." A few students even came up to me and said that they felt it was cruel for me to deprive her of that right. They didn't confuse Tonia's relationship to me with their demands that I be fair to them. They saw things on a deeper level than I had in my anxiety. It was possible to be someone's father and still be a teacher with an equal responsibility for nurturing all the children in the class.

It wasn't that easy for me at first. For a few weeks I watched Tonia out of the corner of my eye, measured her against the other children, worried if she dawdled, wasn't sure whether to push her or leave her be. Tonia works in a slow and deliberate way. She thinks a great deal; her mind is always full of things. She worries about other people, wants to know about everything that is going on around her. On some days she would finish her work without effort — but more usually she took her time, and sometimes didn't even get started. She had her way of doing things, and until I was able to let her alone, there was some tension between us. Fortunately, she liked the student teachers in the room and had no problem coming to them if there was trouble. After a while I learned to observe her and let her grow as she wanted. It was a matter of dealing with my own worries and anxieties — not a matter of dealing with something in her.

Learning to see your own child and not merely overlay your time together with moral judgments and worries about the future helps you look at other things in the world without feeling a need to control them. A good way to step back and analyze how you function with your child is to focus on a situation where the two of you are playing a game together. It is even more productive if it is a matter of your teaching your child to play a new game. Think of how you introduce the rules. How you set the game up. Whether you let your child handle the pieces and improvise with the board. Do you have tolerance for mistakes that are made, or must every move be done correctly the first time? When you get down to playing, do you find yourself competing with your child? Do you let an even match develop and lie back a bit yourself, or do you go all out to prove you can win? Do you make comments that put your child down or look for signs of genius? Is there enough pleasure in playing so that winning or losing does not leave bitter feelings? When the game is over, do you feel you'd like to play again? Can you sit back and watch your child explore and think about the game? Or does it become for the child an unpleasant, nervous situation where he or she is afraid of being jumped on for a bad move?

I've watched a number of adults teaching their children how to play chess and was involved for a while in a chess club for five- and six-year-olds. In one case a father and son sat down to a game. The son had just learned the moves but hadn't played enough to develop game strategy. The father played a fair game of chess, and it was obvious that he could control the game in any way he chose. The very way they set up the board was an indication of what was to develop. The son placed two pieces on the wrong squares and was put down for it. The father's tone was angry, as if to say, "My son should know better than to make such a stupid mistake."

After the first few moves of the game, the father established a powerful position and then proceeded to demolish his son, clicking the pieces together after each capture. The son lost interest in the game after a while, but did manage to finish. As soon as the game was over, the father set the board up again with relish. The boy stared sullenly at the board, and his father realized something was wrong. He softened his tone, assured his son that he would do better next time, almost pleaded with him not to quit, and then proceeded to wipe him out again. The father simply could not lose or give his son the space to explore the game. Not surprisingly, that boy quit the chess club, declaring that he hated games anyway.

It is possible to teach chess in other ways, to introduce the game a little at a time, play in such a way as to keep things even, not care about winning all the time. It even makes sense at times to let oneself be beaten, not as a matter of deceiving a child, but so that he or she can learn to take the game to a conclusion. Let me give an example: I once let Erica win a chess game, and she didn't like it. She felt I wasn't really playing. However, I explained that I had played chess longer than she and could beat her if I wanted to, but that I cared more about her learning and practicing her skills than about beating her. She accepted the fact that playing a learning game with me was not the same as playing a winning or losing game with a player of equal skill. I enjoy playing and teaching games with young children because I can observe them coming to terms with a new system and figuring things out for themselves. That, rather than winning, is my pleasure.

There is great joy that can come from observing children grow and develop self-discipline. This observation does not imply controlling the growth or imposing the discipline. If as adults we can step back a bit, enforce without bitterness or hostility the limits necessary for survival, not take it all so personally, and encourage children to explore the world so they can know it and decide how to live, self-discipline will develop, and with it the ability to think for oneself and feel for others.

The Ability to Resist

The other day I went to a toy store with my children. Tonia had to get a birthday present for a friend, and Erica and Josh came along. The girls quickly picked out presents and then started looking at things they wanted for themselves. Josh was lost in a fantasy game with some cars he found on a shelf. I told the children it was time to pay for the present and go. Then I prepared for the onslaught: "Herb, can't I have that car, that doll, that game; just one; it's cheap; why can't I?" That day it didn't happen. Tonia bought the present for her friend and said she'd come back to get a game she wanted when it was her birthday. Erica and Josh listened to her, assumed very adult ways and discussed how they too could control themselves and wait for their birthdays. The three of them were proud of their ability to resist the desire to buy something for themselves.

It wasn't always that way with us. We went through many scenes in toy stores and supermarkets — tantrums, arguments, whining demands for everything and anything in a pretty package. The phrases "I want that" and "I need that" recall some of the most difficult times I've had as a parent. Showing children the difference between needing and wanting something, and helping them control the desire to acquire everything is a difficult task. This is especially true when children are bombarded by TV and radio messages that are designed to confuse needs with wants and make children feel incomplete unless they own the things that are advertised.

Yet the ability to resist this bombardment, to step back and sort out what is useful or enriching in one's life from what is merely another object to put in the closet or use to measure oneself against other people, is central to the development of self-discipline. In order to take control of one's own life it's important to be intimate with one's own inner needs and have a sense of what activities are intrinsically rewarding; to discover oneself and be able to say, "I care about this" or "I want to learn that for myself."

Without the ability to resist external demands one can never sort out what is valuable from what is incidental. This holds as much for ideas as for things. Children need opportunities to choose among ideas and things, to explore their own personal preferences without worrying about what someone else has or wants them to think. We have to help our children build the confidence and sensibility needed for the development of self-discipline. This means, among other things, talking to children about choices, explaining our own preferences, sharing the problems we have, resisting temptations, as well as letting children know what we honor and value.

One way to begin is to point out to children the difference between needs and wants. Ever since our children could use those words, Judy and I have joked with them about wants masquerading as needs, about the silliness of feeling you need a walking, talking robot or skiing Barbie doll. Children need food, water, love, sleep, community, and some things to play with. They often act as if they need everything. Even though it can be hard to resist children's demands, we have to be sensible with our children if they are to learn how to be sensible with themselves. We have to say "no" to absurd demands. One way to minimize the inevitable disappointment this refusal generates is to have resistance ourselves and demand no less of our lives than we expect in the lives of our children.

There are many things I'd like to have — a video tape rig, a 16mm movie camera, a swimming pool, a country house or farm, for example. However, I don't need any of them nor does it make sense to own them personally when they could get better use by being owned by a group of people and shared. My children are curious to know about those things that I want and deny myself. It's important for them and all children to see adults struggling to resist the desire to buy things they don't need.

For those of us who have been privileged enough to be able to buy many things we don't need or even use, it won't be easy, since we have grown up in a culture where buying things becomes a substitute for getting comfort from other people. It won't be easy, either, for people who've never had that privilege and feel deprived and resentful over not being able to buy what in fact they don't need. Ironically, it is hard to persuade people who've never had an opportunity to buy Cadillacs and Lincolns to buy economy cars.

Giving up buying as a mode of life becomes especially painful if we feel emotionally empty and worthless. When I feel stress, when my writing isn't coming along or when my royalty income seems to be falling, my impulse is to go out and buy things. It's crazy, but under stress of going broke I feel a need to buy, to get security from the knowledge that I can get something I don't need. My children have pointed this out to me and indicated that I can hardly expect them to control themselves if I can't control myself. They're right — it's a struggle I have to go through while they're going through it in their lives too. It may even be that it's easier for them since unlearning dysfunctional habits is probably more difficult than acquiring functional ones in the first place.

The ability to resist goes beyond the realm of material things too. One has to learn to resist acting in ways that hurt others or that are ultimately self-destructive. It is easy to push around someone smaller and weaker, or to manipulate or seduce another person. It is also easy to give in to attempts to be manipulated or seduced or to parrot ideas that are commonly accepted. The hardest thing for people is to take control of their lives, act on their values, and respect other people's right to control their lives. One of the central aspects of self-discipline is this ability to take control over one's life, to learn what one cares to learn, to know what one values and resist taking power over others or taking over the ideas and attitudes of others uncritically. For children the ability to resist external control and coercion is central to the development of emotional, intellectual, and physical strength. With self-discipline — that is, with the ability to be alone, to be patient and willing to make mistakes, to observe something without destroying it, to be with others without controlling them, and to resist being controlled — one can grow strong without becoming violent. However, all of these characteristics of self-discipline are as important for us as parents as they are for our children. I find myself struggling with them every day and find my children and students watching me and the other adults around them. They are concerned with our struggles with power and identity. We are the models, experiments in growing that provide them with a palette of human response out of which they create their own responses. We have to realize that our children watch us, imitate us sometimes, but mostly evaluate us as we try to give them our values. The way we live is a stronger influence on the lives of our children than what we say to them, give them, or wish for them.

3

Strength and Violence

Strength as Learning

The Pee Wees. The Berkeley YMCA has a recreation group for five-, six-, and seven-year-olds called the Pee Wees. One day two years ago a group of five- and six-year-olds went swimming at the "Y." One of the boys tried on a Pee Wee sweatshirt, which came down over his knees. The next day at school Steven announced to a few friends that he had founded a group called the Pee Wees, and before long the Pee Wees became a plague at the school and in Steven's neighborhood.

A Pee Wee talks babytalk, walks around in a squatty position with his shirt pulled down over his knees, and is positively evil. The Pee Wees' national anthem is:

I'm a Pee Wee, you're a booboo.
Get your ass out of here.

Pee Wees always run in groups, kiss girls when they don't expect it, throw water balloons, put tacks on people's chairs, knock over garbage cans, and generally make a nuisance of themselves.

The combination of mischief, cursing, and babytalk is disarming. One day Steven and two other Pee Wees came up to me babytalking, sounding sweet and funny. I relaxed, which I usually don't do when Pee Wees are around. They wanted to show me something interesting, and I followed them around the side of a house, from which another Pee Wee dropped a water balloon right on my head. The Pee Wees were off, laughing raucously, chanting:

I'm a Pee Wee, you're a booboo.
Get your boody out of here.

It was hard to be too angry — the babytalk interested and somewhat charmed me, the con was well worked out. In a sense, the whole show was worth a water balloon on the head.

I noticed the same feelings in the girls who'd been kissed by the Pee Wees. They'd complain, but laughingly, and run back to tease a Pee Wee into kissing them again. They didn't feel assaulted — it was clearly part of a game developed by boys who weren't able to kiss girls without some disguise or role to provide an excuse.

Not all of Steven's friends were Pee Wees. Some boys and girls thought the game was silly. These were the children who didn't need to disguise themselves, to be aggressive, or to flirt. There were other boys who said they wouldn't mind being Pee Wees but they were too embarrassed or shy to do things like that. A number of the girls didn't want to be Pee Wees, they informed me, because they wanted to be kissed and chased. They enjoyed their role in the Pee Wee world.

The Pee Wees obviously play an important role in Steven's life at this point. He is an extremely intelligent and charming person. With adults it is almost as if he's part of the crowd, an adult among adults, able to mix, alert, always listening and trying to make sense of what he hears and feels. With his friends, and especially when there aren't many adults around, his wildness comes out. He isn't defiant or angry so much as playful, challenging, stretching. The Pee Wees use babytalk as a way of informing people that they are acting a bit crazy and irresponsible the way babies do. Pee Wees don't imitate tough-talking teenagers or try to be defiant and threatening. They are more tricksters, experimenting with the patience and tolerance of others under the protection of baby-like behavior. Pee Wees move backward to move forward, use the indulgence given babies to test their own strength and do things that tempt them yet scare them. Steven, as adult as he can be, talks about kissing and sex as if it's a disease or deficiency of the soul. That's his macho mode masking anxiety. But he's also strong enough to try what makes him nervous, to stretch out but under some safe disguise. He's adventurous but not foolhardy. He wants to challenge adults, engage girls, test out his ability to take control of certain aspects of his life without being destroyed or punished severely. The Pee Wees are a solution for him and a few other friends of his to the dilemma children face as they test their power against things and people. On the one hand, they want to learn how to do what they've never done before or what is prohibited; on the other, they don't want to be destroyed.

How do they go about learning things for themselves and extending their control over the world? How do they develop the strength that comes from learning without risking being destroyed or destroying others and having to deal with the consequences of that violence? The Pee Wees is one solution, a temporary one appropriate to this stage of Steven's life, though one that would seem pathological if tried at twelve or twenty.

The Pee Wees point out the central relationship among learning, self-discipline, and the development of strength. The Pee Wees, as wild as they were, had considerable self-discipline. They defined a babyish role for themselves and were able to maintain that role throughout their mischief. The maintenance of the role, the control over the limits and character of their behavior, is what made it possible for Steven and his friends to step out and learn about how other people responded and what they could get away with. As a consequence Steven developed strengths that made the Pee Wee role no longer necessary. After a while he began to relate to the girls as a friend and not a nuisance. However, it was through the Pee Wees that he made his first contacts. The Pee Wees also began to play basketball and managed to give up being silly with each other because through their early silliness they learned to be comfortable together. The Pee Wee role made it possible for that group of boys to learn some socially important abilities and was for them a source of strength in a way that doing something by rote or because someone else told them to wouldn't be. It gave them strength because they were actively in control of it.

The development of strength is an outcome of learning when the learner has taken an active part in the process. Strength goes along with and is grounded in self-discipline. There is an interesting paradox of learning: self-discipline is required in order to learn and become strong, but it is also an outcome of learning. With the Pee Wees, it took some self-discipline to learn and strengthen themselves, and as a consequence of learning, their self-discipline and personal strength were increased. This implies that learning starts with the self, the learner reaching out to master the world, rather than with some task to be mastered. It is the conviction and self-discipline of the learner, as well as the desire to know and be strong, that seem to push children to try to explore and master the world. The drive, the will to know, which is also a manifestation of the desire to put order in one's life and develop discipline for oneself, comes from the learner and is not something that is imposed from without. In studying learning it is crucial to keep in mind the central role played by the choice, desire, and self-discipline of the learner. Children are not passive responders to the world. They imitate action and struggle to master the world in their own ways.

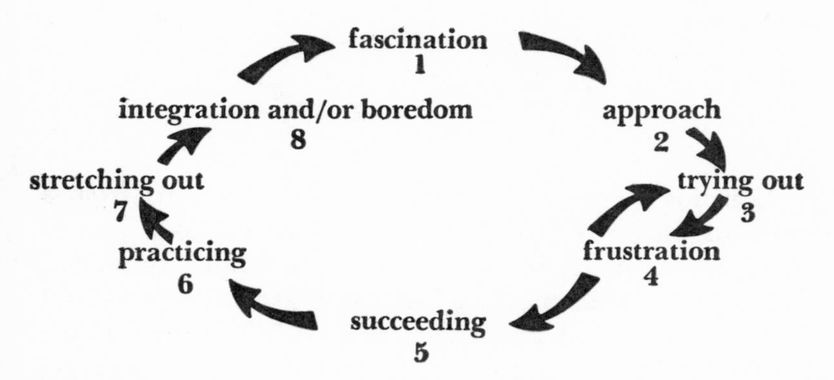

We have to respect and understand these ways if we are to help them.

The Structure of Learning

There seems to be a general form, or structure, to the way people go about learning, and this does not change throughout life, though the content of what is learned and the confidence with which one learns undergo many transformations. The structure of learning can be described by this sequence, which begins with fascination, with a desire to learn that comes from within oneself.

1. Fascination

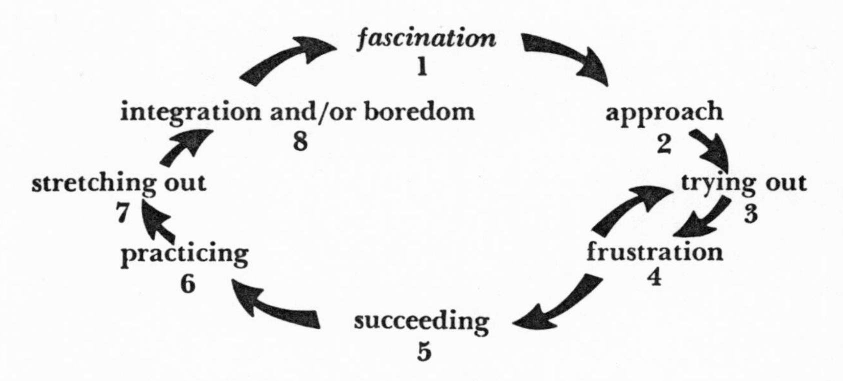

Learning begins with a perceived lack. It starts from a sense of what one can't do or doesn't know and is pushed along by the desire to develop a skill or fulfill a need. Not being able to walk or talk is frustrating to many infants. Not being able to climb or jump or swim is frustrating for two- and three-year-olds and not being able to read is frustrating for four- and five-year-olds. This frustration is not wholly negative, though, for even if young people are aware of what they can't do, they don't have a built-in sense of what they're not able to do. Frustration is usually accompanied by fascination and a sense that one can learn. Not being able to do something is taken as a challenge, not a de facto defeat or sign of inferiority, as it is taken by children and adults who've been badly treated and had their attempts to learn undermined.

I remember watching Tonia before she was able to crawl. She was lying on her stomach and saw a red block in front of her about a foot beyond her reach. She cried and flailed about, trying to move her body toward the block. I felt sorry for her frustration and pushed the block close enough for her to touch it. At that point she really screamed until I put the block where it was originally. She didn't want to be handed the block; she wanted to get it.

A number of parents have told me similar things about their children who expressed anger at being interfered with while they were struggling to walk or stand or crawl or feed themselves. Sometimes children even want to do things that are developmentally impossible at that time in their lives. They still feel the fascination of these things. Driving cars, reading, cooking dinner, building a house are all very desirable strengths. Through play children approximate and imitate these skills. However, the fascination with them remains, and children don't confuse imitation with the real thing. They come back to these aspects of controlling one's life over and over again as they grow until they master them.

How often and persistently they return seems to depend upon the strength of the fascination. I find children capable of patience and understanding that delay gratification of their desires for years. Children patiently learn to read, play games, swing on bars, and climb trees. They understand that sometimes it takes quite a while to develop a strength. Adults often worry too much about their children being frustrated and try to make things easy. They do things for their children or remove challenges that seem too hard. It is important to remember that children are learning many things simultaneously. Some of the things they learn, like a new word or idea, are acquired quickly and others come very slowly. Children understand, as do those adults who have never ceased learning, that learning has many different paces.

Sometimes simplification and an attempt to learn only one thing at a time, and that quickly, causes an impoverishment of experience that can debilitate one for future learning. The pleasure of having learned something difficult is one of the really important experiences of life. If parents break things down too finely, buy too many workbooks or learning toys too early in the children's lives, the opportunities children have to figure things out for themselves become diminished. Children are weakened, not strengthened by learning things in the easiest, quickest way possible.

Most of the examples so far are physical or intellectual, but there is as much learning to be done emotionally as there is physically and intellectually. Young children have to learn to perceive when they are liked or disliked, to develop criteria for trusting others, to deal with anger and develop compassion. They need to understand the way other people feel and to understand how to come to terms with feelings in themselves that they can't yet articulate or don't understand. Children feel the same fascination with exploring feelings that they feel about physical and intellectual challenges. One wants to get closer to new feelings and if possible understand and integrate them with the rest of one's life.

Fascination consists of focusing one's attention on a problem, skill, or aspect of existence that is as yet unmastered. The next step toward mastery consists of approaching what is new and not merely witnessing it. This requires an act of will. Many adults are incapable of making an approach to something new and are paralyzed learners. Children are usually the opposite, and sometimes too careless or trusting in their approach to the new. It is this boldness and trust that is often called the innocence of babes — children don't yet know what they can't do.

2. Making an approach — reaching out

There are many ways to approach something that you want to learn. For two years I taught kindergarten and first grade.

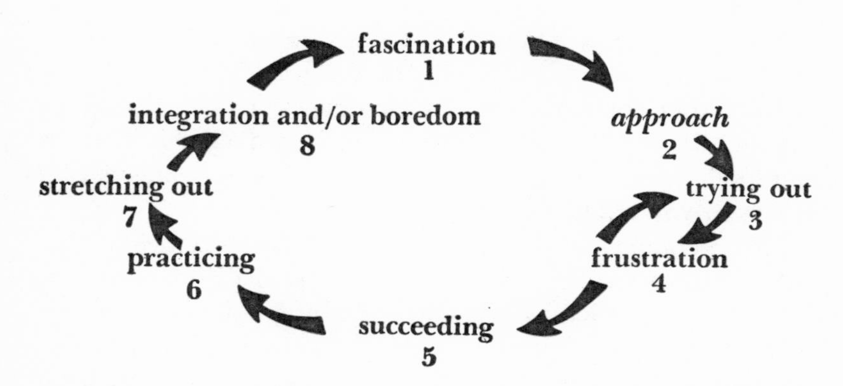

One of my main responsibilities was to teach the children how to read. In watching them go about the business of learning how to read, I learned about the variety of styles they used in approaching the printed word. For example, Mark, one of the youngest children in the class, seemed almost totally passive except that his eyes were always on some of the other children who were reading or playing a game. He refused to participate but insisted on being around where the work was happening. He didn't bother anyone and yet refused to do any of the activities himself, no matter how I pushed him. I decided to lie back — with such active eyes something must be going on. It was. About a month and a half later Mark called me over and said he knew how to read some simple books and could play the word game. I still had not seen him do anything in class (and his mother said he didn't do it at home either), but he read the books perfectly and played the games as well as any of the other children did.

There are people who learn through observation, who practice things in their heads over and over before venturing to display their skills publicly. I've seen children observing others riding two-wheel bikes and then, without taking a fall, riding themselves. There are babies who seem to lie back a lot and observe and try to digest the world. Then all of a sudden they come out with full sentences or pick themselves up and walk. There is a silent mode of learning that involves internal practice and for many children it is as effective as constantly relating to teachers.

Some children enjoy being shown things by someone else, while others want to learn by themselves. Bill, for example, insisted upon teaching himself everything. At times if I was explaining something to the class, he would put his fingers in his ears. I was ruining the pleasure he took in teaching himself. Bill would take science material off in the corner and play with it for hours, coming up with some ingenious device. He would take complicated books and try to figure them out all by himself. Sometimes this led to trouble, as when he chose something too difficult and became frustrated. However, he learned to bear the frustration and usually came back to things after a few days and figured them out. There were times when his lack of interest in being taught was infuriating, as when he grabbed an expensive piece of apparatus without listening to the instructions and broke it. Eventually Bill and I had to come to an accommodation — he could learn as he felt most comfortable, but at times when there was a risk of something expensive being broken or someone being hurt, he would have to listen before grabbing.

Brian was quite the opposite of Bill. He enjoyed being taught and imitated adults' functioning quite often. Once shown a concept or technique, he would practice it and master it. He watched how adults (and often other students) held their pens, walked, threw a ball, ran, or wrote letters and imitated them. This was not like the internal practice of Mark — it involved action in the physical world. Brian seemed to feel most comfortable and to learn most quickly when he was manipulating a physical object or using his body, his mind, and his senses together.

Blair used questions in a way that Brian used imitation. She needed to understand something before she did it, while Brian came to understand through doing. I remember her semifrustrated questions when facing something hard for her: "But what does it mean? What do you mean? I don't understand." Understanding was a very valuable strategy for her. She would stay fixed at a problem for a while, brood, play around at random, and all of a sudden understand. Then she would leap forward, doing all sorts of things through applying her understanding. For example, she didn't understand what multiplication was. Other students didn't particularly care and went on to do 2×2 and 2×4. She wanted to understand the concept and refused to do any of the mechanical calculations. With the help of a student teacher and with lots of thought, she figured out what multiplication was all about. From that point she could do all kinds of calculations, many of which were too complex for other students, who were learning the concept through generalizing from a lot of examples.

The children I've described so far liked to work pretty much by themselves or with an adult. Some of the children, however, functioned best and learned by talking and through dramatic play. Melissa and Miriam worked together most of the time. They wrote books, read stories to each other, developed elaborate theatrical fantasies that at times brought the whole class into their world. When reading they corrected each other; they tried to figure out the sound or spelling of a word together. They pushed their knowledge and, using me as a resource to answer questions they couldn't deal with, they taught each other. Words were very important in the process — they questioned, kidded, tested, riddled each other and learned through the interchange. Their fantasies were grander and more effective than most improvisations I could come up with. For example, they decided to open a Straw Hat Pizza Parlor in class. They used the portable chalkboard to write up an elaborate menu; took the counting chips we used for math and turned them into money; built a pizza oven out of blocks; wrapped up books to look like sandwiches and pizza and garlic bread; used paper cups for beer and wine and soda. They had the whole class quietly lined up waiting to be served. The children had to read the menu and write down what they wanted, to pay for their meal in chips and then, when served, sit down and eat and drink while a puppet show was performed by other members of the class who had been drafted to entertain in the restaurant.

Learning as a social phenomenon is often played down. Yet Melissa's and Miriam's method was effective for them and contributed a great deal to the other students. They provided us with a model of cooperative learning. Both Melissa and Miriam learned how to read. They lost nothing by helping each other, which was somewhat of a shock to the more competitive students who were afraid to share what they knew lest they lose their advantage on the standard school reading tests.

Some adults who visited the class asked me how Melissa and Miriam could learn anything, since they talked so much. They saw learning as coming from books or the teacher. Yet some people do learn most effectively through dialogue and questions, and some subjects (such as politics, psychology, and sociology) can best be explored collectively. Young people enjoy talking, telling stories, picking up casual information, asking questions about things that puzzle or confuse them. And they listen to answers and learn. Words are effective mediators of experience and teach about the world unless we cheapen their value by telling lies and ignoring questions.

Talking as a way of learning need not be a social affair. The year before last, there was a girl in my class who talked incessantly to herself while she worked. At first I was annoyed by the habit and suggested that she try to internalize the monologue or at least whisper. She tried, and I noticed that it seemed painful and inhibited. Over dinner one night I mentioned the problem to my family, and Tonia, who was in the class at the time, reminded me that I talk to myself while writing. I'd forgotten that, since for me talking and the act of writing are so joined to each other that I'm not aware of them as two separate acts. From that point I paid closer attention to Maureen's monologue and learned that talking was a way of exploring ideas or helping herself through difficult problems. She used language as if she were giving instructions to herself, saying such things as "No, that's wrong," "Try to add first," "Don't panic, remember how it worked yesterday." She developed her own feedback mechanism and explored and criticized her work as she did it. Eventually this dialogue would be internalized (she did begin to whisper, and the next school year the voice was thoroughly internalized), but the attitude of continual reassessment and self-criticism was part of her way of approaching growing and living.

Shanti, who loved to engage in Melissa's and Miriam's games, also talked to himself and enjoyed solitude or the company of one adult. Other than in a fantasy situation, he could not function with other children around. His mode of learning was unique in the class. He thrived on metaphors, analogies, images, and stories. Some of the other students in the class thought that Shanti was funny and a bit nuts in a nice way. He tried to understand things just as Blair did. But the way he understood could be called poetic, in distinction to her more scientific mode. Shanti had a lot of problems with reading at the start. He knew the alphabet, knew that certain letters stood for certain sounds, but didn't understand what all those letters and sounds added up to. He also knew that certain people could make books tell stories — that was what reading was to him, and he couldn't connect the letters, the sounds, and the stories. My feeling is that he listened to stories so seriously, was so involved in their images and in the lives of people in them, that he didn't listen to sounds or words. His understanding was too immediate and too deep to attend to the small parts. He didn't learn by induction, but in his own way, by leaps. One day he told me that he dreamed that a bunch of letters was walking around shouting out their sounds and that all of a sudden they crashed into each other, lost their voices and their separateness, and a new voice shouted out the word. Then he told me that that was how letters could tell stories. He then set out to figure out words rather than repeat a series of unconnected sounds when looking at print, and after a while had taught himself how to read.

Shanti always thought in images — subtraction was a number of things stolen away; addition meant throwing things together. Music always conjured up creatures and stories. It is no wonder that when John Oliver Simon, a poet, came to work with our class, he couldn't keep Shanti away.

Thomas was more of a problem at the beginning of the year than the rest of the students were. I had no idea how he went about learning things, since most of his time went into avoiding learning. I assumed that he put so much energy into running away from learning because at some time in his life he had tried to master something and had been brutalized or humiliated for his efforts.

When I first asked Thomas to read, he fell off the chair, called me all kinds of mother-fucker, and threw a tantrum, crying and kicking. There was nothing brutal about my request, it was quiet in the room, there were no other students near us. It was clear that his response was not new. I later found out that he responded to any denial or challenge in the same way. He had to be first in line for snacks, to the lunchroom, or even during a fire drill, or he would pull the same routine — defiance and threats and, if they wouldn't work, a tantrum. The tantrum reappeared on the schoolyard every time he was out in kickball or not allowed to kick first. I found myself faced with the juxtaposition of angry, negative feelings of rejection and with a very positive need and desire to be first. Thomas's face told me other things, especially when I could observe him playing contentedly or doing math, which he loved and did well.

Thomas was kind and generous when he didn't feel the pressure of competition. He grasped things quickly as a whole, but seemed unconcerned with details. He understood all the nuances of a story, could memorize complicated facts in science, yet struggled to remember simple sound-letter relationships despite my having drilled them over and over. I could never decide how much of this apparent amnesia had to do with anxiety and lack of confidence. As the year developed, he felt more secure and seemed to learn quicker though in any new situation he would temporarily retreat to threats or tantrums. In the process of his unlearning dysfunctional habits, it was possible to see Thomas as quick and intuitive. It became clear that since he grasped things so well as wholes, a compartmentalized, structured phonics approach to reading was unwise for him. Instead we started with whole words, sentences, simple stories. I helped him learn words such as *cat* and let him use that knowledge to read *rat, hat, fat,* and so on, rather than having him sound out each word, *f-a-t, r-a-t.*

He operated much more confidently with whole units that had meaning than with parts and segments of meaningful units. At the end of the year, as he became less defensive, I could see more of his most comfortable ways of growing. The attitudes he had shown at the beginning of the year were defenses he had had to develop to avoid being hurt if he didn't learn. Ironically, the defenses he used to protect himself contributed to preventing him from learning things that would strengthen him and therefore make these defenses unnecessary.

As the year continued, I could observe Thomas struggling within himself — curbing the tantrums, allowing himself to be second in line or out at kickball. I responded to his struggles with support, gave him attention, did my best to turn his tantrums into jokes, found ways of changing the focus of his attention when he seemed about to lose control. He manifested in dramatic form what all the children seemed to be going through — a balancing and mediating of their own personal modes of learning with the defenses they were developing to cope with the demands of the adults in their world.

These different ways children have of approaching a new experience indicate different types of strength people use to deal with the world — the strength to observe and to analyze sometimes, the strength at other times to act even if all the consequences aren't predictable, and also the strength to persist in approaching something that seems enormously hard or incomprehensible.

These ways of approaching something one wants to learn are not exclusive to children. We use them throughout our adult lives — we don't learn any differently than children do. This is important to remember when you observe your children and try to figure them out. Children and adults are not much different — children do not do things qualitatively differently from adults.

If the way your child is dealing with a problem puzzles you or makes you anxious, try to think of the ways you could solve the problem if you had the resources and experiences of your child. Think of *ways,* never of one way. There are approaches to problems, not a single way to approach a problem. The difference between children and adults is the factor of experience. We've had more chances to try various ways of approaching new experiences and have developed ideas of what we feel are appropriate approaches. Often by watching an approach to an experience we save time. We know that by observing how someone works a simple machine we can learn to use it more quickly than by grabbing the machine and pushing buttons at random; we also know that by observing and analyzing all the possibilities for developing a relationship with someone we can lose the opportunity to meet him or her altogether. Sometimes jumping in is the best way. We also know that very complex matters are usually best approached in a catlike manner. However, many adults get trapped by their notion of appropriate approaches — become observers so fully that they can't act, so impetuous that they forget how to think, or so catlike that they spend their lives circling about situations in which they should be engaging. Children aren't usually so limited in their ways of approach, and though they make mistakes, they can also make brilliant discoveries. The wider the repertoire of responses one can retain, the more likely it is that one will continue learning throughout life instead of falling into ritualized behavior and predictable responses, as well as avoiding new, unpredictable, and challenging experiences. The wider the repertoire of your own response, the more likely it is that you'll understand the ways your children respond.

3. Trying out something new

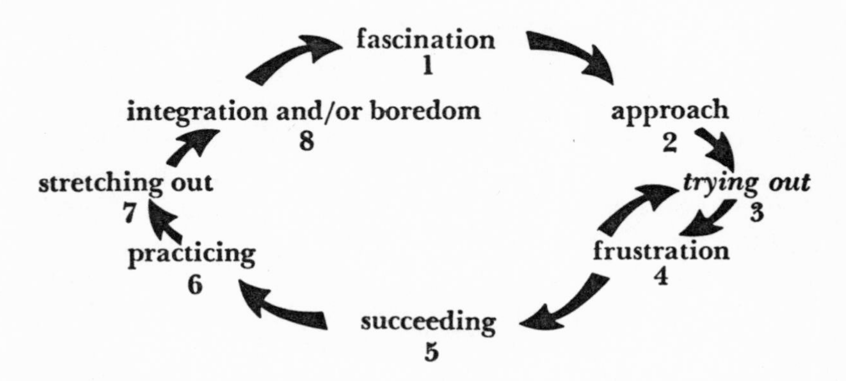

Developing strength consists among other things of making what is strange and difficult familiar and easy. It is not enough to observe or circle around or even to jump into something. A person has also to try out over a period of time a new skill, stay with a relationship, examine a novel idea. After the initial approach comes a period of trying to get the skill right or to understand the nature of some response. For example, think of a baby who decides at a certain point to feed him or herself. Before, the baby was content to let an adult do the feeding, and to bang the spoon on the high chair. When the baby understands that the food gets to the mouth on the spoon and wants to control that process, an approach is made to feeding herself. Let's say the baby jumps in and the first time manages to get a spoonful of food in her mouth. The next time, the spoon hits her nose or cheek. The approach has already been made. Now the skill has to be tried out over and over to figure out the way to do it so it works most of the time. Adults are often impatient with children's efforts to try out new skills. From an adult perspective, it doesn't seem like much to put a spoon in your mouth or pick up and let go of something when you choose, but for infants these are skills that have to be figured out and tried out.

The same tryout period exists in the realm of relationships and feelings. The baby smiles and grownups laugh and respond warmly. At a certain point the baby not merely smiles, but makes the connection between the smile and the response. At that point smiling becomes something that could be used to control the adults in one's world. That control has to be tried out — does the smile always produce the same adult response? When does it work and when doesn't it? The realm of controlling, or at least being able to predict adult responses to oneself, is a difficult one for children, since adults respond differently to the same action depending upon how old a child is. I remember Tonia when she was six trying the same smiles and cuteness that Josh, who was three at that time, was rewarded for by some relatives. They didn't respond the same way to Tonia, told her she was too big for such babyish responses. What she had tried out and mastered in the past was no longer appropriate. A new problem existed: she had to figure out what adults considered to be appropriate for a six-year-old and then to decide whether or not she wanted to do it.

Adults who are too rigid about age-appropriate behavior can cause their children a lot of unnecessary anxiety and confusion. Children do change, but abrupt changes in what you expect from your children create problems that children need time to work out. I've seen these problems in exaggerated forms in families with parents undergoing therapy. A child, for example, learns to expect a cool response from his or her parents, knows that they don't enjoy physical contact and are nicest when they are approached indirectly and can be brought to believe that what the child wants is the parents' idea. All of a sudden the adults change. They believe that their new behavior is likely to make them feel better about themselves and provide a more open and warmer life. So they try out different ways of responding to their children, just as their children try out new things. However, if they haven't prepared their children for changes in themselves, they have created a complex situation for the children. Which behavior is to be trusted: the old quiet form or the new, more physical and demonstrative, form? The children have not merely to figure out how to respond to the changes in their parents; they have to figure out whether these changes represent something permanent and can be trusted or whether they are some passing enthusiasm. The situation can even be further confounded by parents who look to their children for approval. Unmanageable anxiety and confusion can result when children feel such strong and unclear emotional demands upon them. It is important to be wary of asking for our children's validation of psychological changes we undergo. It is more sensible to be patient, explain as clearly as possible what is happening, and give our children a chance to assimilate a new situation. Children can develop the strength to deal with problems and crises of growth in their parents' lives — but they have to be given time to observe and approach their parents, to try out new ways of relating to them.

One of the most difficult responses for children to try out is expressing anger. To express anger is dangerous — one risks the withdrawal of love, physical or emotional retaliation, and guilt generated by the sense that one was wrong or overreacted. Children observe with fascination the ways adults show anger. They know how they are treated when their parents or brothers and sisters or friends are angry at them. They also know how these people respond when they're angry at each other. TV and the movies also provide a whole range of experience with anger. Children see the unambiguously murderous and violent mode of detective stories, as well as the insulting anger of a lot of comedy, and the seething suppression of anger portrayed on soap operas. From this whole repertoire of responses they have to choose their own mode of responding. And anger itself provides another problem: however much you would like to choose the most effective way to let anger be known by the right parties, it explodes out of you every once in a while.

Anger can be experimented with in play, tried out on dolls or in fantasy play with other children. I've noticed my daughters and their friends using Barbie dolls to experiment with a whole range of expressions of anger and disagreement. Usually the targets of these expressions are boys and grown-ups, though other girls are not completely immune. However, there is a qualitative difference between trying out anger in play and trying out a way of expressing anger to other people when one is really angry.

My children express anger in a direct verbal (and in extreme cases physical) way. They don't insinuate anger, pout, or brood. There is something beautiful about that righteous assault on me or other adults. The children are usually right to be angry and I find that directness of expression beautiful. My impulse is to laugh and kiss the children out of admiration for that openness. Once I did, and Erica just about turned red in the face and collapsed in a rage. My response was a putdown from her perspective, a refusal to take her anger on the level where it was intended.

The expressions of feelings must be respected even if it means engaging in argument or struggling to come up with a solution requiring everyone to give up a little. It should make no difference whether the feelings are expressed by an adult or a child. It is essential that young people feel free at home to say what's on their minds; that they don't live with a fear of rejection or punishment for simply letting what they feel be known. Practice with expressing feelings is the only way people can stay in touch with their emotions and learn appropriate ways of communicating them to others. Too many people in our society are inarticulate when it comes to expressing to themselves as well as to others what they feel; they are emotionally impoverished and collapse or become violent under conditions of stress where what is most needed is strength and clarity. Violence is often a sign of weakness, of the inability to focus on the sources of a problem or to articulate one's feelings. It represents a loss of self-discipline. Instead of dealing with a problem, the violent and inarticulate strike out at it, hitting anything or anyone who happens to be in the way. The uneasiness we have to face when our children feel free to express anger and disagreement towards us is really a small price to pay for helping them avoid the disease of violence.

4. Frustration

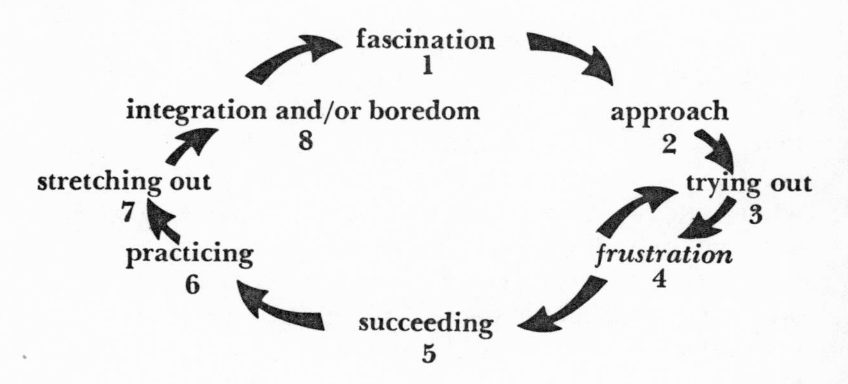

Learning how to cope with frustration is a major component in the development of personal strength. As people try out new ways of behaving, obstacles develop, and there are times when they feel like giving up. This happens to babies learning to walk and to physicists trying to master a new concept. Sometimes one even gets something right the first try and then can't seem to get it on the next few tries.

There are different tolerances for frustration. I've seen some children burst into tears and collapse the first or second time something goes wrong, while other children of the same age can sit and try endlessly until things fall in place. Often fatigue or hunger are major components of the threshold for tolerating frustration for young children. If it's close to dinnertime, late in the evening, or just a bad day after a sleepless night, nothing seems to work for some children. They forget things they knew the day before—can't do a puzzle that is usually easy for them, can't put clothes on a doll they dress every day, can't tie their shoes or button their clothes. Often a diversionary action can ease a child out of a frustrating situation. A snack, some music, a suggestion to do something else with you can become a face-saving device. The worst way to respond to frustration is to attack it, to become angry at your child because he or she is frustrated and can't do what you believe should be easy to do. This attack at a moment when a child already feels weak happens more often than one would imagine. I've seen parents getting angry at their children for stumbling through a book or giving up on tying a bow, or falling too often when trying to walk. Behind this reaction is a fear many parents have that their children might not turn out to be smart. Even before the child reaches the age of one, parents become anxious about where the child will rank. The child's frustration is often confused with lack of intelligence and is looked upon as a negative characteristic. However, the contrary is true. Frustration is a central component of learning to do something one couldn't do before. The anger generated by not being able to get something right can just as easily lead to a resolution to get it the next time as to a desire to quit. The question is how frustration is dealt with and how it is judged by others.

If children can be supported when they are frustrated and shown that all people trying new and difficult things have to deal with periods of frustration, then it will be possible for them to move away from something that's frustrating and come back later. The ability to move away and come back later is a major component of growth.

In dealing with children's frustrations there are two almost contrary and unhelpful attitudes that parents can fall into. One is to assume that frustration is an inevitable aspect of life and that therefore by setting up deliberately frustrating situations the parents will harden their children and prepare them to deal with real life. My feeling is that there is something to the argument that the world is hard and children ought to be prepared to deal with frustration. However, I believe that there is adequate frustration in the ordinary course of living, and there is no need to manufacture problems. More important, children learn how to call upon self-discipline and deal with frustration most effectively when the frustration arises from trying to fulfill goals they've set for themselves. Children need reasons to overcome frustration beyond the attempt to please adults or prepare for some vague future. When frustration is imposed and planned, resentment is as likely as learning to result.

There is a softer way, which is probably no more effective, of trying to deal with children's frustration. This method consists of trying to protect children from frustration and keeping them from attempting things that might be too difficult.

I have a friend, for example, who was pushed into neurotic competition as a child. She remembers her childhood as a long series of frustrating failures. Her parents wanted her to be first in everything, and she never fulfilled their expectations. Reacting to her own frustration as a child, she resolved to protect her own children from frustration. She helps them with everything, does puzzles for them, plays games and makes sure they win. If they can't draw a figure or complete a sum or read a word, she jumps in to help them before they ask. Her protection has had unexpected effects. Instead of freeing the children of frustration she has created frustration of a different sort. Her son and daughter have withdrawn and won't try anything in her presence. They're frustrated with her interference and have carved out a private world where they are free to make mistakes and come to terms with natural frustration by themselves. They've cut her out of their life and she's bewildered by their coldness, since everything she does is motivated by what she conceives of as their interest. Her childhood and the lives of her children are confused. She's created a barrier between herself and the children because she can't understand that their lives are new lives; that what they need of nurturance and support is not what she would have needed. We've talked a lot about this, and it seems that she's beginning to look more clearly at her children and understand what kind of support they're asking for in the present without worrying about her past.

Fortunately most children learn how to deal with moderate frustration and become strong on their own. Some become so unafraid of being frustrated that they are willing to try almost anything. I've found that the most insightful and creative children take frustration as an indication that what they are trying is difficult and worthy of their attention.

There are some skills that are frustrating because they are simply too difficult for a child at a particular stage of his or her life. My children at three and four have wanted to work with Judy's loom, write books in cursive as I do, put together complicated models, play the piano perfectly, and many other things. Often they tried to do these things, plunging into the activity with enormous energy and enthusiasm only to be stopped very quickly by their size or lack of coordination or understanding.

These moments of disappointment and frustration can be quite intense, and children need support sometimes. Because one can't weave on a four-harness loom or write cursive or play a Mozart sonata at four or five or six doesn't mean that one will never do it. I've found that telling stories of my childhood, talking about how long it took me to learn to write, and Judy's telling about how she actually went about learning to weave, helps. Learning about learning helps children set plans for themselves and absorb the idea that there are some things one comes back to time and time again over a period of years to develop mastery. It helps children understand that they are not unique in their frustration or their inability to do certain things. It is one way of turning present frustration into a motivating factor.

Another way of encouraging stamina and persistence is to provide some activities similar to the frustrating ones that children can master. For example, I keep a number of empty bound books, some in the shape of pamphlets, others structured like blank comic books, in my study. I also have pen and markers as well as rubber stamps and stencils. If my children and their friends can't write books in exactly the way I do, at least they can make some books. The same holds for weaving or playing the piano — there are things young children can do that are very close to adult activities and not condescending or childish. Children can work seriously at something the same way adults do, and enjoy it. As one five-year-old told me, "I don't like to be playing all the time — I've got work to do just like you."

As a last note on the problem of being frustrated, there is one way in which children deal with frustration that I find delightful but that seems to worry a number of parents: regression. There are times when children learn to command major aspects of their lives like going to the toilet, getting dressed without any help, being able to make their own breakfast, read without problems, ride a bike, walk to a friend's house or school alone. At these times there often seems to be a resurgence of babytalk, crawling, dependency. Just as some extension of power is about to develop, children seem to jump back to the most immature ways they know how to be. Often this comes at a time of frustration, when they have almost mastered a skill or are about to assume new responsibility. One way to look at this regression is to consider it a sign of defeat, or fear of growing up. Parents who are troubled by their children's acting babyish worry about whether the behavior means that their children are somehow inferior, immature, incapable of normal growth. I see it in another way — regressing is an act of strength at a moment of frustration. It is a way in which a child assumes a mode of behavior he or she has already mastered and shows that mastery by being able to *play* baby instead of being baby. If one could learn to control that mode, then certainly one can overcome the presently frustrating one as well. Playing baby is a delightful way of saying that one is not a baby and feeling strong and secure and capable of learning. My guess is that all of us use this, regress at times of frustration, not because we quit so much as that we concentrate our energies and gain strength from playing our old selves and through that play convince ourselves of how much we have already learned. It is a way of putting present frustration in the perspective of all the frustrations we have already overcome; a reaffirmation of our strength when we most need it. Without this energizing function of regression, I believe many more of us would give up than actually do.

5. and 6. Succeeding and practicing

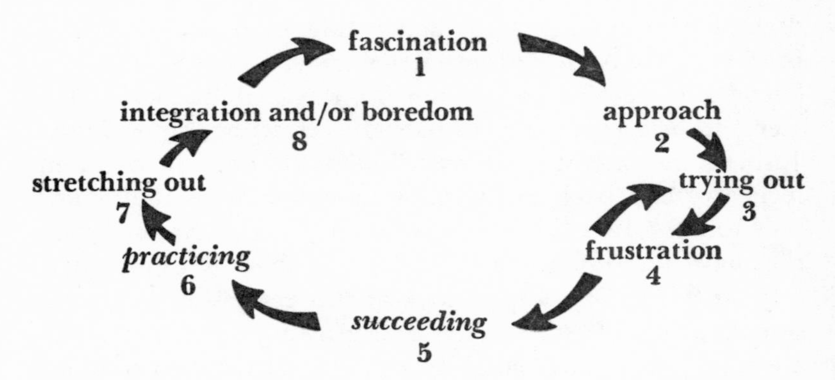

There is a certain time, usually after a lot of trying out and some frustration, when people get what they are trying to learn and realize they've got it. This is usually a time of great satisfaction, something to savor. Recently Josh has been learning to tie his shoes. There was a long time when he would tie a few knots correctly, then mess up a few times, then do it right again. Last week, however, he got it, his hands worked the knot confidently without his having to think about it. For the last few days the house is in knots—everything that can be tied into a bow is. I've even had the pleasure of having my shoes tied for me for several days. There is obvious pleasure on his part in practicing over and over what he's learned. The only impatience seems to be mine.

There are more complex aspects of getting something. For example, after a child has settled on a mode of expressing anger or mastered a way of making others angry, that too has to be practiced and sometimes makes the child seem intolerable. Exercises of new strengths are not always pleasant, and there are times when we have to learn how to be tolerant and sensible about them. I sense a growing impatience on the part of adults with children's doing things that don't seem to imply some intellectual or physical progression. To practice a skill or way of behaving, to repeat something over and over for the pleasure or interest of it, is looked on as some form of retardation. In the schools this manifests itself in a highly structured developmental curriculum, which is imposed upon children sometimes from the time they are four years old. The curriculum moves step by step from one skill to another — as soon as a child has mastered a certain skill he or she is expected to move on to the next level of mastery. This usually applies to what the professionals call motor, perceptual, cognitive, and affective learning — that is, to moving and sensing, thinking, and feeling — to being alive. Life on the move through such a system is a hysterical race with no finish line. There is no time for practice, for savoring what you have learned, for regressing or withdrawing in order to gain new energy. I've seen a number of children in the third grade who've been in such a system since nursery school. These children have mastered all the skills that have been pushed in front of them — but they can't read. They know phonics, can sound out words, can go mechanically through a text, but don't have the slightest idea what it's all about and certainly don't enjoy using those skills. After observing one class for a few days go through skill boxes and fill out forms showing progress, I asked the teacher in exasperation when the children had time to read books. "Read books?" The teacher was puzzled, there was no time to read books because the children were too busy learning to read. This is just like taking piano lessons and having to practice exercises in order to move from one Czerny book to another but having no time to play the piano.

I remember my accordion lessons. Each week I was supposed to do two exercises and work on one song. Practice was to be an hour a day. Last week's exercises were to be perfected, this week's to be mastered, scales had to be played, work put in on the new song. After four years I had become pretty dexterous and competent, but I hated the instrument and the lessons. For a few months before I quit I took the accordion to a room where my parents couldn't hear me, and made up songs, played sheet music, just let myself go with the sound. That's what I needed along with the lessons — lots of time to mess around and learn ways of using what I learned.

Practicing a skill you mastered is a source of pleasure. Children need to do things over and over and over and as adults we have to learn to be patient with repetition, slow down, and not be obsessed with development and progress. We are accustomed to reading books and newspapers once — children love to read and hear stories over and over for the pleasure and mastery of them. Tonia reads some of her comics dozens of times and my fear of her not progressing, getting better, showed in a snippy comment I once made to her about how bored she must be and couldn't she find something better to read. Her comeback stopped me: "How come you listen to that stupid guitar music over and over again? Can't you find something better?"

I think music is one of the few things most adults can take in over and over with pleasure. It is so basic to the rhythms of life that it has mostly been immune from our obsession with change. We can listen to a song or symphony many times, hear it new or feel comfortable hearing it in the same way. There is in the repetition pleasure that at its most powerful somehow engages our whole selves. I think it makes sense to think of listening to your favorite music over and over again, when you find yourself becoming impatient with your child practicing something over and over, learning nothing new for a while, simply letting the power of having mastered something sink in.

Practice is particularly important on the level of feelings and relations between people because that whole area of our beings is less stable and controllable than the physical or intellectual spheres. We can be confident that if we walk today we'll walk tomorrow, that 2+2 will remain 4. But it's not so certain that people will respond in the same way to one's smile or to an expression of anger or a gesture of affection. One has to practice with feelings. At the same time there is always the possibility that practicing and pretending will end up being the real thing. I've seen play arguments between children end up as the real thing and expressions of affection that were meant lightly as play taken seriously and intensely. Children have to develop a sense of the continuum of emotional responses, a sense of what responses are likely from what people. They have to integrate their responses into the whole of their lives, have to practice with anger to see that anger doesn't contaminate their whole being; practice loving and being loved at a safe distance. Dolls and toys and stuffed animals are the stuff out of which practice in the world of relations and feelings is constructed. Adults easily become impatient with fantasy play because it seems so childish and gratuitous. But it provides for children what theater provides for some adults — safe and yet serious explorations of feelings and relationships.

7. Stretching out

There are certain things one masters and then simply forgets about. Once walking is mastered, you don't have to think

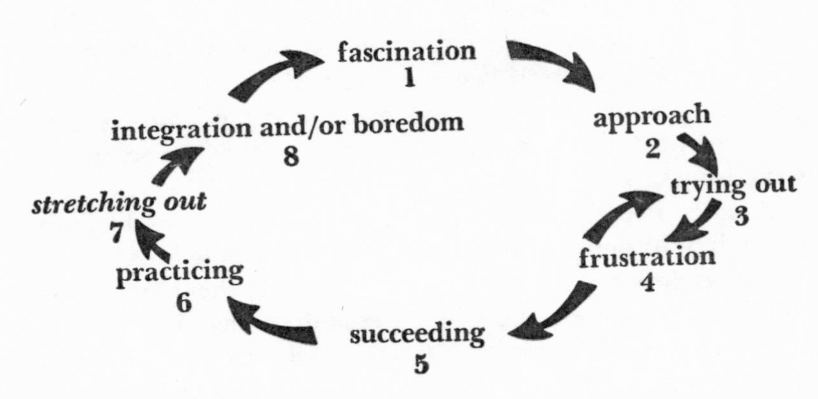

about whether you'll lose the skill or consciously practice how to walk. On the other hand, you can push that skill to discover the limits of its application, walking a bit more every day, going up the steepest hills you can find, even becoming a competitive walker. The simplest skills can be tested, stretched, pushed to limits. Tying shoe bows can turn into a fascination with knots, with ropes and rope tricks, with macramé or rope making, weaving. Emotional testing, which all children seem to do, can lead to many different limits — the limits of tolerance of other people, the limits of one's ability to control or predict other people's responses. In another way it can lead to obsession with expression and nuance of feeling, to a perception of and concern for the behavior of others that lead some people to psychology and others to art. I don't understand what ultimately leads one child to center life around developing physically and another toward developing as an artist or observer; what leads some people to music, others to painting, drawing, sculpting, building, science. However, it is possible to see preferences develop at an early age, to observe children feeling curious about certain aspects of reality and indifferent to others. It isn't possible to predict where the interests and obsessions might lead — the same obsessions can lead a person in many directions. As a child I was obsessed with putting models together and building things. This led me through teaching and writing to build books and create games. Other friends of mine with the same obsessions have become engineers and sculptors. The same holds true for children who draw well and become obsessed with line and color. This can lead anywhere from architecture to drafting to painting to design to a hobby that supplements a life devoted to something else.

There is not one best way of growing nor one most important aspect of experience to be obsessed with. There is no single route to a full adult life. Too many parents are obsessed with the idea that their children will lose out if they become obsessed with knots, or sports, or model building, or collecting, or drawing, or music. All of these activities are looked at as secondary to intellectual development. But these aspects of children's explorations are the very substance of young lives and the material out of which meaningful content develops in adult life.

Many children who are successful in school and are pushed so hard that they have no time to pursue their own interests suffer from boredom and emptiness. When nobody tells them what to do, they are lost. For them the price of academic success is a loss of internal motivation. I've known some adults who were pushed in that way as children and now at thirty-five or forty are trying to explore their own feelings and preferences so that for once in their lives they can do something because they want to do it and choose to do it. In the anxiety many of us sometimes feel about the academic success of our children, we forget what we might be taking from them.

Sometime watch a child exploring at a piano, or with a

pencil or piece of string, or at a sink full of water, or with paints or clay. At those moments there is no other world present. There is only the play of mind and hands and objects — sometimes randomly, sometimes with a plan or form that emerges from the activity, sometimes with a very specific goal in mind and sometimes with no goal at all. Often at those moments you can hear a child talking, either to himself, or to the objects, or to neither, the words being an embodiment of the thoughts passing through the mind or a mirror of the activity. Once or twice I've come upon a child lost in explorations and inadvertently commented, intruded myself into the experience. Each time the child looked startled, as if awakened from a trance, and then embarrassed as if caught naked.

Children should be supported in their explorations, followed in their obsessions, encouraged to pursue things and test the limits of what they can do. Developing skills and interests of almost any sort is a valuable strength that will enrich adult life no matter how silly or useless the skills or strengths may seem from a "serious" adult perspective. It is presumptuous to define what is significant and meaningful in your child's world, based on your notion of what will be useful in the future or of what is functional in contemporary adult society. I find it easier and more interesting to try to understand what my children find significant in their terms, and to understand that some activities are significant because they're fun — because shapes are interesting, water feels nice, colors are striking. One way I've managed to do this is by being childish myself, by playing with toys and games, by doodling and daydreaming, by writing and following the book where it takes me. I'm sure that one reason I enjoy teaching young children is that it gives me a legitimate adult excuse to keep my toys and keep playing.

8. Integration and/or boredom

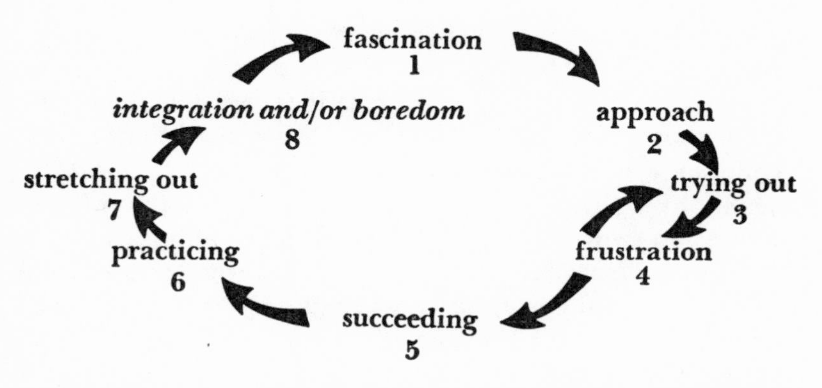

Of course not every skill will lead to exploration, and all the things children learn cannot be tested or stretched by any one child. Many of the things one learns are simply integrated into the everyday automatic functioning of life and do not have to be thought about except in times of particular crisis. Practice of a skill one has mastered becomes boring after a while. There's no big deal about being able to control one's bowels, tie one's shoes, show that one is angry, make breakfast, get dressed by oneself, walk or run or climb. One simply does these things at appropriate times. No matter how interminable the practice period seemed, it ends or is transformed into more complex activity.

As skills become integrated into everyday life, new challenges develop. Often obsessions with skills one has acquired disappear because new frustrations and fascinations develop. Sometimes old obsessions continue over a lifetime even as new frustrations and fascinations develop. Painting can be an obsession while swimming becomes a new fascination and frustration. Children often put aside and seem to forget things as they embark upon new learning. Learning to swim can make one temporarily forget art or reading or worrying about the feelings of others. It becomes the only thing for a while — sometimes causing great anxiety on the part of parents who feel more important things should be happening with their children. Sometimes parents react to these temporary and healthy obsessions as if they feared that their children would never be interested in anything else ever again. I've seen parents panicked because their children wanted to swim all the time instead of pursuing a summer reading program. But even swimming fever eases off and there are new things to learn and old skills to return to and use. Many different learning cycles can be occurring simultaneously with different time patterns. Mastery of a skill is followed by fascination with other things. Some learning cycles end and new ones begin.

Learning cycles. There are some short learning cycles, some extended cycles, and some recurrent cycles. *Short learning cycles* involve the acquisition of simple skills like learning to draw a face or recognize a single word or letter, or tie a knot, or pick up something, drop it, and pick it up again. Sometimes these skills are mastered in a day or hour or minute, sometimes it takes a week or so. Usually they are mastered without much thought or energy expended. At times they are acquired in quick bursts — as if a child had thought about them casually for a while and all of a sudden decided to plunge in and act. Many of these simple skills are parts of larger more *extended learning cycles* like learning to read or get dressed or swim. Some children seem to learn piecemeal, acquiring many discrete skills, going through many short learning cycles before integrating what has been learned into an overall skill. For example, some children learn to put on their pants, then their shirts, then socks, then shoes. Often they forget or neglect using one skill while acquiring another related one. On a given day you'll find these children putting on their shoes, socks, and pants but complaining that they're too tired to put on their shirts.

I remember when Josh was learning to dress himself. He seemed to concentrate so much energy on learning the nature of each item of clothing that he exasperated Judy and me with requests to help him do what we knew he had already learned. In retrospect he may have needed that regression and support. He's the kind of child who thinks everything through step-by-step, figures things out in his mind before trying them out in the world. When his mind was on shoes there was no energy left to deal with shirts — silly, sometimes annoying for adults, yet understandable. After a while he put all the parts together and getting dressed became ritual rather than learning. It made no difference that he spent time and thought on the process whereas other children may have learned more globally without much thought or energy expended.

There are global styles of learning where many things fall in place at the same time and there are slower step-by-step developmental styles. Both are used at different times, and for some people one style predominates. However, neither is better nor more indicative of creativity and intelligence. There are many ways to grasp the world. This is very important. Speed in learning is often mistaken for superiority in learning. If children walk, talk, or read early they are thought to be bright; if they walk, talk, or read late there is always the fear of retardation, slowness, dullness. Yet "early" and "late" are only adult categories. It makes no difference to how one walks as a five-year-old whether one learned to walk at ten months or eighteen months; it makes no difference to the depth with which one reads whether the skill was acquired at four or at eight. One has to fall in with and understand the rhythm of one's children's learning cycles, encourage and support them, and not worry too much about putting them on a comparative scale tied to specious ideas like "learning fast is learning best."

Throughout our lives there are *recurrent learning cycles* as well as short and extended ones. Some things like playing the piano, writing, understanding people, being able to love are not mastered in final ways. There are always more things to learn, revisions and corrections to make, experiments to perform, or experiences to integrate and make comprehensible. We all return periodically to the central questions of how to deal with anger and love, what to ask and expect of other people, the meaningfulness of our lives. We should prepare ourselves and our children to expect and welcome these learning cycles. Love, marriage, having children, getting old are all learning situations. They can be more easily dealt with if we expect them to make different demands on us and require us to go through the fascination, approach, trying out, frustration, mastery, practice, and testing that we can so clearly see our children going through. We need the same patience with learning in our adult lives that we had as young children. As adults we have to learn many difficult and serious things. The psychologists and educators who claim that almost all the learning in life is accomplished before we are five or six years old contribute to an impoverished vision of life that disarms us for strong and healthy adulthood. One gift we can give our children is to help them understand that living and learning are so close as to be almost synonymous; that being an adult doesn't mean that you don't have to learn anything anymore but rather that what you can learn will be more complex and potentially more rewarding. The strongest way this understanding can be conveyed to children is by sharing what you are learning with them and by taking the time on occasion to talk about how you go about dealing with a new situation. It's also fun and helpful to tackle a new task with your children — to learn how to play a new game or repair your car or build furniture together. There is no better way to demystify learning and make children relaxed with trying new and difficult things than to let them watch as you fumble your way to mastery of something. Sometimes a common challenge is fun too — a jigsaw puzzle or some elaborate construction that has to be taken apart and reassembled. Often children are better at those things than adults and can see, working on a common task, that they learn in the same way as adults, and moreover that all people make mistakes as part of learning. As a consequence of learning with adults instead of just from them, children can be encouraged to try new things without worrying too much about making mistakes. They can understand that a lot of fumbling and guessing and approximating goes into learning how to do something difficult and that these are simply normal ways of developing mastery.

It's particularly important that as parents we encourage and support our children as they grope to learn something difficult because in school they usually don't get that kind of support. I remember talking to some children who were having a hard time in school. One of them told me he was terrified of writing anything in class because he was sure there'd be mistakes and he'd be criticized for it. His fear was typical — children are afraid to make mistakes in the classroom because they believe they'll be marked down for them, and worse, believe that those marks are signs of their personal worth. It's ironic that this way of dealing with mistakes discourages learning instead of promoting it. I believe that we should encourage our children to be bold and not afraid to make mistakes. That is the only way they'll be able to learn things for themselves and not confuse learning with doing what someone else makes them do or grades them on.

There are other ways we can support and strengthen children as they face problems and challenges. At times patience is called for, lying back and letting your child experience pain and frustration. On the other hand, there are times when children ask for help, when they want you to do something for them or with them or want you to hold their hands and be near them when they attempt something they find threatening or difficult. At these times it is cruel to refuse help. I've known people who consider requests for help or company signs of weakness on the part of their children. Instead of being nurturing, they lecture on how they managed without that kind of help, and how it's necessary to be hard. Yet hardness shouldn't be confused with strength. Hardness is a bitter assaulting attitude toward things, an aggressive stance that takes learning as a battle, and the development of skill as a conquest. It cuts out the appreciation of the skill itself, the fascination and play with what has been learned, that makes the effort to learn worthwhile. A hard attitude implies finding new battles, and not strengthening one's understanding of the world and one's own capacities. Children don't want to be hardened, to turn into fighters. There are times when they want adults to sit with them or to do something first so that they have a model to imitate. These are times when parents are asked to be active teachers — to show, explain, demonstrate, dissect, display, perform. It can be both a personal pleasure and a gift to your children to teach them, to let them understand that people do help each other and support each other — that the strength of one person can be used to help another.

There are also times when neither patience nor assistance is appropriate. Every once in a while a child builds up a terror of doing something bordering on a phobia — it might be swimming, or climbing, or falling down, or riding a bike, or drawing. At times nothing you try — guiding, doing it yourself, encouragement, patience — works. At those times it sometimes helps to force the issue a bit, to take the child into the water even though he or she is screaming, to put her on a bike and walk her around, to sit him down and force him to look at a book. Sometimes just pushing and at the same time being there, saying firmly *both* "I'm making you do this" *and* "I know you can do it," works.

There is no formula for determining the best way to respond to your child at every moment. All of the responses mentioned above have to be used with judgment and sensitivity. One thing is on our side as parents as we grope for the appropriate strengthening responses to our children — mistakes are not fatal if made with goodwill and readily admitted.

What is important for us is to admit the mistakes we make and learn from them. As our children grow and learn to deal with the world we have to learn how to be parents. Probably the greatest anxieties and grossest mistakes we all make with children are with the oldest of our children, because we are learning the most. Still, it's not fatal nor even particularly serious if we are strong and loving enough to keep from interpreting our mistakes as our children's failures.

The Development of Intellectual Strength

Strength comes from self-discipline and the ability and courage to learn new things. In the intellectual sphere specifically, it consists of the ability to focus one's mind on a problem, analyze different aspects of it, understand how these fit together, and then develop and test a number of solutions. It also has to do with understanding how things work and relate to each other, or how they might relate to each other. This involves fantasy and imagination as well as focused critical thought and the ability to organize information.

Intellectual strength is not an ability that is acquired once and then applied. It is learned, and develops throughout life as it is used. The strength of one's mind cannot be separated from the exercise of it. There are certain techniques and strategies children use as they explore the world with their minds, strategies and techniques not very different from those employed in adult thought. It is worth examining some of these and speculating on ways we can encourage and nurture our children's intellectual growth.

Children's questions. One of the earliest manifestations of the development of intelligence is questioning. In order to appreciate the importance of questioning, try to imagine a language that does not have questions. In such a language you could describe experiences, express your wishes and needs, but ask nothing either of yourself or others, or of the world. Your relationships would be limited to making demands, expressing needs, and describing things. You wouldn't be able to get other people to focus on your problems or ask them to explain and teach things. It would be practically impossible to articulate to yourself what you wanted to find out or where the source of a problem was. Questioning adds a whole dimension to experience — it is a major extension of the self. Words such as *what, when, who, where, why,* and *how* provide you with a means of focusing on people and things, and examining these as a means of bringing them under control or of understanding their nature.

Children as they reach out and try to make sense of the world use language as one way of focusing on particular problems or puzzles or experiences. The questioning mode develops very early. Words such as *mama* or *dada, baby* or *papa* are questions as well as assertions. "Baby" could mean "Is there a me you all call baby? Do you refer to the same person each time?" as much as the simple assertive "Me." "Mama" and "dada" are probably used as questions as well as assertions and demands. A baby sees a person, says "Mama" and waits for a response. It takes a while to sort out mama from the other creatures. The question "Are you Mama?" the demand "Mama, come here!" and the simple descriptive "That's my Mama" are all expressed by the word *mama.* The way the word is said usually indicates what's intended. Babies use and respond to inflection and tone, understand when something is asked of them before they can use words that specifically denote the questioning mode. They question before they master the use of words like *how, where,* and *why.*

Questions strengthen the sense children have of themselves and provide guidelines for investigating the world. They also provide ways of challenging others and comparing what one feels and perceives with the feelings and perceptions of others.

There are many different types of questions that can be asked in our language, among them the following central types:

where — referring to place
who — referring to person
how — referring to mechanical cause or structure
why — referring to will, intent, reason
when — referring to time
what — referring to function or description.

These six types of question focus on space, time, causality, structure, description, persons, will, reason, function — the major questions that philosophy, religion, art, and science deal with. They are instruments we use to make our experiences comprehensible and coherent.

Children, as their worlds expand, try to integrate what they experience and make sense of the world. These questions are guidelines for integration and are posed to others and to themselves as well. Two-, three-, four-, and five-year-olds can often be overheard asking questions to themselves and answering them, or questioning their toys and responding in different voices.

It takes a while to clarify the difference among "what," "where," "why," "who," "when," and "how." The words have to be tested out and often become confused. Children sometimes ask, for example, "When did I get born?" when they mean "How did I get born?" or "Where did I get born?" or "Why does the car go?" when they mean "How does the car go?" or "Who makes the car go?"

Sometimes the persistence of children's questioning drives adults to distraction. Often this happens when adults don't understand the particular question intended because the wrong questioning word has been used. It's important to be aware that questions may be badly formulated when children first experiment with mastering these different forms. Questions such as:

Where does wind come from?
Why is the grass green?
How is there a sky?
What is far?
When did the day start?
Who made the dog?

may actually be:

Why is there so much wind today?

How come the grass is green now when it used to be brown?

Did anyone make the sky?

How far away does something have to be to call it far instead of near?

What time did you get up today?

Who bought the dog?

There are, of course, other possible interpretations of these questions, and sometimes simply rephrasing the question or answering what you believe is intended will be satisfactory in most situations. However, there are times when children mean exactly what they say — when they ask unanswerable questions or questions whose answers are too difficult for them to understand. They try to discover the kinds of answers adults find satisfactory as well as the points at which adults are faced by questions they can't answer. There are times when questions are asked as much to find out about the nature of questions and answers as to answer particular questions.

Children try to figure out what a "how" answer is, and how it differs from, say, a "why" or "what" answer. These aspects of questioning have to be learned. For that reason there are questions that are formulated just to see how adults respond. It's not always easy to figure out whether a question is serious but impossible to answer, or simply an attempt to see how an adult will respond to a particular way of wording a question.

I've found that the best way to deal with persistent questioning is:

(1) be patient;

(2) make the answer as specific as you can and wait for a child to respond to your answer;

(3) listen carefully to his or her response and try to figure out if you answered the wrong question, didn't

answer enough, or weren't really asked a serious question;

(4) at that point either rephrase the question, elaborate on the answer, or drop the issue. At times you may simply claim ignorance and let children know the limits of your understanding. It's foolish to try to explain what you really don't know in order to keep up before a child some image of yourself as strong and knowledgeable.

If the questions seem to go on forever, that is often a sign to shift focus. Usually when this happens to me, I'll get a beer or offer the child some juice or suggest we play a game or take a walk.

I remember a conversation we recently had around the dinner table. Josh wanted to know why water didn't fall off the bottom of the earth. I tried to explain that the earth was round and there was no up and down in the usual sense. Judy mentioned gravity. I talked about the earth spinning. Tonia and Erica elaborated on gravity and the roundness of the earth. Naturally the first questions led to other questions: What is gravity? Why does it pull? How does the earth spin around? Does it make noise when it moves through the air? How come we don't see or feel or hear it spinning? As we tried to explain as much as we could, two things began to happen. First, our explanations were getting thinner and thinner — the limits of our understanding of these physical phenomena were being approached. Second, the questions began to get a bit silly and the children began to squirm and laugh. They had more answers than they could absorb at one time. In order to change the subject, I made some joke about whether the dessert would fall off the table, which switched the focus back to food. That, of course, didn't answer all the questions, but it didn't close any of them. The children will return to them many times in the future. Meanwhile, I've got a bit of research to do.

The ability to pose proper questions is an invaluable intellectual strength. Questions clarify what a person doesn't know, and the willingness to admit and focus on what one doesn't know is an important defense against stupidity. I've seen children in school afraid to raise questions or admit that they didn't understand a problem or couldn't read a word. My initial feeling was to blame the fear on the atmosphere set up by the teacher, but that isn't always the case. One day one of Erica's friends was having a hard time learning a game, so I asked her if she needed help. She got very sharp with me and told me she knew the game, that it was too easy for her and she was just pretending to have trouble. I merely said that if she did happen to need help I'd be around. The next day she asked me if I'd really help her learn the game. I said, "Of course" and asked whether other grown-ups don't help her, too. She answered, "No, they just test me. They think I already have to know."

Children can easily be confounded and become closed if questions are constantly turned into tests, if adult responses are like some of these I've overheard:

CHILD:	"How do you spell 'opinion'?"	ADULT:	"Guess" or "Look it up" or "You should know that."
CHILD:	"How much is a nickel and two pennies?"	ADULT:	"Didn't you learn that in school yet?" or "Can't you count?"
CHILD:	"How far is the store?"	ADULT:	"I told you that yesterday. Do you have such a short memory?"

Some adults ask testing questions all the time. Often doing this intimidates their children and leads them to assuming rigid fearful attitudes toward questioning and learning new things. For example, questions like these are often asked in an aggressive and testing manner rather than posed to help a child reach out and grasp the world:

"Can you read as well as Susan?"

"How do your friends deal with their money?"

"What do you think I do when I can't spell a word?"

"Why don't you practice so you can be as good as Sally?"

A distinction has to be made between questioning and testing. Questioning occurs when one doesn't know something, or has an idea or a hunch. Testing occurs in order to find out what someone knows or doesn't know. Questioning freely assumes that there is nothing wrong with not knowing something; testing assumes that lack of knowledge is a form of inferiority.

It is essential for people, young and old, to be able to face freely what they don't know; to feel that by asking questions they will open up routes to knowledge and strength to themselves rather than reveal ignorance and weakness. It is crucial that children understand that not knowing everything is simply a condition of life for all people.

Unfortunately many adults don't feel comfortable seeming imperfect in front of their children. They cover their mistakes and can't talk about them, fearing that their children will lose respect for them if they seem fallible. But respect has more to do with honesty than with fallibility, and more to do with the ability to confront problems than with the attempt to conceal them. It is strengthening for children to be able to talk with adults about what adults don't know. It is equally important for children to see how not knowing can be turned into a challenge rather than an attack on one's self-esteem.

Children who feel confident challenge people who seem to be wrong, and hold to their questions until they are convinced. This ability is necessary for the development of a critical intelligence. If fear and anxiety pervade one's thoughts, if testing pushes out questions, then what is accepted as knowledge will depend upon intimidation. By questioning and being questioned, a child learns how to deal with criticizing in order to build strength rather than tear something down.

In order to question well and weigh answers, there is one other necessary component — one has to be able to appreciate and respect the skills and knowledge of others. Jealousy interferes with learning. Just the other day I overheard two boys talking. One was eight and the other six. The eight-year-old was commenting on how well the six-year-old was playing ball. The six-year-old said that he really wasn't doing that well, that his friend Jim played much better than he did. He added that Jim was teaching him and that's why he was getting better. There was admiration for Jim in his voice, and clear appreciation for being taught by someone who knew what he was doing. The absence of jealousy in his description was striking. I've almost become accustomed to the seething sound children use to describe someone who does something better than they do. This sound represents the antithesis of curiosity and learning. We don't express unadulterated admiration very often. If a person is talented in one area, we put him down for failings in another. We look for faults, try to measure ourselves against everyone, and often come away feeling insignificant. Our children see this, learn that adults often claim infallibility and confidence and just as often act weakly and defensively. Too often we pass our wounds on. For the sake of our children and the enrichment of ourselves we have to learn to question openly as our children can question, and we have to learn to admire the strengths of others without constantly taking a measure of ourselves.

Developing answers. Children often come up with unexpected answers and explanations that appear silly or cute to adults yet make sense on the basis of the children's own understanding and experience. Last year Josh spent a month teaching himself how to swim. Judy and I encouraged him to relax in the water and demonstrated to him how we floated and swam in a relaxed way. No matter what we did, he wouldn't relax. One day he explained to us that he couldn't relax in the water or he'd fall asleep and drown. That explanation seemed weird until a few nights later when Josh was having a hard time falling asleep. I caught myself advising him to relax in the same tone and language I used at the pool. He had assimilated these experiences and reasoned quite sensibly that if relaxing made you sleep at one time it would do the same thing at another time. The next day at the pool, I explained to him that there were different kinds of relaxing and said he was right in worrying at first since I didn't make myself clear. A few days later he dunked himself and got on with the business of swimming.

Often children guess at answers to questions. They try to puzzle out things for themselves based on their mastery of language, their experiences, and their understanding of what other people say. Sometimes these guesses generate answers that aren't the same as those accepted in the adult world:

"Fog is like steam, so it must be caused by a fire somewhere."

"Some adult is crying, so someone must have hit them or maybe they fell."

"All animals think and feel exactly the way people do."

"The bank gives you money."

Many children's answers are approximations, guesses, hypotheses about the way the world is. They are not properly speaking wrong, and often need further explanation. It isn't appropriate to flatly contradict what a child says and then give the correct adult response. Usually it makes more sense to ask for further clarification, or respond by praising the intelligence of the approximation and adding further information if it is called for. When a child says, for example, "Cars go by themselves," this can mean any number of different things ranging from a sense that cars don't need to be pulled or pushed (you can't see the motor, and a child might not know cars have motors), or that cars can go without being told to go, or that cars are like people and might be able to function all by themselves since they're not plugged in or attached to anything and are often talked about as if they were people. None of these answers is strictly wrong—they are intelligent guesses, attempts to make analogies from different areas of experience and generalize from limited experience. To reject these answers and simply make a "correct statement" is to take the risk of making your children afraid to appear silly or wrong in adult eyes. This can have the consequence of their trying to parrot adult responses rather than using their minds to figure things out. The magic of the mind is that it does make bold guesses and can be self-correcting. We should encourage this stretching out.

It is wonderful to engage in conversation with children who are not afraid to guess at answers. They usually don't have deep stakes in their answers, which seem to be part of an internal dialogue. If you ask them to explain themselves, you might be rewarded by seeing the world in new ways yourself. Children, for example, try to figure out how things are made when we take them for granted. I remember questions like "How is ink made?" "What types in a typewriter?" "How does a whole book come out of a pen?" "Where do the wheels on a car come from?" "Who gets the money you give in a store?" "Where do the people go when the TV is shut off?" "Where is the voice in a tape recorder?"

Children not only ask these questions but make up answers to them, which is more than we do. Many children's questions challenge us to learn more or rethink our ideas.

There is an extension of guessing that children make use of in developing answers, and that is fantasy. They hold imaginary dialogues, imagine themselves flying or inside machines, fantasize secret powers. If they want to swim or ride horses or fly or drive cars, they can, as my children call it, do it in their heads. They can work out a problem in their heads, imagine and practice fights and reconciliations, trips, games, roles. They can farm and build and live in their own homes and have jobs. Fantasy and imagination are central parts of young lives and the boundaries among what is real, what is possible, and what is impossible are not clear.

I tell my children a story about Mimi, Tutu, and Jha, three children with magical powers who are looked after by a formless power named Overall, who has female and male characteristics, can take any form it chooses, and speaks Yiddish. These stories have been going on for at least five years. Usually the demand for them is greatest when our family is on vacation together. I can't remember most of the stories, but among the three children no detail seems to have been lost. Tonia knows it's just a story, but she recently told me that when she was younger she couldn't tell whether it was real or not. Erica still isn't sure, though she knows she isn't really Mimi. Josh has to be reassured at times that he isn't really Jha since occasionally he dreams about Jha. Sometimes the story becomes so compelling that the children seem to live it.

I never know where the story will go and find that some active fantasies of mine take over and stories focus on problems the children have with each other or I have with them or my work. There isn't a plan — the stories begin with a problem like Overall forgetting how to write, or Mimi, Tutu, and Jha visiting their grandparents, or the quest for new enemies and secret powers, or dealing with other children with other magical powers who try to hurt them. I follow the story wherever it goes and often the children contribute as much as I do — speak as Mimi, Tutu, and Jha and make decisions for them. We are engaged in collective fantasy making and problem solving at the same time. This is the closest I get to the fantasy games with dolls and toys children play all the time.

A number of parents worry about their children's fantasies, and about all the imaginary friends and creatures and situations they seem occupied with. The usual complaint is that their children will stay removed from reality, won't be able to cope in the real hard world, but will become accustomed to retreating into fantastical or imaginary worlds. It is true that some people are driven so far out of the everyday world that all that sustains them is fantasy and imagination. But the word *driven* is the important one. Most children are not driven out of their everyday worlds, though all of them have problems dealing with that world. Adaptation to the world as given is one possible response; imagining better worlds and learning to change the given one is another. However, even in the best of worlds fantasy and imagination should be nurtured. They are great sources of personal pleasure and powerful problem-solving techniques. There are times when no rational and analytic approach leads to a solution, where things have to be stood on their heads or turned inside out or placed in different worlds. Resolving human conflicts, developing caring social organizations, inventing new ways of dealing with energy, and with our environment, and making technology work for people all require fantasy and imagination as much as analysis and technical knowledge. We have to reawaken them in ourselves as well as to nurture them in our children.

Storytelling. A magical part of childhood is listening to stories and making up and telling stories oneself. I've never met a child who couldn't be captured by a story and who didn't also have some story to tell. Stories transport children into worlds they hadn't imagined existed, provide ways of testing out relationships and feelings, and of identifying with the weak and powerful, the beautiful and ugly, the loved and the rejected peoples of the world. They also provide bonds between children and adults. While listening to a story, children give themselves over to the teller — the listening and telling create a closeness that goes beyond the story itself. Often when I tell stories to children, I can feel love coming from them that is transformed somehow into the energy that goes into making and telling the story. If you can do very little else with your children because of the circumstances of your life, I suggest you find a way to tell them stories in the evenings when you do see them. The gift of your voice is greater than anything you can give them materially and more lasting.

Many people feel they don't know how to tell stories or read them in any interesting manner. However, you don't have to be an actor to convince a child to listen to your stories. There is no good or bad, just the story and the warmth generated by the telling of it. If you feel very awkward, don't know where to begin, read *A Treasury of African Folklore,* edited by Harold Courlander (Crown, New York);

A Harvest of World Folk Tales, edited by Milton Rugoff (Viking/Compass Books, New York); *A Treasury of American Folklore,* edited by B. A. Botkin (Crown, New York), and pick out a story you like. Tell it. If you're too shy to tell it, read and don't worry about whether your child will understand every word. If the language begins to bog you down, stop reading and elaborate yourself or ask your children what they think happened. Start with short stories, ones that can be told at a single time, and move on to what we call in our family "chapter stories," the kind that end "to be continued."

Another source of stories is the ones you might remember from your childhood. Try to bring up a few of those and tell them. Also ask your parents, if they're still alive, to refresh your memory or tell you stories they remember from their parents.

Every once in a while suggest that your children tell you stories. If they don't know where to begin or say they're too shy, it helps to ask them what their favorite story is and ask them to tell that to you. You can also ask if they would retell one of the stories you told them. There's no need to push the issue; if the first time you make the suggestion, there's no response, go on to your story and come back to the suggestion in a week or so. Often children will come back to it before you do; they'll have thought about a story and practiced it in order to surprise you.

Storytelling is one of the first exercises in extended thinking for children. They have to think in terms of sequences, put parts together in an order that makes sense, move through an action. At first for three-, four-, and five-year-olds it's not that easy. They forget parts, get things in the wrong order, make up new parts of the story to make sense out of the jumbled order. It takes patience to listen to these efforts at drama and coherence. Sometimes it's best to lie back and let a child struggle through; at other times you have to offer help if anxiety seems to be building up. The thing to watch for is signs of fatigue — stumbling, stuttering, clenched fists, tears about to flow. Sometimes a simple reminder is all a child needs to finish a story. At other times the situation can be rescued by suggesting that at any point your child would like it, you'll finish the story.

Being told stories, being read stories, telling stories yourself, and pretending that you're reading them provide a strong intellectual foundation for children. It expands their sense of the world, enables them to develop their capacity to think logically and put things in order at the same time that it uses fantasy and imagination. It is an integrating experience and one that prepares children to think things through for themselves, carry on an extended argument, and tie many threads and themes together into a single fabric.

Making models. Making models is both a childhood hobby and one of the most powerful and sophisticated of adult intellectual techniques. Children make models by building things that are structurally similar to things actually used by adults. Making a model can consist of building a car out of Lego blocks, making a walkie-talkie out of a piece of wood and a nail, building a city out of blocks or sugar cubes, making a movie camera out of a shoebox. Most of the models children make have some function in their worlds. You don't merely make a car or walkie-talkie or a movie camera — you have to use it in play, to model adult activity. Creating these models and articulating them into games often involves considerable thought and ingenuity. It involves taking what is at hand and transforming it rather than expecting everything to come ready-made and store-bought. It's good to keep a scrap box and a set of tools around for children to use. A carton full of wheels, plastic scraps, fabric, nails, nuts and bolts, rubber bands, cardboard, buttons, cans, and boxes makes a wonderful toy box. Glue, a hammer and a screwdriver, a coping saw, a pair of pliers, several paintbrushes and watercolors, scissors, a small stapler, masking tape, some spoons, and perhaps a knife can be stored in a fishing tackle box and provide all the tools children need.

Many parents worry about four-, five-, and six-year-olds using tools. I was reluctant to let my children use knives or saws, but Judy persuaded me to let the children try and not hover about them nervously when they were working. I tried a few times and realized that if the material is soft enough (balsa wood, cardboard, thin pine, Styrofoam), children can handle knives and saws if they are given some basic information like how to hold the handle and which part of the blade is sharp (something I discovered many children don't know).

Drawing and sketching. There is one particular form of model making that is common to young children and the most sophisticated mathematicians and scientists — and that is drawing and sketching. The importance of these activities is hard to underestimate, and yet in school, drawing and sketching are relegated to "art" and are not considered basic skills. It is worthwhile considering these skills, which also represent ways of thinking and modeling, in some detail.

If you observe children drawing or painting for any length of time you'll be able to discern two fundamentally different kinds of activities. At times children will struggle to make something look right. They will have a goal in mind — to make a circle or a face or a house or a rainbow or a tree. The entire effort will be focused on developing some representation that will satisfy them.

Other times the painting or drawing will be more of an open-ended activity, the development of a theme or the telling of a story. I've seen children draw a person, add someone else, and develop a conversation between them while adding more to the picture, perhaps drawing a house around one of the people and then completely coloring the figure over, putting it to sleep by drawing a night sky, setting the house on fire, drawing a fire engine, drawing water all over the page until there's nothing recognizable in the scene. To someone who looked at the finished product rather than witnessed its development, the work would be a hopeless mess, a failure.

Both of these forms of using visual images contribute to the development of intelligence. Trying to get a drawing to look like something in the world helps children organize what they see and coordinate what they see with what they can describe. Letting a story flow in visual form is a form of problem solving, of working out relationships and adding and subtracting elements until a resolution emerges.

Children benefit from having paper and pencils and pens available as they grow up and from being encouraged to continue drawing as they get older. There is so much that can be done with a pencil and blank paper — sketching a person or object, drawing a comic strip, making a working diagram of a machine, developing fantasies in visual form. Four- and five- and six-year-olds have no problems trying to draw monsters, airplanes, people they know, places they visit, and places they imagine. As school sets in and children are expected to become more like adults, there is rarely any time left to draw — especially if doing so is not considered serious work in school and if one's parents don't draw either. The atrophy of visual sensibility is characteristic of many young people, who by twelve or thirteen don't look at things, are often afraid to draw anything or even describe how something or someone looks. There are a number of ways to encourage drawing— one, of course, to draw yourself. Other than that there are a number of How-To-Draw books that young children enjoy using:

The Big Yellow Drawing Book by Dan O'Neill, Marian O'Neill, H. D. O'Neill, Jr. (Hugh O'Neill Associates, Box 1297, Nevada City, California 95959).

How to Draw Cartoons by Syd Hoff (Scholastic Book Services, New York).

Ed Emberley's Drawing Book of Animals by Ed Emberley (Little, Brown and Company, Boston). Emberley has done many other drawing books, all published by Little, Brown. My favorite is a small paperback entitled *Ed Emberley's Little Drawing Book of Weirdos.*

How to Draw Monsters, by Larry Evans (Troubador Press, San Francisco). For young people who can read and have spent time drawing.

One caution about using these books — they do not and cannot teach *the* way to draw. They provide techniques and tricks that are useful, but the eye above all teaches drawing. If techniques acquired in books aren't informed by a personal eye and sensibility, drawing becomes merely copying, a repeating of other people's models without regard for what one sees or wants to represent. For these reasons, getting several different books, which have different styles and different approaches to drawing, is a sensible strategy. Then there won't be a single model. Children with many models to learn drawing from practice over and over to get each right, and then feel free to use and change whatever they care to.

The second type of drawing — what might be called action-thinking drawing — is hardly encouraged at all and usually degenerates into doodling or manifests itself as elaborate war pictures or superhero stories. The reason why it is probably not developed in any way is that it doesn't lead to a final picture but is open-ended play on paper. I remember doing thousands of drawings like that and have watched my children and students do it, too. And I've noticed something else that leads me to believe it is an important intellectual activity. All the mathematicians and most scientists I know work with pencil and paper or chalk and chalkboards. The same is true of other people whose work involves organizing a lot of materials or exploring ideas or developing models for complex phenomena. Sketching and drawing become part of the thinking and organizing process. Let me give several simple examples:

(1) When you set up a problem, it is often easiest to draw a picture of the conditions given as you plan a strategy for solving it. A math problem might say: Imagine three sets, one with five objects, one with six objects, and one with two objects. The first two have two objects in common, the last has no objects in common with either of the other sets. This situation can be condensed into this drawing:

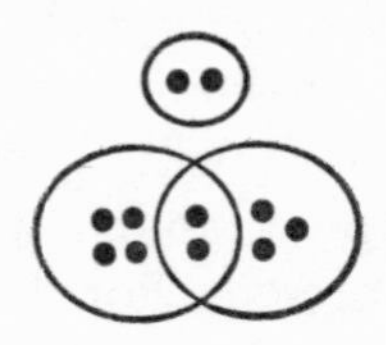

(2) When you have a lot of material to organize and the relationship of the parts to each other isn't clear, a visual representation of the situation is very useful. For example, when I was thinking about the aspects of learning, I began with this list of different activities that seemed relevant:
Then I started drawing arrows between phases that seemed to represent similar ideas:
From this initial grouping I ended up with eight headings,

boredom **mastery**

frustration **interest**

practice **getting close**

trying something out **sniffing around**

approach **figuring out**

testing **pushing an idea**

stretching out

which I wrote randomly on a piece of paper and then tried to organize according to which activity preceded which other activities:

I came up with this cycle, which, when straightened out and thought through, became the structure of the section on learning.

(3) In planning a trip there are always a number of factors to be considered. It is possible to write down all the aspects of the trip — time, money, where you want to go, how much you want to take with you, how little you could get along with — and draw up a plan. This approach is more global than trying to set out things in final order right off. It lets you see all the factors you can think of, and to move things around, make adjustments, erase, add, reconsider — think with a pencil in hand and an eraser on the table.

(4) Imagine planning to build your own house. What

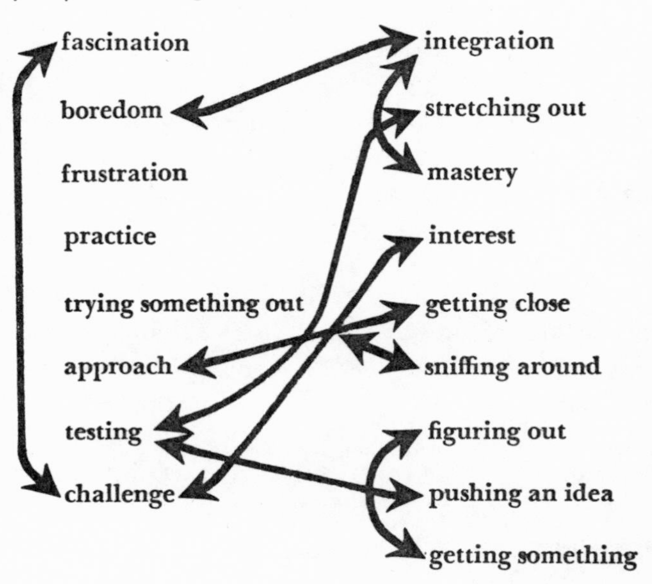

factors are important: what do you want, what are your resources, what ways can things be organized? The value of sketching is that there is no final commitment, that many sketches can be made, many opinions considered before developing a final plan.

Children can benefit by being encouraged to think at times with a pencil and paper — by being able to map or sketch out something that seems too difficult or complex for them to keep in their minds. This strategy for children is not much different from drawing an organization chart, developing a flow diagram, or sketching out a diagram representing the structure of a society. Here are some examples of how this might develop.

(1) A child has twenty-five cents to spend and wants to buy comic books, a small toy, gum, candy. Every attempt to explain that twenty-five cents won't do it all might be resisted

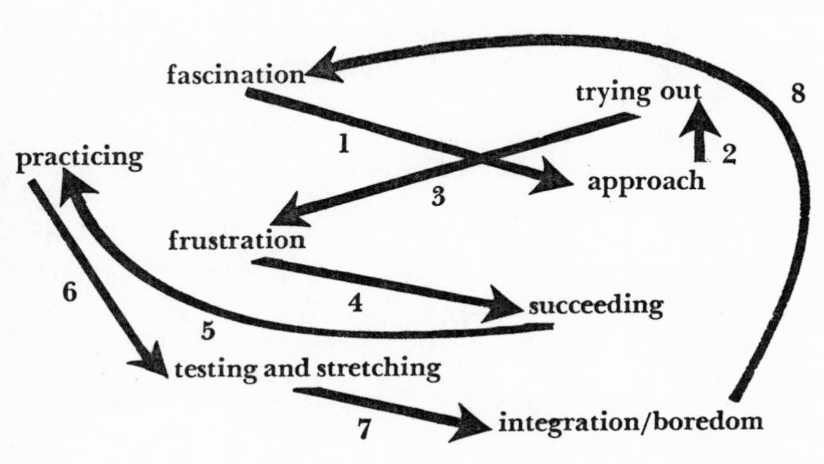

— either because the child doesn't want to hear or can't keep all the factors organized in his or her mind. A drawing is a useful aid to thinking through the problem:

25¢ = ooooooooooooooooooooooooo

Comic = ooooo	Gum = oo	Toy = ooooo
ooooo		ooooo
ooooo	Candy = oooo	ooooo
ooooo	ooo	
ooooo	ooo	

By drawing arrows, filling in the circles, or using a number of other techniques, a child can see what the possibilities are. The phrase "I see" often means "I understand" in English, and for many of us things do become clarified when we can see a drawing, map, plan.

(2) Two children have to share a room. How is it to be organized? The furniture can be moved around as the children discover how they want to organize their room. Some-

times moving it here and there isn't possible, and models or drawings can help clarify what people would like.

(3) There are times when children would like adults to build a certain structure for them or make them a particular mask or cape. Often the words used to describe exactly what is wanted aren't adequate. Asking children to draw a picture of what they want often avoids a lot of frustration and clarifies for the children themselves as well as for an adult what they want.

(4) Sometimes a four- or five-year-old wants to tell a very complex story and finds her words inadequate. She acts as if she has thought out exactly what she wants to say, but it all comes out wrong or disorganized. Drawing often helps here too — children can with great ease tell a story they have drawn. The pictures provide an underpinning to the words and ideas.

The older children grow, the more they need devices such as drawing and sketching problems, writing out conditions and attempting to organize them, sketching or planning out a paper or a story, making a diagram of the conditions of a problem. Unfortunately, though these devices are used easily and thought natural for young children, and somehow persist for a small number of creative adults, they are lost in school and not something we as parents think or know about. Yet I believe they are invaluable aids to problem solving in almost all areas of life. There are a few books that go into the specific aspects of using visualization and drawing as techniques of problem solving, and they are worth looking at.

Visualizing and drawing as thinking:

Thinking with a Pencil, by Henning Nelms (Barnes & Noble, New York).

Lateral Thinking, by Edward de Bono (Harper & Row, New York).

Children Solve Problems, by Edward de Bono (Harper & Row, New York).

Playing strategy games. Strategy games are powerful aids to intellectual growth. These games are ones that do not depend upon chance devices such as dice and spinners, but involve the players in choosing their moves and developing overall strategies for the games. A simple and familiar strategy game is tic-tac-toe. However, there are dozens of such games that children four years old and older love to play, and that two- and three-year-olds love to mess around with and pretend to play. Spending a little time teaching and playing these games is a good way to help strategic thinking develop. These games develop concentration and the ability to think ahead and to anticipate another person's move, and provide a challenge to develop and perfect these skills over a period of time.

If you don't play many strategy games yourself, there is a wonderful opportunity for you to sit down and learn a game with your children. Here's a list of games and books on games with an indication of the youngest age at which children seem to be able to handle them:

Chess:

An excellent beginning book for adults is J. R. Capablanca's *Chess Fundamentals* (David McKay Co., New York). There are also two good books for young children: *Chess for Young Beginners,* by William T. McLeod and Roland Mongredion (Golden Press) and *Chess for Children Step by Step* by Grand Master William Lombardy and Bette Marshall (Little, Brown, Boston). I see no reason why six- and seven-year-olds can't learn chess. It is a matter of helping them to become familiar with the moves and realizing that the goal of the game is to kill the king. If your children can't read any of these books, learn how to play the game yourself and teach your child how to play as you learn.

Go:

Introductory book: *Stepping Stones to Go* (Tuttle, Rutland, Vermont).

Diplomacy:

This is available as a commercial game.

Checkers

Mancala (or Wari or Ayo):

Perhaps the most popular game in the world, played from the southern tip of Africa through Asia and to the Philippine Islands. The best introduction is in Claudia Zaslavsky's book *Africa Counts* (Prindle, Weber, and Schmidt, 55 State St., Boston 02109).

In addition to these games there are three wonderful books of paper and pencil games created by Sid Sackson and published in paperback by Pantheon Books, New York: *Beyond Tic Tac Toe, Beyond Solitaire, Beyond Words.*

I don't know the youngest age the books can be used with. I like to try everything with a young child, and if some game is too complex for the children I'm with, I try to simplify the game on the spot. For some ways of making up and simplifying games my book *Math, Writing and Games* (Review-Vintage, New York) might be interesting.

Also, Cynthia Brown and Ray Nitta's book *How to Make Your Own Educational Materials* has many interesting strategy games as well as instructions on how to make puzzles, bind books, and set up a work space in your house or garage so you can make materials for your children instead of buying them. The book is also available from P.O. Box 9434, Berkeley, California 94709.

Understanding other people's ideas. One afternoon I had a long loud argument with a friend over whether economic growth should be limited on ecological grounds. My children were in the room, half playing, half listening. When my friend left I commented to Judy that he was wrongheaded, stupid, and uninformed. Erica ran up to me and objected: "But Herb, Mike is nice. He can't be wrong."

Nice people have correct ideas; mean people have wrong ideas. Young children often accept foolish or dangerous ideas because of this identification. It's natural to want to believe someone you like or feel that someone who has been mean to you is stupid. However, experience is more complex. In this case Tonia and Erica liked Mike but they also liked me. Our ideas are completely opposite in the area we were fighting over. I use the word "fighting" because the issues were not frivolous and we both acted on the basis of our analysis and beliefs. I tried to explain this to the girls and they had to struggle with the notion of two people liking and respecting each other and yet disagreeing so strongly. Erica's first response was "You mean we shouldn't like Mike anymore," but she caught herself. "No, it's more like what you said: You and Mike are two different . . ." The words weren't there, so she tried an example and asked if it were like arguing over which movie you wanted to go to or which color was prettier. She said some students in her school argued over food all the time, made fun of each other's lunches even though they played together and liked each other. Then she hesitated — and added, "But sometimes they fight over things like that and aren't friends anymore. Could that ever happen to you and Mike?"

I had to stop and think. Over the past few years I've become alienated from a number of old friends because of ideological differences. We had disagreements over Vietnam and about the urgency of the need for social and political change. At times I find myself getting very sentimental about these old friends. I can't bring myself to dislike them and yet we don't speak to each other and even find ourselves on opposite sides of bitter social and political battles.

The relationship between ideas and personalities is not simple or direct. Mike and I could become enemies, I told Erica, but not easily or stupidly. That seems to be the crucial point — to resist becoming stupid.

Stupidity is to me thoughtlessness: action without reflection. When children become bitter enemies over the issue of their food preferences, they are allowing themselves to be made stupid. I remember witnessing what could be called a taco war between a group of Anglo and Chicano five- and six-year-olds. The Anglo children made fun of the Chicano children for having tortillas in their lunches instead of slices of processed white bread. They called the Chicano children taco heads and laughed until they found all the Chicano children on top of them.

After breaking up the fight, I asked some of the Anglo children what was wrong with or funny about tortillas. Most of them didn't have the slightest idea — they just had heard older children and adults make fun of Chicanos, and food was the recurrent symbol that was used. Several of them had even tasted tortillas and loved the food at Taco Bell. Their whole provocation was thoughtless and stupid. They didn't think of what they were saying, couldn't step back and look at themselves and the situation they were creating before it was too late. As we discussed what happened, the children seemed more bewildered than anything else. It was as if they were asking themselves what made them do such a dumb and silly and mean thing.

Children in our society are rarely reflective. They aren't accustomed to thinking about their words and actions. They tend to plunge into things and hurt or get hurt. Yet they are enormously responsive to reflection and discussion when they are offered the attention of a caring adult.

It seems to me that one of the most crucial strengths we can provide our children is the ability to step away from a situation and reflect on it, to separate an idea from the person who advocates it and consider its intrinsic merit.

We have to help our children overcome fear of thinking. That doesn't mean that all ideas are equally valid. I am a partisan — racism is wrong, pollution is insane, poverty should not be tolerated. However, it is of no more value to have children parrot sensible ideas than to have them parrot their opposites. Helping them think is worth the risk of having your children disagree with you. I have no sure idea of what the guiding moral, social, and political principles of my children's lives will be. However, I do feel confident that they will be developed through reflection and informed by sensitivity, and that as much as possible the children will resist acting stupidly or cruelly.

There are a number of specific ways of encouraging reflection that are worth trying.

(1) This could be called *the lollipop game* and has endless variations. It is a way of getting young people to think about how they make choices. Start with a range of things — many different flavored lollipops, a series of cards of different colors, or pictures of many different types of dogs or cats. Ask your children if they would like to play a game and then tell them to arrange the things from their most to their least favorite. Include yourself in the game. Once preferences are stated, try to compare different people's choices. Then see if you can determine why people chose as they did. It is probably best to start by analyzing your own choices. Talking about the reasons you can uncover for your own preferences is the best way to set up a situation where others will feel free to talk about themselves.

(2) Ask "Why?" a lot. Children are always asking adults why things happen the way they do or why people behave the

way they do. It makes sense to ask children the same question. At the same time, it is important to be sensitive to the limits of someone's ability to answer a question and drop the issue if things seem to be getting too tense or too boring. A conversation that is meant to be congenial and reflective can often turn unexpectedly into a test situation in which a child, instead of thinking about the issue, worries about what answer the grown-up wants.

(3) Guessing at other people's feelings, motives, and ideas encourages reflection. Why do people like each other? Why does someone share and another person get selfish? What does it feel like to be on trial, famous, in jail, rich, hungry all the time, indifferent, different? The newspaper provides a wealth of material to speculate about every day. The pictures provide a rich focus for conversation and reflection.

(4) Discovering contradictions among thoughts, feelings, and actions is a sophisticated and powerful technique of thinking. Children are sensitive to ways in which people say one thing and do another, or talk about certain feelings and then reveal totally different feelings through their behavior. Most adults try to smooth over contradictions, to tidy up their views of life for the sake of children, who are usually not deceived. Critical thought requires a sensitivity to contradictions. One of the main themes of the development of intellectual strength should be to *seek contradictions and reflect on ways of overcoming them.* This may seem like a very abstract issue for young children. But there are many specific instances where this idea can function in everyday life.

In order to analyze contradictions with young children I've found it useful to call them "yes-no situations." If you answer "yes" and "no" to the same question you are creating a contradiction. If you try to do something and its opposite you are creating a problem for yourself.

Here are some examples.

There are times when children feel rejected by people they initially reject. For example, if they insult their friends, they might find themselves friendless without having made the connection between their actions and the consequences they lead to. This situation can be analyzed with a young person, using this simple form:

YES (+)	NO (−)
I want my friends to like me.	I insult my friends.

The "yes" moves me toward my friends; the "no" moves them away from me. The contradiction has to be resolved by the child's changing either the "yes" or the "no." There are a number of choices that the "yes-no" form brings out: (1) if you want your friends to like you, don't insult them, or (2) insult them but don't be surprised by rejection. There is a third possibility, which incorporates both the "yes" and "no" and yet presents a qualitatively different situation: (3) insult only a few people who you feel have provoked you, and be prepared to be rejected by them.

A similar situation arises when children refuse to share their toys and at the same time expect their friends to share with them. The consequence is usually that these children are avoided. Nothing is said often. The selfish children feel lonely, sad, and rejected. Through "yes-no" analysis it's possible for them to see how they contribute to their condition and how they can get out of it if they choose. Here's one way the situation could be broken down:

YES (+)	NO (−)
I want to play with my friends and share their toys.	My toys are only for my use.

The contradiction lies in the imbalance of the situation, in wanting others to share without having to share oneself. The resolution can come through forcing oneself to share or through learning to accept being alone.

There are many occasions where "yes-no" situations develop, and it's worthwhile at some point to talk with children explicitly about the difficulty of living with contradictions. I've found that four- and five-year-olds can understand that you can't hit someone on the head with a brick and expect her to love you for it, or that you can't be selfish with your own things and expect other people to be generous toward you. Often children are trapped in contradictions — they haven't had an opportunity to think out the consequences of their actions. At other times, they want everything and don't see that it is impossible and painful to try to control everything. It's a service at times to sit and talk analytically about contradictions, to show *in concrete instances* how selfishness produces resentment, violence begets rejection, and manipulation creates resistance. The important point is to help children think through the consequences of their actions.

The ability to analyze the contradictions in our own behavior is no less central to developing healthy lives for us as adults than is the "yes-no" analysis to helping children avoid confusion and neurotic pain. I've found that by spending time with my children talking about their behavior, I've developed a useful technique to use in getting perspective on my own behavior. It's an ironic truth that sometimes we learn ways of coming to terms with our adult lives by offering help to our children.

I.Q. and intelligence. There is no direct relationship between I.Q. and intelligence. I.Q. can be trained, while intelligence develops throughout life. I know a number of school psychologists who spend most of their time administering I.Q. tests. The children of these people tend to do very well on

I.Q. tests. Someone suggested to me that the reason was that psychologists were probably very intelligent and passed the quality on to their children. After a while I discovered that they indeed pass on high I.Q.—not genetically, however. They trained their children to perform well on the tasks that make up the WISC and Stanford-Binet. Naturally, when these children were tested, they did extremely well. Any of us can do the same thing with our children. It is always possible to find old test samples and familiarize children with what is expected of them in testing situations. However, in my experience, overanxiety about performing well on tests can interfere with other, more important, learning. If youngsters learn to read thoughtfully and with pleasure, they can also acquire test-taking skills without too much effort. However, if they do well on tests and reject reading because they perceive it only as related to being tested, they've lost a lifelong source of pleasure, knowledge, and enrichment. It's important to keep I.Q. and achievement tests in perspective, and to distinguish test-taking skills from the skills and understanding that lead to an intelligent life.

Intelligence develops throughout life. It manifests itself in how people deal with other people, analyze events and experiences, develop and perfect their work, learn from others, and learn to teach themselves. It is neither a single skill to be obtained once and for all early in life, nor a series of hierarchical developmental skills each to be acquired in the correct order at the appropriate stage of life. Rather it is a continual integrating and questioning of experience.

Intelligence consists of curiosity and openness tempered by analysis and informed by past experience. To live and to act and to think intelligently are all part of the overall development of personal strength. Intelligence is not merely smartness or cleverness. It is informed by emotional strength, by courage and resistance to stupidity, dogma, and thoughtless imitation. The development of intellectual strength goes along with the development of emotional strength, which all of us have to be sensitive to as our children grow.

The Development of Emotional Strength

Emotional strength is as much a manifestation of self-discipline as is intellectual strength. It consists of the ability to deal with a reasonable amount of stress, to control wide swings of emotion and recover from occasional loss of control, as well as the ability to sustain affection. None of these things develops effortlessly. Stress, moodiness, occasional loss of control, and inconstant affection are all normal aspects of growing up. We have to support our children as they develop emotionally and accept the fact that there is no easy and painless way to become strong.

Acting like a baby. Mr. Spock on *Star Trek* is a calm, somewhat mysterious, alien. He hardly ever expresses feelings and is usually invulnerable to emotional appeals. On one program, however, a woman he loved was transferred to another Starship. At the moment when he realizes he'll never see her again, his usually expressionless face begins to quiver, and then wholly unexpectedly tears begin to flow and he cries out, "I want my mommy!"

Our whole family was watching the show. Josh, who was five at the time, immediately began crying with Spock. Tonia and Erica laughed in a way that was close to crying. I was moved too by that unexpected expression of vulnerability and dependence. We talked about Spock for days, and now several years later still remember that episode and are moved by it. Usually my children ask me after talking about it whether I ever feel as if I want my mommy. They know my answer — of course I cry and sometimes things hurt so badly that I want to be a child held and protected by my mother. But they like and need to hear it said over and over — that growing up doesn't mean invulnerability or that there won't be times when you need and get protection.

The development of emotional strength does not consist in eliminating all dependency or controlling all of one's expressions of emotion. Occasional regression is a source of strength and not a sign of weakness and neurosis. It is important to keep this in mind when thinking about the growth of emotional strength in young children. Tantrums, crying, sulking, sucking on a thumb or pacifier, curling in a lap, and playing baby are recurrent ways of behaving, especially in times of stress. They are returns to the source, as it were, brief escapes from the drive to change or be responsible. Often it pains parents to see their children falling into modes of behavior they had assumed had been outgrown. However, we only need think of ourselves facing conflict, change, or tragedy to see how silly it is to even want children to be free from regression. Somewhere within us we have to find sources of emotional strength. We have to withdraw from the world, cry or rock ourselves to sleep, dream or suck absently on a pipe or cigarette, or sip something the way we used to sip milk as infants. This need can be psychologized away — we can see the dependent child drawing strength from a nurturing parent as something to be eliminated. Or we can take it in the opposite way and treasure that child in ourselves that makes emotional rebirth possible when we feel we have been drained of all our resources. At times when your child throws a terrible tantrum or cries uncontrollably or seems to regress into formless dependence, see the experience through patiently and observe your child's face when the storm passes. I've often seen a relief and freedom, a surge of power and energy, emerge from what seemed an aimless overreactive regression.

Emotional strength does not develop in a linear manner. It does not consist merely of one stage replacing another, of moving, say, from dependency to independence or from uncontrolled crying to controlled verbal expressions of feelings. It consists more of the sorting out and eventual integration of different modes of expression. Dependency is not so much replaced by independence as tempered by it. There are times when dependency is appropriate — one is dependent upon people one loves, work one cares about, a community one builds. There are also times when independence is necessary — when one has to struggle on one's own. The same is true with the expression of emotion — if one can't cry at all, sorrow itself disappears as a response. However, if one cries at everything, there is no balance or depth to one's responses. Emotional strength is integrative; it consists of balancing and sorting out feelings, of tempering control with naturalness, of accepting one's own complexity and developing ways of calling forth strength and energy and expressing sorrow, joy, and compassion. When you observe your children, it helps not to speculate on what behavior your child must be induced to outgrow so much as to think of how that behavior can be balanced by other behavior or organized into a comprehensive and coherent whole life. Temper tantrums might be out of place in adult life, but not temper. Pacifiers have to be given up, but there have to be ways to induce a steady calm under pressure. The way in which this organization develops can be seen by noticing how people deal with certain stress points that exist throughout emotional development. These points could be called: *breaking points, weak points, sore points, soft points,* and *points of maximum and sometimes outrageous strength.*

Breaking points. Breaking points are those points at which people collapse and can no longer function in coherent ways. They vary from person to person, and from age to age. Two of the most common and earliest experienced breaking points involve fatigue and hunger. Many children cannot function if they are hungry or very tired. One sees this readily with infants. However, as children get older it's sometimes hard to determine the effects of hunger or fatigue. As breaking points are reached, skills that have been mastered seem to fall apart. Everything seems frustrating — puzzles seem to fly apart by themselves, blocks become heavy, books that were easy to read become impossible. Children sometimes fumble and cry, or explode in anger without realizing they are simply tired or hungry.

Children respond in different ways when they reach breaking points. Some fall apart and scream, attack objects, accuse people of hating them. Others sob quietly, while some children withdraw into a corner with a favorite stuffed animal, a pacifier, or blanket. Often children aren't aware of what's causing them so much frustration. If hunger is the problem, an offer of food usually brings the feeling of hunger dramatically to consciousness, and a little food helps the storm pass. Things are more difficult when hunger isn't the problem and food doesn't help. It's hard to know when you're too tired to function, especially if you're resisting fatigue. That's as true for adults as for children — we often don't know when to quit when we're tired and trying to do some work. The ability to become aware of one's own fatigue and allow oneself to rest is an important aspect of growth. It takes a while for children to realize that fatigue produces frustration, and they need to have that connection pointed out over and over.

I don't know how many times Judy and I have had to deal with frustrated angry children trying to do their homework when they're fatigued. The simplest adding problems seem impossible; a sentence seems like a Victorian novel. Sometimes a fifteen-minute rest is all that is needed, a withdrawal once it becomes clear that a breaking point has been reached.

We all have breaking points and will continue to have them throughout our lives. We have to learn how to anticipate them, be able to deal with our responses at those times, and integrate them into the flow of our lives. Not all breaking points are as simply analyzed or alleviated as fatigue or hunger. Some people, for example, cannot function at all if they are in pain. Others cannot live with emotional pressure, and their whole lives disintegrate when a love affair or friendship breaks up, or when they feel rejected by their parents, children, or friends. We all need to inventory our breaking points and those of our children as well as of the others we love and live with. Then we'll be able to support them when they fall apart, and develop some strategies for dealing with our own emotional stress points.

I know, for example, that I cannot live with unresolved emotional conflict. It becomes impossible for me to sleep, or work, or even read a newspaper. I've found that the only way to deal with such dysfunctional tension is to blurt things out, insist on resolving things. It relieves the tension and allows me to return to the normal pace of my life. However, that doesn't mean that impatient attempts to resolve emotional conflict are always sensible or are a valuable mode of functioning for everyone. Because of my particular breaking point, more often than not such attempts help settle problems and restore life, especially if the people around understand my way of dealing with tension.

There are many different types of breaking point I've observed in children. Some children are extremely vulnerable to criticism, and the slightest negative word paralyzes them. In those cases, one has to be loving and supportive while still being truthful. Most children can learn to integrate criticism of their behavior or work if it is given in the spirit of love. The supersensitive child often hears a simple comment like "You sure made a mess out of your spaghetti" as "You inferior and worthless person, why did you ruin my life by making such a mess with your spaghetti?" Of course, some adults give criticism in that manner, but one doesn't always have to offer it harshly for it to be taken that way. Children who are so fearful and insecure have to be supported as they learn to bear criticism. Sometimes I find myself saying silly things like "You've got nice jeans on, you look very good today and you drew a wonderful picture, but you made a mess of your spaghetti." The sillier and more absurd you make things, the more easily criticism made with the idea of helping someone become stronger and less vulnerable is taken. Sometimes even though breaking points are not totally eliminated, they can be brought under some conscious control and create less disruption in life.

Some children don't mind criticism at all, although they are vulnerable in surprising and unexpected ways. For example, there are some children who are inordinately sensitive to the organization of space and time. If something is moved around in their room, or something they planned on doesn't take place right on time, they go to pieces. It is easy for parents to respond to these seeming overreactions with anger. Yet when someone has reached a breaking point and collapsed, anger and assault just increase the intensity of their paralysis. Sometimes it helps to restore order, to simply accept supersensitivity as a factor in life with both positive and negative aspects. It can be important to give privacy, time, and space alone to someone who has broken apart so he or she can recompose him or herself. The best time to help strengthen children and make them less devastated by their breaking points is when no problem is occurring. The worst time to try to help someone become more flexible is while the person is broken down and needs more than anything else the strength to restore an emotional balance.

All of us experience moments and perhaps days and weeks of emotional perturbation. There are times when being troubled and blue seems to define our lives; there are other times when we walk around euphoric. These highs and lows are part of the fabric of life — neither good nor bad. They define the depth and intensity with which we live. And it shouldn't be surprising or disturbing that our children experience highs and lows as well as steady times no matter what we do to make their lives free of frustration and pain. In fact, the range and variability of children's feelings is the stuff out of which emotional strength can grow. Depression, breaking down, exploding, being joyous all come together in a centered meaningful life. Too many parents want to protect their children from the painful, the negative. Children need to know and experience those aspects of life if they are to grow strong. That doesn't mean, of course, that unhappiness has to be manufactured or frustrations created. There are enough difficult things in the world to fill anyone's life. The point is that we need to be prepared to understand the points at which we break down and are vulnerable, and receive support and build strength there. It is a much greater gift to help people than to impoverish their lives in the futile attempt to protect them from vulnerability of all sorts, internal and external.

Weak points. We all have weak points that are not quite breaking points. Some people cry too easily; others get upset with minor uncertainties or eat or drink too much or can't take a joke or feel uneasy with new people. Some of us travel poorly and become rigid in new places until anxiety wears off a bit. All of these weaknesses are part of our characters. Usually we can keep them under control, accept them as part of us, and work to minimize their effects on our functioning. It's easier, however, to accept one's own weaknesses than to accept the weaknesses of one's children. Yet children, being people, neither are nor can be perfect no matter what their parents do. Wishing for purity in one's children can lead to turning minor weaknesses into neurotic habits or breaking points. I've seen many parents irritated by their children's weak points and tearing their children apart just when they need most support. There are many examples of this:

- Your child is anxious about getting hurt and so climbs and runs cautiously. Instead of running and climbing with him and trying to create a situation where he is too happy to be annoyed, or just letting him move at his own pace, you pounce on him, call him a weakling, or talk in his presence about how inept he is.
- Your child has breathing problems and minor asthma, which worry you so that you both chain-smoke and overprotect her, thus intensifying the asthma.
- You can't help yourself from bothering your child about eating too much. The anxiety that creates causes a hunger that increases compulsive eating.

There are images of perfect carefree children that interfere with loving and supporting children as they are. Emotional strength shouldn't be confused with some images of calm perfection and control. The struggle to understand and come to terms with our weaknesses is the process by which strength and maturity grow. Perfection is a burden — children who pretend to be all good to please their parents have no time or space to grow. It seems to me that our fullest and most creative moments come out of disequilibrium. A lack of balance — too many tears, too much anxiety, uneasiness about moving or feeling — is full of challenges, occasions for understanding oneself and others in a respectful way and for making one's world.

This sounds like my grandparents talking. Their understanding of people and events grew in the midst of pogroms in Poland and Russia, during the early union struggles of working people, through the Second World War and Hitler, and ended with the economic success and cultural devastation of their family. Through all this, it always amazed me how strong and hopeful they seemed. Once I asked my grandmother how she could bear up to all she had experienced. It seemed logical that she would be hateful and unkind, and yet it never happened. Her answer was that she never expected that much from people. She knew the worst and was always surprised and delighted by how much people struggled against the worst in themselves and others. She wasn't romantic. It was just that imperfections didn't bother her.

This kind of attitude makes it possible for people to actually negotiate conflicts and think about their own worst selves. In the years when I taught kindergarten and first grade it seemed that most parents had wholly different attitudes toward their children. Each parent's child was perfect. When anything happened, it was always done to somebody but never done by anybody. If your parents deceive themselves into believing you have no weaknesses and are pure, you're absolved by them for the responsibility for any pain or trouble you may cause. I found a large number of children using their parents' unreal attitude toward them as a weapon. It makes more sense to put weaknesses such as selfishness, jealousy, or a sense of inferiority in some perspective, to look upon them as aspects of the self which along with our strengths help define us as unique. They generally can be managed and their impact on our lives minimized if we do not deny them or let them possess us. My grandparents' attitude seems to me to embody a healthy, humorous acceptance of the imperfect condition that life is, open as it is to growth, and to dialogue.

Sore points and tantrums. There are points at which we explode at a person or thing. It is as if we all bear some open wounds, and when they are touched we respond as if we have to fight for our lives. Sometimes these wounds exist in such unexpected parts of the self that the explosions seem irrational, pointless, without focus or will. In some children these sore points manifest themselves as tantrums. A suggestion or remark like "Clean your room" or "It's time for dinner" will set off an explosion. Sometimes refusing a request for a friend to sleep over or for a toy or game has the same effect. Tantrums have the appearance of uncontrolled rage and frequently show a fury we don't usually associate with children. They can make us forget that something triggered them. The first time one of my children threw a tantrum I was flustered and scared. The screaming and crying and writhing around distracted me so much that I forgot all about what caused it. First I tried to reason about the tantrum, suggest patiently that we be reasonable. This of course increased the intensity of the tantrum. Then I got angry and started yelling about being reasonable, becoming quite unreasonable myself. I can't remember how it ended, but probably after a while we both got screamed out and fell quiet, then shyly apologized and laughed at how absurd we were. That of course didn't prevent future tantrums. However, there seem to be two possibly effective ways of dealing with tantrums as they are happening. One is to let them storm themselves out and to be quiet and patient. The other is to pick up a child and put him or her someplace where he or she can live out the tantrum alone. Any exchange that I've ever seen midtantrum only exacerbated the situation. Sometimes it's hard to do either of these things. One of the most emotionally difficult things I've had to learn with my children is to be patient with their pain, frustration, and occasional loss of control. There are times when growth is painful, learning involves frustration, when tears in your child have to be borne patiently. There are hard moments when you have to say either in words or by your actions, "I can't help you now. You have to do it yourself." Being available yet not interfering as a child tests out emotions and struggles to acquire control is extremely hard, yet I believe is a part of needed emotional strength of adults. There is a fine line here. I don't mean that you should abandon your child. It is more that you have to be patient and accept tantrums and other forms of sorrow as part of living and growing.

Tantrums end. However, the sore points that set them off usually don't disappear. For example, one boy I know cannot stand to be second in anything. He is charming and bright, and seems very mature. Usually he also seems happy and uncompetitive. Yet if he doesn't get first on line to the ice cream truck, first up to bat in a ball game, or if he doesn't get the window seat in a car, he falls apart and throws a tantrum. The first time it happened in my presence was at a park where I'd taken a number of children to play kickball. He was second to kick, so he lay down on home plate and screamed. I made the mistake of giving him his way and letting him kick first just so I wouldn't have trouble in the park. My giving in guaranteed that the next time he didn't get what he wanted from me, he'd throw a tantrum my way. Sure enough, it happened as we were getting ready to go home. He wanted to carry the ball and I asked someone else to take it. There was Thomas on the ground kicking and screaming. I just walked on; he wasn't going to oppress all of us with his demands. I decided to let him cry himself out, a little fearful that he might go on for hours, but nevertheless determined. The rest of us walked slowly to the car. When we were halfway there, Thomas got up, dried his tears, and raced off ahead of us, jumped into the car, and claimed a window. If he couldn't have the ball, at least he'd have the window. It was sad to watch such a driven child. There were so many sore points in his life that he must have had a dozen tantrums a day — a good sign that someone somewhere in his life was giving in a lot. Thomas and I saw a lot of each other during the year when he was six. We were together at the park or at my house when he was playing with the children on the block. He tested me with tantrums over and over. Usually I refused to give in but let him know that I liked him and wouldn't chase him away. I also let him know that I admired his desire to be first. There was strength behind it. He could stay and play and talk — but he had to give and take in a world of equals rather than manipulate things and make everyone else resentful. He gave a lot — managed to accept the same rules as everyone else, take a turn batting or kicking, not grab so anxiously at everything. Every once in a while he'd throw a tantrum — just to stay in practice, I suppose — but they became like a private joke between us. Once he was writhing on the field, claiming he wasn't out when he obviously was. I walked over and was about to pick him up and carry him off the field and let him cry out of bounds. He knew exactly what was going to happen. As I approached he looked at me through his tears and smiled shyly. The tantrum had become theater. He could control it. I played the scene out and put him down off the field. In a second he was back ready to play.

This reminds me of a game my children made up, called "Doing the Fake." What it consists of is one of the children throwing a tantrum or bursting into tears, or two of them fighting or screaming at each other. The crucial thing for play is that the activity has to be done so that Judy or I can hear or see what is going on. As soon as we get drawn into the action and respond, the three children immediately drop their roles and break into a soul dance while singing "Doing the fake, doing the fake." There are times when the acting is so convincing that I can't understand how that intensity and that genuineness were generated. The children have a lot of stake in playing the game well — probably because it's the strongest confirmation they have that they've developed power over their emotions, that they can control and discipline their own lives in ways that "little kids," who do throw tantrums and cry uncontrollably, can't.

Soft points. Most people have soft points — moments when they become pliable and insanely generous. Sometimes these moments are caused by personal guilt, other times by death or the termination of some work or the discovery of a new love or the renewal of an old one. They are times when our actions reveal parts of ourselves that children don't usually see, and therefore they can be special moments for children. Sometimes one just sees in a child something so beautiful and fulfilling that one wants to give her the world. These generous moments initially can seem strange to children. Something is happening to you or something your child does sets off a soft, loving, almost metaphysically giving response, and you act out of character.

Let me try to make this clearer. There are periodic times of celebration — birthdays, anniversaries, religious or national holidays — and there are private unique moments that make one feel alone and lonely and needing to affirm life by making other people, especially children, happy. Recently my grandmother died. She was quite old, at least ninety, had lived fully, didn't suffer much — but she died and left a great vacant spot in the world of her children and grandchildren. We mourned — death is horrible, even the best of deaths at the end of the fullest of lives. The mourning, the sadness, reached an intensity and depth where there was nothing to do but be generous and loving, to be soft, to heal wounds, pretend the family and the world could be made eternal. At that moment we all turned to the great-grandchildren, to my children and their cousins, with a sense that the world will be theirs, with a need to give them things, see them happy and fulfilled in the present.

These soft moments are part of being mortal. They aren't all produced by such major events as death. There are times when little things are symbolic of the whole, when feeling depressed seems to define life as depression, or when lying makes the world seem a lie. At those moments, if we see a child, and are not hardened and bitter at the center of our being, a feeling of what could have been, of conceivable perfection and joy, can overcome us. At those times, our children seem to be all that we can hold on to, and of course we try to communicate through gifts and through giving an acknowledgment of our mortality and our love.

Upon first experiencing these soft moments, children feel

presented with a puzzle and a challenge. Children can easily become overwhelmed and tempted by a generosity that might seem to them to be without adequate or apparent cause. What causes such an overflow of gifts and affection? How can it be controlled? Insane generosity begs exploitation and courts frustration. One day you shower your children with gifts, give in to their slightest whim, feel driven to make them happy — the next day life settles down and you restore the usual flow of time and emotion; only your children don't forget those moments — they want today to be like yesterday and try to do something to evoke that surge of love and generosity again. Their behavior seems staged and annoying. What was soft in you yesterday becomes hard and closed today.

A number of times I've found myself blaming my children for the fluctuation of my moods when I should have been explaining those fluctuations to them instead. The only way to deal with periodic excessive generosity, which is a reaffirmation of life during a time of stress, is to articulate what is happening and acknowledge within the family the existence of nonusual times. Children can readily understand, for example, that when someone you love dies, from your sadness a desire to make someone alive happy can arise. They can understand surges of love, depression that becomes transformed into generosity. They can understand that life consists of nonusual, nonpredictable, nonmanipulative moments as well as the usual, more transparent and controllable, time of everyday life.

Points of maximum and sometimes outrageous strength. There is a need in some part of our selves to be tough and resistant to external influences. The strength and quality of inner convictions determines to a large degree how people deal with the historical and social context into which they are born. There are dramatic examples of the importance of this emotional and intellectual toughness. In Germany in Hitler's time, there were people who resisted the powerful emotional appeal of fascism; in our own country and more recently, people overcame the fear of death and rejection to become part of the civil rights movement or the anti–Vietnam War movement. That kind of toughness, which is informed by compassionate morality and a complex analysis of current situations, is to me a treasure. It is basically an affirmation of living, of dreams of harmony and health that are difficult to sustain in our present condition.

Most children I've known have that toughness. It is part of their sense of who they are; of where they end and others begin. The defiant and resistant behavior that children display is often justified. If a child questions you or challenges you, catches you out in a lie, it is important not to respond to the child as "only a child." The issue itself has to be dealt with. As a rough principle, it's a good policy to stop before reacting to your child's statement and consider whether it's true or not. The way you weigh statements is a crucial element in how your child learns to deal with moral and social dilemmas. It's not that your child will necessarily be like you. He or she may turn out to feel quite differently. It's more that your actions set up a climate of trust or one of suspicion, and that atmosphere will pervade your life together.

Another aspect of inner toughness is the ability to focus one's emotions. We all occasionally feel mad or depressed or elated without knowing what's causing us to feel that way. Sometimes it requires a lot of thought and discipline to think through to the cause of these feelings. At times one just can't tell — but by thinking of the way one feels, it is possible at least to gain some control. Children are often even more unfocused. They sometimes feel hungry but don't know it, feel angry but aren't sure why, act hastily without realizing it. It helps to talk about feelings, especially at times where no judgment is involved. Children are fascinated with stories about adults' being out of control, love to hear about how you felt during the day, about your falling in or out of love, about the time you got angry or the day you were so depressed you couldn't function. Stories help focus on realities. The richer the stories, the more children have to draw on as they try to understand and focus their feelings.

Toughness is a paradoxical virtue. It serves the gentlest, most compassionate feelings. It provides a focus for feelings and convictions, informs them with a sense of what is real, what is possible, and what is worth taking a risk for. It is an indispensable component of emotional strength, and yet, carried to extremes, can turn into a coldness and hardness that negates emotional life itself. The line between toughness and violence is hard to draw. Without compassion and sensitivity, toughness in fact is violence, the destruction of the self, which manifests itself in the destruction of others.

Strength and style. It is easy to confuse the quality of emotion with style. Some people are louder, more forceful, than others. Others are quieter, and emerge more slowly. Some children, for example, can appear confident and focused, seem articulate and sensitive, and yet act in cruel and selfish ways under stress or when an adult isn't present. Other children can seem nervous and self-centered, yet over a period of time act in ways that make it clear they are compassionate and don't fall apart under pressure.

In addition to personal differences in style, there are class and cultural differences. I've had many opportunities to observe children with different cultural backgrounds and social classes encountering each other for the first time. Initially a lot of misunderstanding develops. A friendly gesture is taken as a threat, playful language is interpreted as an insult, a friendly look is considered to be a challenge. Often some children have a hard time seeing beyond these cultural and class differences to the individuals. It is important to help children observe others and not be too easily taken in or put off by initial impressions. Once again, it is hard to underestimate the value for the development of sensitivity and intelligence of stories and reminiscences and of the conversations they can lead to. Children are curious about what people are like, how they act in different circumstances, how you can tell whom to trust and whom to suspect or fear. Examples, tales, stories about friends and relatives all help build a complex human world a child can draw on as he or she reaches beyond the family and learns to relate to people in his or her own way.

It is also enormously valuable to provide opportunities for your child to meet as many different types of people as possible. Visiting your place of work, going to an occasional "grown-up" party, a political meeting or convention, to the theater or a live sports event builds up a sense of how people behave in different contexts. One way people develop judgment about others is by observing how they behave in different situations. Some people change faces all the time, are overbearing with their children, subservient at work, charming when on the make. The best way to know about people is by seeing them in different contexts and seeing how constant or changing they are.

Children love to compare the different faces people wear and can usually imitate grown-up masks beautifully. The search for personal identity consists in a large part in looking for a constant face that doesn't need to be masked. As children grow they can be pressured into having different modes of being or can learn to be themselves in all situations. For example, they can be pressured into being submissive and obedient at school even in the face of an intolerant and unloving teacher; they can be pressured into behaving sweetly to an important person, or contemptuously to someone who is poor or culturally different. This pressure can be seductive as well as oppressive. There are rewards for being many-faced. Children can be bribed to be on good behavior, or to do well in school, or in some other way to meet unpleasant adult demands. They can also see their parents acting inconsistently and hear them talking about how their masks are necessary in order to make money or get a good job or survive. There are many ways in which fragmented identities develop. At some point we as adults have to face the problem of whether we will encourage our children to assume many masks or strive for one consistent face to present to the world. To me, emotional strength can only emerge from continuous growth toward consistency and wholeness. Each mask we assume has its associated moral values and emotional setting. The more masks we wear, the less coherence there is in our beings, and the less consistency in our feelings and values. Strength comes from wholeness, from knowing who you are and struggling against the temptations to give up part of yourself in exchange for power or money. None of us are pure. It is through the struggle we make, adults and children, in all the areas of our lives, to be whole and consistent and caring that emotional strength develops.

The Development and Use of Physical Strength

There is no single model of physical strength nor an ideal body to strive for. Children are built differently and enjoy moving in different ways. Some children like to run, others like to walk, swing, climb, skip. Some move quickly, others deliberately; some have their strength concentrated in their arms and shoulders, others seem centered about their legs or backs. The development of physical strength is as much an individual matter as is the development of intellectual style and emotional maturity. It consists of understanding your own body and learning to move with your own grace and at your own pace. This implies being on good terms with your body, feeling content with the way you look and move, and knowing how to discipline yourself to master a physical challenge. Physical strength shouldn't be confused with physical aggressiveness, a mistake I made as a teenager.

Being a punk. In 1950, when I was thirteen, Ike jackets were in. For less than five dollars you could buy a jacket just like the one Eisenhower wore and strut around the neighborhood exuding military presence. I had one hidden in the hall of my house behind the empty soda and seltzer bottles. My parents wouldn't have a child of theirs wearing such a thug jacket. Their child was not going to get involved in gangs and fighting and hanging out on the street. They were right, of course. I didn't want to get involved in hanging out or fighting. However, I wanted it to appear as if I was. A number of us used to sneak out on Friday nights wearing boots and Ike jackets and wander around looking for girls to impress. One Friday quite by chance we happened to wander right into another group of thirteen-year-old males on the prowl, only they were the real thing. They belonged to one of the Fordham Road gangs, and did fight and did hang out. They were prepared to have a battle over territory with us. I remember one of them walking up to me and staring at me. My face felt like dissolving in twitches, but I managed to look back into his eyes, meeting them but at the same time expressing submissiveness. He must have seen that I didn't want to fight but wouldn't back away, because he looked away and told his friends that we were nothing but punks and advised us to clear out, which we did.

I remember this now because of how confused physicalness is with sex and class in our society. My friends were all from working-class and lower-middle-class families, and we were all bookish despite our pretenses. We were trying to impress girls who weren't supposed to be physically tough themselves but who were supposed to love that characteristic in boys. And when faced with really tough young men, we felt inadequate and acknowledged our weakness.

I also remember another part of my life those days. On Saturdays my uncle and cousins and their friends went to the schoolyard to play basketball. My cousins were on the City College basketball team and most of their friends were high school and college players. They let me and a friend or two of mine play with them. I don't know whether I've romanticized those days, but in my memory the games lasted for hours with no one keeping score. It was a running, talking, shouting game that was played with joy and respect. People admired each other's performance whether they were on the same team or not. And when it was all over there seemed a closeness and warmth that often dissipated that same night when the same players would play against each other in a League game and be violent and fiercely competitive. Basketball seemed beautiful or horrible to me, depending upon the spirit with which it was played.

I've thought about these aspects of my growing up while watching my children and their friends grow. Erica competes as fiercely as any of the players I knew; Tonia sometimes plays at being tough, and in many ways is tough. Josh runs the range from being fiercely competitive to simply taking joy in playing for its own sake. All these ways of coming to terms with their bodies are not simple matters of getting the right amount of exercise. They have to do with how physical strength and coordination are used socially. I see some young girls and boys, for example, withdrawing from using their bodies at five or six, and defining themselves as intellectuals or as delicate people to be served by others. Other children use their strength brutally to bully or terrorize weaker children. And some take their strength calmly and joyfully, as if movement and play were intrinsic sources of pleasure. The balance between competitiveness and intrinsic joy in using one's body, as well as the problem of how one learns to defend oneself without becoming either a bully or a terrorized person, is a matter that parents and children have to face.

Competition or joy. As very young children begin to control their physical movements, you can observe an interesting combination of personal competition and joy. A child seems to set goals for him or herself — to stand, or walk, or run, or climb up on something and then work toward the goal. Then practice sets in with pure delight in exercising power that has been acquired. After a while new goals are set and the child competes fiercely to become more powerful once more. The situation is structurally the same as the intellectual learning cycles I discussed in the section on intellectual growth, and the competition is internal. It takes a while for a child to look out and begin to compete with another person in order to do something better or quicker than the other does. Before that social competition develops, there are times when children simply attempt to do something like someone else. I remember my children trying to throw a ball like me, or catch it the way I can, or walk with the same gait I have or swim with the same pace. In fact, last summer one of the greatest pleasures I experienced was to swim alongside of Tonia and Erica, adjusting my pace to theirs and doing something in synch with their movements, not trying to be faster or better than each other so much as together.

Imitation and slight variation are wonderful ways to develop physical strength. They mean walking or running or swimming or hiking or playing ball with rather than against someone. To function in conjunction with another person, whether a child or adult, involves a mutual setting of pace. It may mean slowing down or speeding up; the crucial element is collaborating on how to move together comfortably. That's where the imitation and variation come in — one person begins, another imitates; after a while someone varies the pace. It requires a physical sensitivity to the way someone else is moving. No words need be said in the process. With young children, the adult has to be particularly sensitive to the child's pace or else what starts out to be a pleasant time can turn into competition, with the child as guaranteed loser (at least for a few years). I've seen parents, especially fathers, who seem incapable of adjusting their pace to children: a hike becomes a race to the top of the hill, a casual swim becomes training for the Olympics. We simply have to learn to move for the pleasure of moving and for the pleasure of our children's company.

Physical competition, however, is not always damaging. There is no contradiction in running with someone a lot and racing him occasionally, nor is there anything wrong with competitive team sports (with the possible exception of football and ice hockey, which can be excessively brutal). The question is how one thinks and feels about the results of competition. If you lose but have played well, there can be satisfaction in your performance as well as appreciation for how well your opponent did. If you did poorly, that can merely be a challenge to function better the next time. If you won, that can be satisfying, but you can also feel an appreciation for the efforts of your opponent, without whom there'd be no game anyway. What turns competition into judgment of the worth of people is the attitude that somehow someone who does something better than another person is superior, and that if you lose a particular event you are a failure as a person.

Children can play team or individual sports with joy and forget the outcome of a game half an hour after it's over. It's the adults who teach them that self-hatred and the right to look down upon others are appropriate attitudes to develop through games. Next time you play with your children, or watch a sporting event on TV, think of what your children are learning from you about the values obtained from physical activities. Unfortunately for them, many people in our society use their bodies only to compete. For many people there is no such thing as a friendly game of tennis or golf, a relaxing run, a solitary walk. Everything becomes oriented toward results, times, sets or points won, miles covered. Relaxing movement for itself becomes an alien experience, especially for people who live in large cities.

Getting to know your body. The students at Hillside School, which is a few blocks from my house, love to swing on the rings. The rings are made of steel and are hinged to metal bars about six feet off the ground. Every day at lunch time you can see ring contests — who can swing fastest, who can hang upside down longest, who can twirl around and do the fanciest tricks. Some children are the acknowledged school champions; most children try the rings at one time or another; and a few boys and girls avoid them completely. One night around seven-thirty I walked by the school. One of the children who never went near the rings was on the playground by himself. I stood back and watched for a while. Frank jumped up and tried to grab one of the rings, but he missed. Then he tried to climb the metal bar that held the rings, but he slipped down. He was short, compact, a bit heavy perhaps. He stood back and picked up some sawdust, which was under the apparatus, and flung it toward the school. Then he turned to walk away, stopped, saw a wooden crate, grabbed it, and pushed it under the middle ring. Then he climbed on the crate, grabbed the ring, and swung back and forth slowly.

The next night he pushed off a little bit, used his legs to get some momentum, and tried to jump from one ring to another. He fell, but three nights later (watching him had become part of my evening ritual) he succeeded. After a few weeks he managed to swing from one ring to the next ponderously and with effort. Then he stopped coming evenings.

About four months later I got to know him a bit and told him I had watched for several nights while he was trying to master the rings. I asked him why he stopped coming. His answer was "I got to do enough for me." He explained that he didn't want to be the best in the school or even show the other children what he could do. He just wanted to know whether he could do the rings at all; he wanted to learn about his own strength.

Frank was a secure person. Many children at the school made fun of him for being short and stocky. He dealt with the situation by withdrawing from physical activity at school and developing his physical strength in private. Once I noticed two boys making fun of him because he couldn't swing on the rings. He took their mocking for a while, then walked away smiling. He obviously took more pleasure in knowing secretly that he could swing on the bars than in proving that the other boys were wrong.

Many children aren't as strong as Frank. They become self-conscious about their bodies if their parents or other children criticize them for the way they look or move. Often they retreat from physical activities, which in turn has the consequence of making them weaker and less at ease with their bodies. I've had children ask me whether it was better to be thin or heavy-set, to be tall and loose-jointed or short and compact. Those are sad questions, denials of the intrinsic strength and beauty of all of us. It makes more sense to ask how to make one's own body strong than to turn it into an object and measure it against some external standard of strength and beauty.

Sometimes it isn't easy to do this. There are some parents who can't bear to see their children short or fat. Others feel the same visceral repulsion about thinness. It often requires a great deal of parental self-discipline to accept the way a child looks and moves, especially if a parent is insecure about his or her own body.

There is a technique that can be used to help perceive children without judging and rating them against other children. It could be called *looking for strength* and consists of temporarily suspending negative perceptions and focusing on what children do well, feel comfortable with, and enjoy doing. Here are two examples of the value of looking for strengths.

(1) Heath is seven. She moves very slowly, hardly runs at all. Her bearing is stiff and angular; it almost seems as if she can't move in any flowing way. However, she is enormously serious about the world and will try anything if she is given the time and support to do it in her deliberate angular way.

When I first met Heath her parents were concerned about

her slowness and stiffness. They kept urging her to loosen up, and she responded by withdrawing and becoming more tense. After talking for a while, her parents agreed to work at ignoring her weaknesses and concentrate on her strengths. Soon they realized that her slowness had many unexpected strengths. She would try anything but never get too crazy. She could climb steep slopes but she moved slowly; she could catch very fast-moving insects and rodents but slowly; she could become competent at tennis and basketball, but she mastered one small skill at a time.

Heath's parents came to see her as a strong self-paced young girl who acted with caution and intelligence. They told me recently that they even have a hard time now reconstructing what upset them so much about Heath before.

(2) Here's a more dramatic and exceptional case of the power of looking for strengths. Tim lost his right arm in a car accident when he was eight. His parents panicked and could think only of all the things he wouldn't be able to do in the future. He was right-handed. He wouldn't be able to write or throw. He wouldn't be able to drive. No one would like him or fall in love with him when he grew up. They developed a whole philosophy of deprivation in their despair.

A counselor they talked to suggested they become obsessed with Tim's strengths, starting with writing down a list of all the things Tim could still do. In that process they discovered that he had already learned to use a fork and spoon with his left hand and had colored in several pages in a coloring book when he was in the hospital. They came to watch how he was teaching himself to function again, and in a funny way their seeing him strong helped them realize how their pity was undermining him. After a while they were able to see his handicap as a minor fact in the perspective of his whole life.

If you do worry about how your children look or move step

back a bit and try to make a list of the strengths they have. That doesn't mean being blind to their weaknesses. It implies instead learning how to support and respect them where they are strongest and help them become strong and comfortable with their own bodies.

"Playing rough" and defending oneself. Fear of being physically hurt by another person operates everywhere in our society. Poor people have to deal with ghetto violence, the violence that comes from many people being forced to live with resources that cannot nurture them all. Middle-class and wealthy people live with fear of the poor, of people who will hurt them or take their possessions, and who have nothing to lose by making the attempt. The fear of violence is common to all children in our society, though for different reasons. That fear prevents communication, impels children to insulate themselves, or become outrageously tough in order to defend themselves. It is the price we pay for inequality and can be overcome only through a redistribution of resources and a change in the way people understand each other.

On a personal level, fear can be dealt with only if children are confident that they can defend themselves from the assault of others. For that reason it is important that children have an opportunity to learn self-defense. This can be learned through play, or it can be done in a structured and disciplined way. My preference is for play though I know a number of youngsters who have begun judo or aikido at five and who have managed to master them without becoming violent and aggressive toward other children. One of the dangers of young people's mastering some martial art is that they can use it to oppress other youngsters. There is so much romance in the movies and on TV about kung fu and karate that they are used indiscriminately and without any self-discipline. The main reason I prefer learning self-defense through play is to break away from that image of smashing walls and breaking necks associated with the martial arts. At a time when a youngster is old enough to decide to subject him or herself to the discipline of formal training in martial arts, it's vital to select a teacher carefully. The spiritual aspect of the training is crucial — what is the teacher's purpose in having students master such techniques? Is it for inner self-discipline, self-defense, and play, or is it to turn out killers? I'd suggest never taking on a teacher without first observing at least a full session, and, if the teacher is for your child, observe the teacher at work with youngsters. I've known of excellent teachers but also of brutal ones who enjoy the violence of martial arts techniques for its own sake and treat the ability to perform controlled violence as their main goal.

Learning to defend oneself through play is quite different. It is similar to playing rough with your child, wrestling or boxing with him, rolling about on the floor and getting to know each other in that physical sense that is part aggression and part love. Playing rough is often a boy's or girl's first opportunity to test physical strength against another person in a nonthreatening or nonserious situation. Children know that you're stronger than they are but they're not sure how much. Two-year-olds love to pounce upon adults they feel comfortable with and see whether they can push them or knock them down. Playing rough reminds me of the way cats teach their young to fight. They let their kittens pounce on them, then a mock fight begins, and soon the parent has a kitten by the scruff of the neck. In a real fight, that's triumph. In play fighting the cat lets go and the kitten starts pouncing again. The parent seems to know just how far to stretch the kittens out without actually hurting them.

Watching cats teaching their young to fight gave me the

idea of approaching self-defense with children in a similar way. The idea is to play fight with children with a strict control on what you as an adult will do. First of all, no real attempt should be made to hit or in any way injure a child. Play boxing consists of throwing punches and holding them before they hit, or of tapping someone gently. In wrestling no holds are barred — however, none are really made. An arm is almost twisted, a headlock held for no more than a second. Just a little pressure is applied to present a challenge. The crucial thing is to set up a situation where four- and five- and six-year-old children will learn to attack and defend.

Usually I kneel upright and tell the child to come at me. She or he can circle around and jump on my back, or scream and jump right at me or keep her or his distance and jab away. Initially I just stay still and relaxed, and let the child make the first contact. Different children approach the attack in different ways. Some jump right in; others try to feint at you. Some are initially so shy that they stay out of your reach and hesitate to do anything. Usually with the really shy ones I set up a free-for-all situation, where two or three youngsters play fight with me. After a while even the shyest child will jump in.

Over several years' play fighting occasionally with my children and their friends as well as my kindergarten and first grade students, I've developed a few tactics in order to preserve my body and insure that I don't hurt anyone.

(1) I roll with the movement of the children's attack. If someone jumps on my back, I bend over letting the thrust carry the child over me. If someone runs at me, I usually move to the side and give him or her a gentle push in the direction in which he or she is running. This way, I don't get exhausted, since most of the energy used up is theirs. Also, it creates a challenge — can they be quicker or hold onto me

better next time? This can all be done in a very small space.

(2) Whenever I flip someone over I catch the child to ease the fall, or make sure that he or she falls on his or her own movement rather than being slammed by me. Young bodies are very malleable, and as long as you don't introduce unnatural force or put too much pressure on them, falling and tumbling won't hurt them.

(3) I wrestle exactly the same with girls and boys. After several minutes of the children attacking, we switch roles. I try to catch them and sometimes let them get away. I don't make it too easy, but I don't always win either. I remember that I'm a teacher and not a combatant.

Sometimes the whole routine can be varied; I play box instead of play wrestle, or I referee two children play fighting. There it's important to make it clear beforehand that it is play fighting, because an accidental hit or trip can turn it into the real thing. During play boxing I always make myself the timekeeper as well as the referee so I can arbitrarily end any round that seems to be getting out of hand.

If you feel shy about engaging your children that way, you can start a little at a time. A nice way to begin is to get on all fours and ask your child whether he or she wants to climb on a bucking bronco. Tell her or him to hold on, and then buck a little. You'll find that if after bucking a little the child is still holding on, you'll be able to buck her off without hurting her by simply raising up your legs and lowering your head and arms. She'll roll right down your back.

Play fighting isn't all that children need to learn for self-defense. However, it's a good beginning. Beyond that, children have to be supported if they fight to defend themselves rather than punished for fighting. Fighting, from my perspective, is not necessarily bad. It depends upon how one fights, when and whom one fights, and what one fights for.

Fighting to defend yourself, your relatives, friends, or other people from some oppression is healthy and sometimes necessary.

Violence

Children encounter violence and have to decide how to deal with it. They also have to learn how to deal with temptations to be violent themselves.

Violence fundamentally involves learning how not to care — how to destroy or steal something without regard to its use or ownership, and how to hurt or control another person without worrying about how that person feels. It requires becoming hard and blind. Sometimes it is quite disciplined and focused. At other times it is merely a chaotic and desperate flailing about in a hated world. It can be provoked or planned, self-destructive or murderous. There is no single form of violence nor any single best response to violent behavior. A strong self-disciplined person has to know how to defend him or herself from violence and then to make an effort to uncover its sources. One way to do this is to study the inequalities that underlie acts of violence.

Inequalities. Underlying the manifestations of violence in children's lives are basic inequalities. Consider the following instances of violent behavior.

(1) Sally is a kind and lovely and intelligent girl of eight who lives near us. One day I came across her beating a little dog and screaming curses at it. She stopped as soon as she saw me and burst into tears, explaining that she was getting even. It took a while to get the whole story from her. There were a

group of boys in the neighborhood who tormented her every day on her way to school because she was fat. They poked her with sticks and said mean things about her. Sometimes her best friends even laughed. She was miserable and full of hate, which poured out on that little dog because he happened to be in her way and because she was afraid of the other children.

(2) One of her tormentors, an eleven-year-old boy named Billy, acted the thorough bully with everybody. He organized the six- and seven-year-old boys in the neighborhood into a little army and drilled them and pushed them around mercilessly. Yet at times he wandered around lonely and friendless, looking for kind adult attention. He wasn't physically brutalized himself, but no adult was ever home. He was a victim of what could be called middle-class neglect — both his parents were nurturing their careers instead of their children.

(3) Here's another case altogether. Ricky is small, almost runty, and seems to have a constantly running nose. He is physically withdrawn and prefers to stay in the house reading or playing chess or doing workbooks. At school he is considered a genius. He is usually a few steps ahead of the teacher and takes great pleasure in shouting out the correct answers before anyone else has a chance to think. He also enjoys telling people how stupid they are. He is intellectually violent. You get the feeling he doesn't enjoy what he's learning except as a weapon to put others down. He fights like crazy to keep his position at the top of the class. He also stays next to the teacher all the time because there are people out gunning for him on the schoolyard. Several times he has been beaten up in retribution for the violence he initiated in the classroom.

(4) Peter is unlike any of the children I've described. He

spends all day silently muttering to himself, putting puzzles together, coloring, eating — doing everything mechanically in a fixed order. Whenever something unexpected happens — a puzzle is misplaced, there are Ritz crackers instead of graham crackers, a doorbell rings when it wasn't expected — he falls into paroxysms of self-hatred. At those moments he tries to hurt himself, blames himself for the world falling apart and punishes himself accordingly. He is the only one he ever hurts.

(5) Juan is the opposite of Peter. He is quiet, independent, intense, loyal — serious beyond his ten years. He lives in a poor and rough community, has been abused, often hungry and cold. He is tough and only violent when attacked. At those times he is out of control and has occasionally hurt people quite seriously. Yet he never initiates a fight. His older friend Steven, who is just as tough, uses violence in a calculated and measured way. Steven, who is fifteen, has seen his parents hungry, spent days with his father when he got turned down for job after job, has a focused and controlled hatred for wealthy people. He plans to take from them everything he believes has been taken from his parents and ancestors. Violence is merely a tool, a way of getting what he believes is his due.

(6) Finally Bryan, a special beautiful child, is a loner and a looker. He knows the same poverty and misery as Juan and Steven, but for ten years he responded with resignation and a quizzical smile. In school his teacher screamed all day and he spent hours hunched down on his desk hoping he wouldn't be seen. At home there was no space, seven people in two and a half rooms, often no heat in a New York winter, life lived on the margin of survival. Bryan spent a lot of time sitting quietly in the corner or watching TV, the family's single luxury. One day Bryan couldn't bear it anymore and at-

tacked the TV, then his younger sister, then anything in sight. He tried to obliterate his world and calmed down only when he was put under psychiatric care—and only temporarily then. He accepts an impossible world until it becomes too intolerable, and then he explodes. He has not yet been able to break out of the cycle and make life bearable.

A typology of violence. These sketches provide a glimpse of some of the ways violence manifests itself. Generally they could be described as: *violence from above,* which functions to maintain power; *violence as response,* derived from a position of weakness or relative powerlessness; and *violence as despair and self-destruction.* All these forms of violence have intellectual, emotional, and physical verisons. Sally, responding to emotional violence inflicted upon her, turned around and used physical violence against the dog. Billy responded to a different form of emotional violence by trying to control others physically and emotionally. Ricky used intellectual violence in the classroom, and others responded to it physically on the playground. Peter turned against himself in every way, and Bryan exploded and tried to destroy everything he cared about in the world out of too much love burdened by too much despair. Juan used controlled self-protective physical violence, and Steven used controlled aggression through intellectually and emotionally motivated physical violence. In each case there was some basic inequality in the situation, which led the children to act to either maintain power over others, seize power themselves, or give up and try to destroy themselves. It's worth looking at these forms of violence more carefully.

Violence from above. People do not like to lose or give up privileges they have. This holds as much for children as for adults. However, privileges, as opposed to intrinsic emotional, intellectual, or physical qualities, have inherent problems, since the existence of privileges implies that some people have them and others don't. Consider the following.

(1) Tracy is gifted in math. At eight she can solve algebra problems in ways that her parents and teachers find uncanny. She seems to see directly to the center of a problem and understand what its solution has to be without going through all the intermediate steps she needs to use to demonstrate her answers to others. She doesn't consider her gift unusual — it is what she does. However, there are problems she has to deal with. Her teachers marvel over her work; she's constantly showed off by her parents. The other youngsters in her class resent all the attention that flows her way, and she has to deal with their hostility as well as all the adult approval she gets. What are the choices open to her?

She can accept the adult praise and show off her talents. This means drawing closer to the approving world and allowing herself to be cut off from her peers. She can expect protection as well as praise from the adults. When other children make fun of her or exclude her from their games or in other ways slight her because she has chosen to cut herself off from them, she can fall back on what the grown-ups offer her. However, the price is loneliness and hostility, which can easily turn her to violence. She can use her special status to put down other children, call them stupid, laugh at their mistakes. She can use her gift to claim superiority and privileges, and transform it into a weapon to hurt others.

Another way she can respond would be to refuse and perhaps reject the praise she gets and even deny her talent and refuse to exercise it in order to remain in the world of her friends. Possibly she would not merely deny her talent but cultivate other skills, become an athlete or gymnast instead of a mathematician. As an extreme response, she might become expert at defying and denying adults as a way of proving solidarity with her friends. In this way she would avoid perpetuating a kind of intellectual violence at the cost of denying some central part of her being. She would do violence to herself in order to prevent herself from doing violence to others.

There is a third way, which Tracy chose, to nurture her talent and at the same time refuse to use it as a weapon to hurt others. She accepted it as a rewarding part of her life that she could use to help other children. She became generous with her friends, explaining math, assisting people with their homework, or playing math games. She also refused to claim any special privileges no matter how much adults offered them. This is a difficult thing for a child to manage, but some children do have the inner resources to accept their gifts and not use them as weapons.

Yet many children and adults do seek and claim privilege without thinking of what they are doing as violent at all. They think only of what they have or can get — the other, the deprived or excluded, is not part of their consciousness at all. If they then become victimized they look on the other person as violent and themselves as injured. It is characteristic of people who create violence from above not to think of themselves as violent.

The other day one of the boys in the neighborhood was beaten up by several boys who live in a poorer part of Berkeley. For several weeks before, this boy had been showing off his ten-speed bike on the playground. He proudly rode it slowly past other children, though he refused to let them try it out. He also brought his basketball some days and controlled who played and how long the games lasted. After several weeks of this control and ostentation, several of the boys resolved to get him, which they did. His parents and other neighbors were up in arms about the violence, about "them" being in "our" neighborhood. The boys were caught and taken to juvenile court. They were the only ones branded as violent in the situation, though they were responding to the more subtle violence from above that was unacknowledged and perhaps even sanctioned.

I find that whenever there is an outbreak of overt physical violence there is usually some form of prior covert violence. One child makes fun of another's hair or clothes or family; one person has more than another; some inequality exists and explodes into physical violence. Sometimes the victim of the explosion just happens to be in the line of fire by chance. Some children reach a breaking point and explode at whoever's around even though their real tormentors might be elsewhere.

When dealing with violence I find it useful to examine whether there is any underlying violence from above, and to weigh intellectual, emotional, economic, and political violence against overt physical acts. That doesn't mean that these acts are justified — it just means that in order to understand and prevent them from recurring, underlying inequities have to be dealt with.

The alternative to ignoring or sanctioning violence from above is to become repressive. Think of a family in which one child is treated better than another. Perhaps the older child is good in school, a fine athlete, full of confidence and arrogance. The younger one is constantly urged to be like the older one and put down for not being able to. At a certain point an explosion occurs; the younger one hits the older one with a hammer or stabs him with a pencil. Immediately the response is to punish the younger and protect the older. The responsive violence is dealt with but not the violence from above. This not surprisingly generates another attack, and the younger becomes a problem child to be suppressed or, in enlightened families, be sent to a therapist. The underlying inequality is never dealt with; the situation continues to be uncomfortable for everybody. One of the consequences of repression is that no one can be comfortable in the situation.

Violence as response. There are some injured and deprived children who dedicate their lives to violent response to a world that they find hostile. These children often come from poor families, but that's not exclusively the case. There are many forms of deprivation, and one sane response is violence. To become a thief, to get even for injuries to yourself and your family, to try in any way possible to get what has been cut off from you is a way of maintaining the self in a destructive world. The problem with most violent responses, however, is that they are self-destructive and don't deal with underlying inequities, either. To hit someone who has too much because you have nothing, or to steal a little when you need some constant source of support gets nowhere. Curiously, responsive violence, though understandable, does as much harm to the self as to the other.

I remember once walking in Times Square with Judy. Quite by chance we came upon some of her fourth-grade students rolling a drunk. They looked half-delirious, as much delighted because they had power over an adult after having suffered so much abuse and deprivation as because they got a little bit of money. As we passed, not knowing who they were, all the boys stopped what they were doing and in kind and affectionate ways said, "Hi, Mr. Kohl; hi, Mrs. Kohl." I was astonished by the instant change in mood and tone. Those boys knew and liked us; it wasn't a game. Their delirious violence and the gentle respect lived side-by-side within them. They were trying through violence to solve genuine problems they faced — poverty and racism. They were acting from a rage that kept them sane. They refused to accept powerlessness, which was an obvious possibility in their lives. However, their choice was self-destructive. They had to fight the police, never had enough money to give up their violent responses, set themselves up in a situation where there was no winning for them. And there were no adults around at that time to help them see the whole, to help them organize for community action that dealt with the fundamental inequities that drove them to the streets and to hurting someone who was fundamentally as helpless as they were.

Violence as response to genuine inequities can be channeled into political and social action. It cannot be eliminated unless the inequities that motivate it are also eliminated. All of our children will suffer from the inequities we tolerate. When adults indulge in privileges and ignore the deprivation of others, they prepare a world in which their children might be attacked and abused out of rage and despair.

Violence as despair and self-destruction. There are some individuals who accept the role of being inferior. When violence is done to them, they accept it as something they deserve or at least make no counterresponse. There are other people who simply give up and try to destroy themselves and the world. These self-destructive forms of violence manifest themselves in children as well as adults and are tragic to witness.

Pat, a boy I've been attempting to help, refuses to try anything. He won't play, sits looking warily about most of the time, though every once in a while he'll throw himself against the wall and try to hurt himself. He was badly abused as a young child, beaten into submission, and brainwashed to believe he was worthless. He's no longer living at home, but when he was at home his brothers and sisters used to push him around and give him no support when he was assaulted by his mother and father. They were abused as children too but fought back and are tough. They know how to be violent if necessary. Pat is different. He was the youngest and most vulnerable of the children and seems to have been crushed. He needs a fresh start, a new life, a rebirth. For a while he needs consistent loving care and an environment where he can step out without being hurt. He is one of the children who simply will not survive in the context of their families. He needs to be in a place where he can develop the inner resources and strengths that make it possible to deal with violence without being overwhelmed by or becoming a party to it.

Not all self-destructive children are so overtly abused. Sylvia, a nine-year-old I've been helping with reading, tells you as soon as you meet her that she hates herself. She's heavy and constantly pinches her cheeks and tries to make her face as grotesque as possible. She wears baggy clothes because she's ashamed of her body and always seems about to flop on the ground. She also believes she's dumb and because she often acts stupidly, other people confirm her view of herself. Her father, a bitter man with a great deal of self-hatred himself, calls her "our little mistake" and she thinks of her life as a mistake. She isn't physically punished, is given food and books and dolls and toys. It's just that she's tolerated, not loved, and can't tolerate herself. Words can be violent and damaging. Children can be devastated by being called stupid, by being mocked and baited — especially those who don't know how to be violent themselves. It's important not to tear at your child's soul even in a joking sense or mock or reject her. Sylvia's working with a friend of mine who's had similar problems as a child and has come to terms with her self-hatred and turned it into a joke she makes on herself. By mocking herself, my friend takes the force out of others' aggression, and little by little has begun to build strength and self-respect and to dare to love things in the world. I see her helping Sylvia too by sharing her vulnerability and showing her how it is possible to turn self-hatred into inner strength. On a certain level, all of us have a little of Sylvia in us and the transformation of violence and self-hatred into strength is part of growing.

Desensitizing children to violence. I'll never forget something I saw in Spain about fifteen years ago. It was six in the morning. From our window we could see a hill overlooking a barnyard that had several pigs and a flock of sheep. On top of the hill was an old woman, the grandmother of the two boys who were standing on either side of her. They were looking down into the barnyard. All of a sudden I heard a horrible squealing sound. One of the boys started jumping up and down. The other hid his eyes with his hands and started crying. His grandmother grabbed his hands and held them, making him look down into the barnyard, where his father had just slit a pig's throat. She was teaching him to accept the violent act, to look directly at it and know that it was a necessary part of their life. Her intent was practical and caring — in that town the meat from one pig had to last all year and feed two families. In addition, her family provided most of the meat consumed in the town by raising and slaughtering sheep.

Our children look straight at violence and are desensitized to it also. TV is our barnyard of violence, though our children are not exposed out of goodwill or a communal sense of what is needed to survive. The violence on TV has a curious quality. There are people trying to get away with something and others trying to prevent them. There is no sense that there are underlying inequities that can be resolved. It is as if violent confrontation is taken as a nonreducible, and therefore noneliminable, basic.

With few exceptions, TV shows avoid dealing with the human consequences of violence; with the pain and anguish it causes. Violence is prettified or at least neutralized. The boys who saw the pig slaughtered heard the moans and saw the blood. Their father did not enjoy his task — he did it out of necessity and there was no pleasure in it. Many TV detective and adventure series are more casual toward death and injury. A bullet is fired and someone dies, a body falls off a building and is presumed dead. The detailed face of violence and the grief it produces are not portrayed in any serious way. Judy and I simply don't watch and don't let our children watch shows that exist to desensitize people to violence and create an attitude of inevitability and acceptance toward horrible abuses of life.

Strength and violence. The poet Wallace Stevens said in one of his essays, "The mind has added nothing to human nature. It is a violence from within that protects us from a violence without. It is the imagination pressing back against the pressure of reality. It seems, in the last analysis, to have something to do with our self-preservation; and that, no doubt, is why the expression of it, the sound of its words, helps us to live our lives."

Intellectual, emotional, and physical strength are components of mind in its broadest definition. They provide what Stevens calls inner violence and I refer to as strength. They enable people to resist becoming violent and to work to eliminate the inequalities that generate violence in others.

They are counterforces that make it possible to become a centered whole person.

Their development is not incidental to childhood but the essence of it. They lead to the one trait of character more than any other that counters violence from above as well as uncritical violent response and self-hatred — that is, self-respect.

Self-respect develops as personal strength grows. The stronger a child becomes, the more he or she becomes aware of being a person of value, someone who has power and can come to terms with the world. This authentic sense of personal worth and power, which constitutes self-respect, underlies the development of caring and strong children.

Without self-respect it is easy to become violent and resentful toward others, or to fall apart under pressure and succumb to other people's violence. With self-respect it is possible to continue learning, growing, and developing new strengths throughout life.

4

Respect and the Problem of Self-Image

Images of the Self

WHEN YOU THINK of yourself, what comes to mind? Is it your name or your children? The shape of your body or your sexual role? Does work come to mind or the secret things you enjoy? Are there times when images of yourself are bound up with your parents and their culture or with politics and friends? Or with the ways you mess yourself up? I find at one time or another all these aspects of life provide images that clarify me to myself. There is no single articulable self-image so much as a constellation of images that change and evolve over time yet that cohere enough to define a person that I recognize as myself. Sometimes these images provide contradictory aspects of the self, show me ways I want to be like and unlike my parents; to be a nurturing equal of Judy and babied at the same time; to look upon success as incidental to work and yet crave recognition and approval.

These images flit in and out of life. The question "Who am I?" is usually a crisis question. Yet in everyday life the images we have of ourselves affect the way we act and the choices we make. Our actions and choices in turn change these images. A few examples will make this clearer.

A friend of mine, who is a very gentle and loving man with children, is harsh and demanding with women. He sees himself as part of a traditional macho culture whose values and style he respects. On the other hand, he understands how foolish it is for him to encourage his students, both male and female, to liberate themselves and struggle for sexual and political equality while he resists the change he encourages. He has contradictory images of himself, which often pervade his dreams — the liberator and the tyrant playing with each other.

Herman runs up against himself every time he begins to take a woman seriously. He has to decide who he will be. A number of times in his life he chose to act to preserve the macho image of himself and ended up alone. Recently he has decided to replace that image of himself and imagines himself as free as he hopes his pupils will be. On the basis of that image he has backed down on many demands he used to make on women. He thinks of himself in a new way — as a person in transition. The image of the person he chooses to be has begun to change who he is. In turn, he no longer thinks of himself in the same way: the old sexual image of himself has been replaced by new images of his struggle to reconcile what is valuable in traditional culture with the need to give up all forms of dominating others.

I experienced similar conflicts over who I was and who I chose to be. For me, college was a focus for many of the contradictions that were building up in my life as I became a successful and popular high school student chosen to skip from a working-class community in the Bronx over the middle-class suburbs straight to Harvard.

I remember my first day at Harvard. My parents and I drove up to Cambridge from the Bronx. I was dressed according to my image of a Harvard man. My parents bought me a Brooks Brothers suit, a thin subdued tie, and a pair of white bucks. That morning was the first time I put the whole costume on. How was I to know that white bucks were supposed to look dirty and elbow patches were the signs of an authentic Harvard type; that thin ties were out that season? I was clearly identifiable as an imitation, but not to myself.

When we arrived in Cambridge and got to my dormitory, a deep shame overcame me. I was embarrassed by my parents' presence. They gave me away; there was no mistaking them for old Harvard and Radcliffe grads. I think they were embarrassed and awkward too. They had to go, I wanted them to go — the whole contradiction between who we were and who we wanted to be was too painful to face at that moment. They went home, and I was left to try out my new image.

That night I met my high school friend, who was assigned to another dormitory. His roommate was from Boston, an authentic Harvard man. He invited the two of us to go to dinner with his parents at the Harvard Club of Boston. We were picked up by his father, who drove a Mercedes-Benz. I found myself angry, thrown off — I'd never seen such an elegant car before, realized I wasn't wearing my clothes quite right, felt powerless and violated though no one had said or done anything to offend me. I felt a need to control the situation, to show people that I knew how to do things. We arrived at the Harvard Club and pulled into the parking lot. I jumped out of the car and looked around. It was an opportunity to take charge. I spotted a tall man wearing a fedora and a chesterfield coat, obviously the doorman or parking lot attendant, just like at the fancy restaurants in the Bronx. I ran over to him and imperiously commanded him to park the car. He looked down at me with a disdain I'd never experienced before and said, "Excuse me." My friend pulled me away — it was Senator Leverett Saltonstall. I could barely eat or look at anyone on the way back to the dormitory.

During my years at college I could never reconcile two images I had of myself: Harvard intellectual and Jewish boy from the Bronx. It never occurred to me that these two aspects of my personal history could be brought together — they were at war with each other, it had to be one or the other. It seemed a personal problem those days, just my struggle. I thought there was something wrong with me. Why couldn't I be content being a Harvard man or return to the Bronx and go to City College? If I had been able to cry, I think that there was probably some moment during every day at Harvard that I would have. Instead I drank a lot of beer.

Several years after graduation I was still faced by these same contradictory images of myself, and I chose to be my parents' and grandparents' child, not a Son of Harvard. The first time I realized that I would have to make that choice was the last day of commencement ceremonies. I went out for a beer with my tutor. He asked me what I intended to do with my life. I told him my dream — to teach fifth and sixth grade in the New York City schools and be a writer. He laughed; Harvard men don't do that. When I returned from my year at Oxford (I had just won a fellowship), graduate school was the obvious thing for me. Why, in five or ten years, if I was lucky, it was even possible to become a professor at Harvard.

Working with young children had been a dream of mine since junior high school. Yet that laugh kept me in graduate school for two years until I decided I wouldn't do what other people expected me to do anymore. I quit graduate school, got a teaching credential, and was hired as a fifth grade teacher in the New York City public schools. It was the first time in years that I felt I had come home.

For most of us the images we have of ourselves overlap past and future, mingle reality and dream, embody resignation and aspiration, and are full of love and rejection. They represent who we think we are, what we expect will happen to us in the world, and who we hope to be. These images develop through our lives and sometimes hinge on events; sometimes are felt rather than embodied in a scene or idea. For example, when I think of myself, I think among other things of the year Judy and I spent in Spain living in a small town gardening and teaching me how to write; asthma and my continual flight from people and things that try to smother me; the way my grandfather looked toward the end of his life; toys and games, the toy store my mother used to take me to, the Gilbert Hall of Science, where my father took me; eating a Bialystok roll in a cafeteria with my grandfather while he talked to his friends in Yiddish; walking down Riverside Drive in a snowstorm pretending I was a Jewish peasant in Poland trying to find my way home; stationery stores and piles and piles of fountain pens; fat, the struggle to keep my body healthy; the Masked Rider, a combination Lone Ranger and Plastic Man I used to make up stories about before going to bed when I was in grade school.

There are other images and scenes too, some that occur in times of crisis only, others which appear like dreams, uncalled and unexpected. Taken as a whole, they provide a fairly accurate portrait of who I think I am and who I'd like to be. They also portray the contradictions that characterize my life.

I remember taking a class at Teachers College, Columbia, on the self-image of disadvantaged children. I tried to apply everything the professor said to my students and myself. Did we have positive or negative self-images? Could our images be improved? The more I listened, the less I understood. No one I knew had a simple way of looking at him or herself. Everyone had burdens and longings, was loving at times and cold at other times. *The Self-Image* was an unreal abstraction, a way professionals used to talk about people who were strangers to them.

There is not one fixed and consistent image we have of ourselves. The same is true for children and infants. They do not have *A Self-Image,* but rather a number of images of themselves, which are sometimes contrary and always complex. They develop around central themes in children's lives and reflect who children think they are or are supposed to be as well as who they wish to become.

The Emergence of a Sense of Self in Infants

One can only guess how an infant thinks and feels, or what an infant's earliest sense of self is. I imagine a number of things happen simultaneously as an infant becomes aware of the division of the world into Self and Other. These things happen to the infant and are initiated by the infant — from the very beginning, life is a matter of exchange.

Imagine yourself lying on your back unable to turn over yet, having no command of language, no focused control of your arms and legs. There are still ways to take in the world and control it a bit. Your eyes take in what surrounds you, you smell and feel. Your nerves respond to what comes in contact with your body. All that is mostly passive, but move your eyes and the world shifts, turn your body and you may feel something different, turn your head and the smells may shift with the sights. There is a you that focuses, shifts, turns, grabs, hears, and makes noises. Imagine the power that an infant must feel upon first realizing that he or she can decide when to cry, that the making of sounds can be controlled.

As most infants grow, an integrative process takes place. Sounds, sights, and feelings are put together into wholes, and objects and people emerge. It's even possible that this integration starts with life. In either case, the infant has to figure out the nature of the objects and events in the world about it and in doing so also has to come to a sense of him or herself as the clarifier, the point of reference. Without this sense of the self as point of reference, space, time, objects, and living beings make no sense and become unpredictable and fragmented.

One can see this with some severely disturbed children, who seem to have no sense of who they are or where they are. They act as if objects might fly away or explode at any moment, are often confused about where their bodies leave off and the world begins, and are terrified of the world because there is no stability to people and objects.

The sense of oneself as reference point seems to develop very early. Young infants lie in their cribs moving their eyes back and forth, over and over; practice making sounds; grab things and practice letting them go. As they get older, practice and repetition remain central activities. They hold or push things, drop things, say words over and over. These events seem to have dual purposes — they confirm the power of the self and the stability of the world outside the self.

The ability to practice, to control one's eyes and head, to repeat a sound, or to grab something is not a mechanical function. Perhaps there are times when repetition does take place in a machine-like fashion. However, machines don't laugh and feel pleasure at the exercise of their power, nor cry when they are frustrated or not allowed to function. When infants exercise their power, there is some sense in which they are aware of what they are doing and exercise their wills. The sense infants have that they can do something is probably the earliest sense of self. It is preverbal, and it might be similar to the unselfconscious feeling of wholeness and control adults sometimes feel when singing or dancing or creating. When I write, I feel that way, like an infant — in control and yet not thinking of controlling, completely in my pen and on the paper and at the same time thoroughly myself.

Another early sense infants get of themselves comes through a recognition of their names, through understanding that certain sounds other people make stand for them and no one else.

Naming and Disrespect

One of the earliest images a child has is tied up with the name he or she is given. That name* defines the child as a particular and unique individual at the same time that it places him or her in the context of a family and culture. One of the surest ways to offend young children is to forget or fail to learn their names.

When a child learns to recognize and use his or her name, it is not merely a matter of memorizing another label for something. To know your name is to recognize yourself as a separate entity, a person in a world with other persons. It is an act of self-identity that at the same time is an act of separation.

* For a more in-depth look at naming, see my book *Golden Boy as Anthony Cool* (Dial Press, New York, 1972).

However, very early in life children can learn to hate or become ashamed of their names, or to hide them or wish for new names. People can make fun of their names, parents can be ashamed of their own names or embarrassed by the names cultural custom has forced upon their children.

For example, a child born José can be turned into Joe, Moishe into Morris, Herschel into Herbert, Rivkah to Rebecca. The anglicization of names that occurs in many immigrant families can come as a shock to a young child and be taken as a violation of the self. I was born Herbert Cohen and my parents changed the name Cohen to Kohl when I was four or five. It was a shock to me, a sign that something wasn't right in our family, that being ourselves somehow wasn't good enough. In my mind it was bound up with being Jewish and not wanting certain people I never saw, but whom my father saw at work, to know that we were Jewish. It raised questions about myself as a Jew, as a member of a family that felt insecure about itself, and as an American who didn't really belong. That change of name became an image for me of a whole number of things about myself that I couldn't articulate. I was Herbert-Cohen-Kohl. Or perhaps I was none of those. The change of Cohen to Kohl opened up the possibility that I might not be Herbert either. In those days I had a fantasy friend, the Masked Rider, who was me and independent of me. Every night before I went to sleep I would make up a story about him. He had no name, didn't know who his parents were, and roamed about helping people Lone Ranger–style. He remains for me an image of the problem of roots that many of us in this country face.

A change of name is not always a negative thing. Many Black people I know have abandoned the names they were born with, which originated with slave-owners, and have chosen names that indicate their roots in Africa. The change of names is an affirmation of self rather than a denial of it in the service of assimilation. A number of five- and six-year-olds I know whose parents have changed their names can tell the meanings of their new names and explain how these new names provide positive images of their selves.

Children treat names as if they had some inherent power and listen very carefully to how people use other people's names. They quickly pick up on the fact that adults find some names strange or silly, that some names seem appropriate for girls and others for boys, that some identify a person as a foreigner and others as an American.

It is important for adults to understand that children are always listening and trying to sort out what adults talk about. Sometimes casual remarks or jests about people's names — about the Cohens, Goldbergs, Rufuses, Sambos, Juans, and Josés or Giovannis — set the scene for deeper prejudices and begin to get children to sort out people by types rather than to know them as persons.

The way you talk about your own name and the way you refer to your child while talking about him or her to other adults also make deep impressions and generate images of the self. In pathological situations, where for some reason parents hate one of their children and refer to his or her name with scorn, a child can learn to hate that name. This may sound harsh, but a number of years ago I took care of a child who hated his own name so much that he became schizophrenically deaf for about five minutes after he heard anyone use it. He never used his own name and referred to himself as an embryo. He insisted he had not been born yet. I could understand after being around his parents for a while why he hated the sound of that name so much. "Henry," they would snap out at him, "go to bed; you're in the way." "Henry is a strange boy," they would tell visitors. "Thank God, Henry isn't here," they would say when he was out of the house. After a while I grew to hate that name too, though I cared very much for the boy. He had to be renamed; he was right, he hadn't been born yet. His so-called madness (childhood schizophrenia, the psychiatrists called it) was sane — he was protecting himself from becoming the person his parents thought he was. Before he went to bed every night, he read a number of Dr. Seuss books over and over, pronouncing all the weird and funny names Seuss uses, speculating on which one might fit him. He once told me that he'd find the right name one day and then he'd be born.

Children are very sensitive to how their names are used and know they can hurt others by twisting or making fun of their names. There are times when my children become annoyed at each other and tease each other by distorting their names: Joshie, Moshie, Poshie; Tonia, Bonia, Ammonia; Erica, America, Dereka. Sometimes it can simply be fun, but often such taking of people's names in vain provokes real anger.

Once I remember calling Joshua Joshawoodie. It seemed silly and affectionate, but he reacted very angrily. "I'm Joshua!" he screamed, and I laughed, he seemed so grown up and serious. My laughter angered him even more, and he swung at me. I realized that my perception of the situation and his perception were not the same. By playing with his name and by not taking his response seriously I was showing disrespect, and he fought me to command my respect.

Respect in this situation meant my taking seriously his image of himself, of not playing with his name against his wishes. Many adults want to command the respect of children without realizing that they will be respected only if they, in turn, respect their children.

I've noticed a lot of fathers who enjoy teasing their children, making fun of their names, making up nicknames that their children don't like, and carrying on without any regard for the feelings of their children. Sometimes it's a power game — an attempt to reduce a child to nonverbal rage or tears. At other times it is more harmless, like playing with a pet whose feelings you don't believe you have to respect.

Children are people and dislike the same kind of mistreatment and disrespect that you dislike. For example, adults like to be called by the names they accept as appropriate to a given situation and are offended if they are made fun of to their faces. At home it is usually quite acceptable to be called by an affectionate nickname, yet many people find it inappropriate to be referred to that way by a stranger or by an employee.

There are many other ways of showing disrespect to children. Grown-ups don't like to be pinched arbitrarily, to drop whatever they are doing and perform for someone else, to be asked to show off what they know. Neither do children. I found it useful to compare my ways of talking to or being with children to my ways of being with adults in order to undo a tendency I had when I first began teaching kindergarten, which was to talk down to my students and not take them seriously on their own terms.

It is easy to forget to take children seriously — to pay no attention to their opinions, to undervalue what they care about, to manipulate their friendship, to talk about them in their presence. All of these ways of being disrespectful to children undermine the respect the child might feel for you. To be treated disrespectfully introduces an element of distrust and resentment into a relationship. It shows up the adult to be manipulating and lacking in authenticity.

I remember sitting on the floor as a child, pretending to play with a toy and listening to the grown-ups talk about me in the third person.

"Herbert is such a doll."

"How is his asthma?"

"Doesn't he ever give you any trouble?"

It went on and on. I learned a lot from the way I was talked about but wished that people would talk to me, ask me about my asthma, find out from me the ways in which I was wicked.

In my family I was usually referred to in loving terms. I've known children, however, who've spent hours listening to their parents complaining about how difficult children are, about how boys are such a bother, about how they wish their girls were only more active, about all the frustrations and difficulties of raising children in our society. When speaking directly to their children, except in anger, they are all positive and saccharine, never raise any issues or ask for opinions. The children hear all of this and their image of who they are, the sense they have of the meanings and associations of their names become weighted with all these burdens. It is no wonder that so many people in our society find excuses to change their names or dream of doing so.

It is important to use people's names respectfully, to be sensitive to ways your children care to be addressed, and acknowledge their presence by not talking about them in the third person in their presence. Children listen carefully, and what they hear is as influential as what you tell them.

Pretty Babies

Another source that generates images that last throughout our lives is our body. Infants and very young children are not self-conscious about their bodies except in extremely pathological situations. They are more concerned with getting control over their body and using it than with how it looks.

And at the beginning of life adults are very open and accepting of the way children look. There is probably a universal cultural convention to look on babies as beautiful or at least pretend that those seemingly helpless and uncoordinated creatures are lovely. I remember when my three children were first born. I badly wanted to see something special and beautiful in them, but only saw the beginning of life. That in itself was beautiful, but until after a few months, when I came to see the infants as people, I pretended they were beautiful and said so to friends and family, who naturally agreed.

For at least the first year of life, adult tolerance for the physical appearance of normally formed children seems to hold. Fat infants are cute, skinny ones are strong, bald ones are cuddly, hairy ones are mature. Any characteristic can be accepted, even praised, up to a point, and then we begin to educate our children to be self-conscious about their bodies. I'm not sure exactly when this begins, probably when children are between the ages of two and four, depending upon how a child looks and how the parents would like their child to look. Excessive praise or criticism, or some mixture of both of these, begins children thinking about their bodies as physical objects for others to judge and not just organic parts of their selves. The body begins to be like a painting or sculpture, an aesthetic object to be judged on the basis of culturally bound ideas of beauty and ugliness that are also often confused with equally culturally bound ideas of good and bad.

Fatness is a good example of a physical characteristic turned into a personal and cultural problem. As a baby I was chubby and remained so until adolescence. My grandparents loved me to be that way. For them fatness was a sign of wealth, a tribute to the parents who could feed and protect their children, a sign of sturdiness and heartiness, which were of great value where they grew up in Poland. My parents weren't so sure about fat. They loved me as I was but also wanted an American child, a slim, tall, handsome prince who would make any middle-class family proud. My grandparents would feed me chocolate bars, and my parents would urge me to diet. My body became a battleground, and at times I tore it apart. In the fourth and fifth grade I got into the habit of thinking of myself as little fat Herbie, an image that has stayed with me in the same way that the Masked Rider is still alive. Once I saw a comic book called "A Little Fat Nothing Called Herbie," which said it better than anything. On a bad day I am that little fat nothing who wants to pinch his belly and sides, squeeze the fat out of cheeks, and cut off his double chin. On other days I roam like the Masked Rider. Most of the time, however, I'm not particularly self-conscious about my body.

I've been thinking about fat recently because Tonia is a bit heavy. I see me in her: the best and the worst. Not surprisingly, I don't mind seeing in her parts of me that are sources of pride. But when I see parts of me that are weak or confused, it becomes difficult to control my anger at her. Why does she eat so much? Isn't it bad for her? She should wear dark clothes, since they make her look skinnier!

I'm not talking to her, but to myself. However, it has been a problem for me to control my impulse to change her. I'm sure if it were left to me, she would have a problem. Fortunately, Judy and I know and can talk about the worst in each other. She has shown me how I was beginning to get down on Tonia, to make her worry about her body when, in fact, she was active and lively and quite comfortable with herself. I was able to pull back and look at Tonia not as me, but as herself, to leave her alone and then take her for herself and not provoke the same confounding physical self-consciousness I had as a child.

At Harvard I learned that problems can also develop for people who are looked upon as the embodiment of the dominant cultural ideal of beauty. There are a number of men who fit the model of a blond, handsome, thin, tall prince of democracy. The physical perfection that is attributed to them in the culture also generalizes in people's minds to an emotional perfection. I imagined the first time I met people like that at Harvard (they were the first Protestants I'd ever seen in real life) that their inner life had to be calm, untroubled, full of contentment, as emotionally perfect as their appearance was physically ideal. I discovered after a while that they were people more often than not pained by the burden of other people's assumption of their perfection. It took a while to understand the pain of people I pinched my body to be like. It's as if they suffered the same pain over the worth and dignity of their minds as people who aspired to be like them suffered over their bodies. In fact, some of these people I knew at Harvard came to despise and destroy their bodies too, since their bodies masked their souls. It was crazy, and yet it brought me back to myself. The slave imitates the master only to discover that the master is miserable too and that there is pain both in being the cultural ideal and in wanting to be it.

It is important to learn how to look at children without ranking or comparing them. Instead of wondering about who is best or most beautiful, it makes sense to look for the uniqueness in each individual. This requires practice — some children emerge slowly, some give a first impression that quickly changes, others are admirably constant. Some children are easy to find attractive; there are others who seem too sloppy or nervous or extreme in one feature or another to be attractive. It is hard for many adults to look at or be with children who don't show an easy charm or grace or who don't conform to their stereotypes. Yet all children who are not deprived of love show a grace and uniqueness. It is a question of adults' learning to look into children's eyes, to encounter them face-to-face, to show respect and love, and therefore to allow mutual respect and regard to emerge. There is no formula that can show one how to do this. As a teacher I find it useful to look for children's strengths and relate to them through these strengths. If a child can play ball, draw, tell a good story, relate to animals, enjoy memorizing facts, or whatever, I focus on that strength and try to resist defining or describing people through their deficiencies. It is possible to describe a child as "the fat boy" or "the girl with the pimples" or, on an intellectual level, as a "dummy." It is also possible to describe the same children as, for example, "John, who knows everything about fighter planes," or "Susan, who's the best jacks player in the school." I've never known children who didn't display strengths and who didn't appreciate their being acknowledged. And after a while, looking for strengths instead of pouncing on weaknesses becomes a habit.

Comfortable Bodies

We have images of ourselves as active or passive, as mobile or clumsy. Some children learn to be afraid to move and to distrust their bodies or overprotect them. I know a couple who married the year they graduated from college. They immediately set themselves up in a fancy decorated apartment. Every object was carefully chosen and artistically displayed. Unfortunately, a year and a half later a child was born into this fairyland. There was no place for the baby to move around. They roped off the living room, put their bedroom and the dining room off bounds. A small study was turned into a nursery, and that was where the baby lived when he wasn't brought out and displayed to friends and relatives. That worked out well for a while, but a child needs more space at two years than at six months. As the little boy started moving out of the nursery and exploring the house, he was met with a barrage of no's. Don't climb, don't touch that, good children don't swing on furniture. All of that would have not been too bad if the child had lived in a house instead of a city apartment; at least the outdoors would have been available. But it wasn't, and I could see the child becoming afraid to use his body. He couldn't move without wondering whether he was being bad or not. After a while he took to sitting and watching TV most of the time, and when he got a little bit older and went to school, he took to being a little brain, a child who used his mind because he didn't know his body. It wasn't curiosity he showed his teachers so much as aggressiveness and competitiveness. He relished verbal assault, shaming and embarrassing others for their errors. All this was rewarded in school — he had straight A's, was told over and over how good it was that he didn't fight and run around like so many other boys. His parents were pleased too — except that he was a little fat, didn't seem happy somehow. When he quit college after two years to live on a farm with some friends and, as he put it, "get into his body," his parents were shocked. Yet he claims that this time is the happiest and fullest in his life. He told me that this is the first time he has respected himself and that he no longer needs to make other people feel uncomfortable.

Hating your body or finding it a problem is a form of

disrespect toward your self and a source of resentment toward others who make you feel uncomfortable. Children who are too confined or restricted, who cannot move around, who are expected to behave in too controlled and respectable ways too early in their lives can easily become frustrated and seem snotty and disrespectful toward adults. It is as if a basic need were being denied and a wedge being driven into the self.

Children don't have too much choice about the conditions they are forced to live with. They don't choose their parents, don't choose poverty or wealth, don't choose at birth their language or their food. However, they do react to all these conditions and can choose to respect the world they live in or reject it. Often the decision to reject the world adults force on a child is a healthy form of disrespect, a decision to remain oneself despite the efforts of grown-ups to mold and change one. When you find a child acting disrespectfully in general or with disrespect toward certain things, it is necessary to go beyond the particular act into the conditions of the child's life to understand the coherence and motivation for disrespectful, defiant, insulting behavior.

For example, children who feel uncomfortable about being fat are always attuned to the way people refer to them. If they are praised for looking lovely, they tend to react with scorn toward what they interpret to be a polite lie. If they are made fun of, even in a good-natured way, they become resentful. If nothing is said about fat, they become suspicious because it is such an obsession that they can't believe other people aren't thinking about that. Children whose self-respect is undermined in some way simply cannot respect adults who seem to be in complicity with their parents or others who make them feel uncomfortable. That might explain why so many young people look toward adults as different as possible from their parents to be their teachers and gurus and leaders. It is often an attempt to develop self-respect, to escape from damaging images of the self and randomize things and start living all over again.

Hair and Personal Appearance

There are many absurd ways in which people feel their bodies in our culture. Hair is a focus for many of them, since it is in the peculiar position of mediating what is natural and what is culture. We are born with hair; that is natural. What we do with it is cultural. There is no way to avoid making a cultural or personal statement through the way you deal with your hair. Even never combing, brushing, cutting, or touching your hair is a statement.

It used to shock me how much my parents worried about how my hair looked. My hair is black, part curly, part frizzy, and thoroughly disorderly. When I was born, it was sandy brown and straight, good Protestant-type hair. I've always liked to wear my hair moderately long and brush it only for hygienic reasons. I have cultivated a moderately wild and disorderly look ever since the time I spent in Paris enjoying the pretense of being an artist and a free soul. There were times when this way of wearing my hair would drive my mother and father wild. They responded to it on a visceral level, and there were times when I fancied them getting sick looking at me. Looking back, I think I enjoyed seeing them becoming so upset by something that seemed superficially so simple. It was a way of having power over them and making me feel strong at a time when I was feeling lost and powerless, in between finishing college and finding work that was meaningful.

It took some time to understand what was so upsetting to my parents, and it wasn't the same thing for each of them. My father saw in my hair the curls and earlocks of the Orthodox Jews he and his friends tried to dissociate themselves from. It was a symbol of European Jewry, of shtetls and pogroms, of confinement and poverty. For my mother the same hair was a symbol of Bohemia, a rejection of the middle class she was trying so hard to join. The hair embodied different cultural contradictions for my parents and was a source of power and self-respect for me.

It is fascinating to watch as young people take control over their own hair. There is a whole range of styles to choose from. But these styles are not simply ways of dressing hair so much as of identifying oneself with a particular way of living.

I've seen parents practically disown their children over fights about the way the children chose to wear their hair. In some families it was long hair that provoked the struggle; in others it was wearing an Afro instead of a "process." Recently the same thing has happened in some "hip" families, where the children of long-hairs choose to wear their hair Marine or Buddha style.

Usually until children are seven or eight years old parents have control over their children's hair. They decide how hair is to be worn, adorned, cut. Sometimes there are monumental battles over haircuts or over not getting haircuts. In my kindergarten class the boys were particularly sensitive to their parents' changing their hair styles. Generally there were two hair styles for the boys: Afros and medium long hair. I remember Saul having his hair cut short and keeping his coat and hood shut tight for weeks. I tried to flatter, cajole, charm him into showing himself instead of hiding. He refused, and the one time I took the coat and hood off despite his protests, he acted so devastated that I pulled back and let him cover his head.

The same thing happened to another one of the boys, whose parents gave him an elaborate set of corn rows (closely braided hair in traditional West African style). The hair was beautifully done, the design intricate, but he couldn't show it to the other children. It was too different, and he didn't choose it. For days he wouldn't take his stocking cap off.

I'm a little that way with my own children's hair. Generally my identification goes back to a 1950s Bohemian style. I feel most comfortable with shaggy-haired men and long-haired women, though I realize that it's my form of provincialism. Recently Erica, who has long straight hair, wanted to get a haircut with a friend of hers. I panicked inside at the same time that I realized how foolish my feelings were. Yet a short-haired daughter didn't fit my image of her being a beautiful young woman at all. I realized that despite my attempts not to mold her against her will, I had very strong feelings about who she should be and how she should look. Short hair seemed unfeminine to me on a gut level. I braced myself and she did get a haircut — not a short one, but a medium one that didn't bother me much.

Recently around Berkeley lots of women and girls have been wearing their hair short. At first the style repulsed me. I couldn't look at women with short hair without feeling tense and angry, much the way my parents felt about long-haired men. On an intellectual level I understood that people had a right to wear their hair any way they wanted and that long hair and female submissiveness were tied up in parts of our culture. However, on a gut level I was upset and angered by "these women turning themselves into men." This anger and revulsion had to be dealt with, has to be by all of us who want our ideas and dreams and beliefs to also be embodied in our feelings and our daily lives. I began by looking at people's faces and avoiding their hair; then, little by little, working myself back to the hair, remembering that it was I that was silly and overreacting.

Cultural forms, even oppressive ones, get all tied up in feelings. If culture is violated, we get sick to the stomach, get headaches, nausea. Wear hair too long or short, listen to unfamiliar music, eat with different utensils, wear strange clothes, and we can tolerate and rationalize it, but we can't control our feelings. Parents often act irrationally toward their children's style or preferences, even when they know better. We have to get better control of our feelings, which are as likely to be deceived as our minds.

There is a current therapeutic attitude that masquerades as sensitivity and implies that if you feel something, then it is all right. I find that as dangerous as the attitude that people have a *right* to believe whatever they want. People do not have a *right* to believe that they are superior to others and have a *right* to oppress them. Nor do they have a *right* to reject people on the basis of feelings of disgust.

We have to be able to work with our feelings when they are tied to intolerance and rejection. We have to learn to accept changes in style, differences in behavior and culture, even if this means living with a bit of discomfort. It is amazing what one can get used to — long hair is no longer a problem for people who used to be repulsed by it; pork is eaten by many Jews who felt nauseated at the mention of it; atonal music no longer sounds strange to many people. Feelings change as well as ideas. This is important to understand when your child does something that is unusual to you but not dangerous or threatening, and yet you find yourself sick or angry.

It is healthy for young people to experiment with style, to discover ways in which they feel comfortable. Experimentation of this sort is not defiance or rejection, as many adults interpret it. It is a reaching out to the world, an assertion of self, an attempt to come to terms with the world on one's own rather than simply imitate one's parents. It's a stepping out that involves making mistakes, developing judgments about people and confidence in how one appears in the world. It is fundamental to the development of self-respect that young people experiment and take chances, try out things short of those which are clearly suicidal. It is also fundamental to the development of young people's respect for their parents that parents support their children's efforts to develop autonomy and show self-discipline in dealing with situations that are new to them. How can a person respect someone who loses all control over a hair style, much less a political or sexual act?

Of course, it is easier to want to be supportive of your child than actually to do it. The earlier one learns to respect the integrity and autonomy of one's children, the easier it will be to support them when they become older and move away from the family. There will always be mistakes, times when you can't stand your children's friends, when their clothes or hair styles seem bizarre or ugly, and when you can no longer contain yourself and explode over nothing. I see it in myself and have come to realize how important self-discipline is for creating a safe nurturing environment for my children.

Parental Images

If you ever wonder how your children might turn out as adults, remember that your life is before your children, with all its pain and inconsistency, funniness or grimness, self-destructive habits as well as creative ones. Children form images of their parents but have to keep them secret, because they represent more truths than can be politely spoken.

Think of the images of Mommy and Daddy that your children might form, and those you had of your own parents. And think of the materials that these images are created from — the fights, the casual kiss, the time you lost your temper, the time you told stories about yourself as a child, the way you leave the house in the morning or return in the evening, the way you talk about other people and the way they talk about you, the way your body looks and feels, the things you do to punish or praise, the way you relax and the way you respond to pressure. Five-year-olds, maybe even two- and three-year-olds, take all this in and attempt to sort it out, to get a sense for themselves of who Mommy is and who Daddy is. As very young children they will accept almost anything as the way things are. As they grow, however, judgment sets in and children sometimes get very severe with their parents. This is especially true if different standards are applied to adult behavior and child behavior. Children are fanatic about fairness.

One can imagine how a child's images of his or her parents might develop. Suppose, for example, that a young boy's father is a skilled writer who has not been published very much. The father, whom I'll call Robert, loves to write and is fanatic about having a place to write and a time for writing free of all other responsibilities. An hour before writing time, Robert paces frantically, smokes, talks almost incoherently. After writing he is ecstatic, friendly, gentle — for an hour, that is — then he becomes bored and depressed, feels no one will ever care about his work. At times he seems on the verge of crying; at other times he rants and rages against publishers and editors. His son sees him in many ways — as a worker who enjoys his work, as a gentle man, as a nasty, bitter, selfish man, as a depressed and babyish man, as an artist and crazy person, as a ritualist. All of these images exist, some dominant and some minor. Children sort out all the images they have of their parents and different children in a family form different constellations of images of the same parents. If Robert's son highlights the work, he sees a special person, a literary martyr perhaps; if he highlights the frustration, bitterness, and the selfishness about space and time to work, he sees a mean and egotistic man.

Children have all these images to sort out about both their parents, and often the very process of sorting them out and choosing how to perceive parents is part of a child's development of his or her image of self. I chose to build my image of my grandfather over his obsession with work, his generosity, and his fairness. The impatience, crankiness, intolerance for things done in new ways, and the fear and scorn for the non-Jewish world were present but played down and often forgotten. I turned my image of him into a model for myself, an image of the kind of person I wanted to be.

It was more complex with my father, of whom I had conflicting and equally strong images. He was demanding, a perfectionist, the boss of Herbert Construction Company, the boss of my mother, and the boss of me. He also was a soft touch, someone you could get presents from and get to do what you wanted. One image induced fear, the other a sense that people were manipulable if only one were clever enough. I admired the boss and feared it, chose not to be one. It was not part of my image of myself. However, I see myself as a hustler, a manipulator for what I believe to be just causes, more like my father than I like to admit.

As a child I used to have long discussions with my friends about our parents, about what we liked and didn't like in them. None of us imitated our parents uncritically — we accepted what seemed of value to us from what we perceived of them. We also rejected a lot and tested a lot. I remember my parents worrying about my inconsistencies just as I find myself worrying about the inconsistencies of my own children — one day cruel, the other day loving, sometimes bossing, sometimes cooperating — trying many modes of functioning, picking and choosing from the examples around them ways that they find comfortable and that minimize their own pain and problems.

To get a sense of how your child sees you it's necessary to have an honest and complex vision of yourself. If you can develop this, it will be easier to understand and accept the ways in which your children choose to be like you and the ways in which they choose to reject aspects of your life.

Sex Stereotypes

Children use the images they have of their parents (and of their siblings too) as palettes out of which part of their own images are composed. One component of these images is sexual. Most boys and girls in this society have a very strong sense of themselves as either males or females. In my neighborhood there is a group of boys five to eight years old who call themselves the Girl-Haters. They go around teasing and sometimes tormenting girls their age, refusing to play with girls, and generally strutting around. They play with guns, race down the street on skateboards, and take a very aggressive and competitive stance toward each other. Some of the boys are gentler, more able to relate to girls or adults away from the group. Within the group their image of themselves is as tough and independent men.

There are a number of girls the same age in the neighborhood, but they don't have a club. In fact, they seldom play in groups larger than two or three. They seem to spend a lot of time manipulating each other, stealing friends, or ganging up on someone. They don't have the same pack loyalty the boys show and seldom run around or climb. Their lives are lived more indoors than the boys', and they are occupied with fantasy play, with dolls and doll clothes. They do a lot of reading, too, which the boys find sissyish.

Among the girls there are also children who behave differently, both more gently and more physically aggressively, when the group is not around.

These children have defined sex roles for themselves. Some of them are not happy with the roles and will have to come to terms with what it means for them to be boys or girls. Others, actually a smaller number, seem to enjoy the roles they have created from their observations of their parents, other adults, and TV.

What is interesting is that most of these children are willing to act in stereotyped ways within the group and know what the stereotyped images of boy behavior and girl behavior are, and yet have not completely assimilated them to their private images of themselves. Most of these boys and girls don't want their worlds restricted. They all want to experiment with feelings, with their bodies, with being aggressive and being loving. The images of boy and girl squeeze them. It is possible to help children escape these stereotypes and avoid the pain of having images of themselves that are stifling and frustrating. There is a problem, however. You cannot enable children to develop images of themselves that go beyond the traditional sex-stereotyped ones unless you are discontented with those roles yourself and doing something about it in your own life.

I have a friend who teaches the use of power tools to women. Often mothers and their children come to learn together. The women who come usually confess to being afraid of the tools and uncertain whether they can master them. Power tools are bound up with images of male aggression. The children are also afraid because the tools are dangerous. As people learn to use the tools with skill and caution, the tools become desexualized. They become instruments to make things, no more nor less. A number of times I've seen parents and children laughing at each other's mistakes, building things together, engaging affectionately in common work. Learning something new with your child can be an adventure for both of you. Making mistakes together, and developing mastery together, can create trust and affection the way words cannot.

The desexualizing of objects and tasks is an important part of developing a wider range of possible activities and responses for children. If dishwashing, cooking, and serving are desexualized, the issue of who does them is a matter of time and competency rather than sexual identity. Sometimes a shift in definition or a redescription of toys can make them interesting to both boys and girls. For example, a dollhouse redefined as a haunted house lends itself to broader use. There are also physical activities such as bike riding, ice-skating, and swimming that boys and girls can master together.

Presenting boys and girls with a challenge they haven't faced before also helps overcome the segregation of activities according to sex. Camping, hiking, hunting for insects, learning first aid, working a microscope, building a geodesic dome can all be mastered equally by boys and girls. What is important is to pick activities that are new to both the boys and girls so that they can observe and help each other learning.

As you attempt to overcome the identification of certain activities with sex roles, there are certain facets of daily life in our society that have to be dealt with sensitively. All of our children are aware of traditional sexual roles and most of them are tempted by them. Boys and girls all know about sexy women and virile men; about dolls and fancy dresses being girls' stuff, and trucks and racing cars boys' stuff. Moreover, many children find what the culture offers somewhat attractive — my daughters love to play with Barbie dolls and my son prefers racing cars and knights and Superhero dolls. There are times when they play together or when they change toys, but there are clear preferences they show that are none of my business to manipulate.

On the other hand, my daughters both play with Barbie dolls and consider themselves feminists. They believe that they can play with any kind of toy they want, that they can do any work they choose, and that they can enjoy both being physical and being fancy.

Josh in his way also believes that he can do anything his sisters can do and also that he has a right to make his own preferences.

It is important that choices be opened up to children, that they be assured that they can become anything they choose, and that they will be supported in the choices they make. Over the last four years Tonia has said at one time or another that she wanted to be a pilot, an artist, a writer, a nurse, a doctor, someone who fixes cars, a mother, a ballet dancer. These choices shift, but the palette is broad — she can see herself doing so many different things. Her images of herself as a girl are enriched by other images of work and play.

There was a phase I went through that could be called the penitent male chauvinist stage. I saw in myself all the evils of machismo pointed out by the feminist movement and even made up some more. It was an indulgence in male guilt, almost a slipping into the man-as-baby role. I took to washing dishes with a vengeance, cooked dinner, made the bed, and watched my children for signs of sexist contamination. I got the girls cars and building sets, read Josh *William Wants a Doll* a thousand times, and bought him a baby doll. The girls were encouraged to be physical, play ball, and run around and be tough. Josh helped me with dinner and the dishes. For a while it was fun for the children. But then the girls wanted something else — to be girls with all those abilities, but still to be girls who played with dolls and sometimes dressed fancy. In fact, they preferred dolls, as they let me know when birthdays and Christmas came around.

They identified themselves as girls, not boys. And Josh thinks of himself as a boy, not a he/she or a "him or her." It has been fascinating for me to watch my children sort out sex differences without confusing them with limitations imposed by one sex on the other, or with one sex exploiting the other. Sex-role identification seems to me to be very healthy for children as long as it's not confused with the real problem of sex-based limitations on life functions.

Sexual Images

The images children have of the sex roles they play are tied up with sexual images as well as with play, work, and style. Children quickly get a sense of whether people consider them plain or pretty, ugly or handsome. They also sense when some people think them attractive and others think them plain. Adults flirt with children all the time, and children as young as three understand flirtation as a particular mode of relating to people. One whole facet of the images children have of themselves is dependent upon the tone and emotional quality of the attention adults give them. In a family of many siblings, the children are aware of who gets the most attention and who the least, of who is paid attention to by men relatives, of whom women go toward. Parental preferences are even more carefully scrutinized. However, the way children react to being flirted with or kept away is often quite complex. In some families where the children are close to each other, the "pretty" child can suffer guilt for being liked so much, the "plain" child can learn to play sexy to gain attention. On the other hand, the "pretty" child can use the attention he or she gets to manipulate adults and can come to have an image of his or her body as a weapon. The "plain" child can feel rejected and come to hate his or her body, or can compensate and become supersmart or superstrong. It is important for adults to be aware of the quality of attention they give to their children. For example, do you treat boys and girls differently in terms of physical contact, joking, rough-housing, showing off, punishing, praising?

Just think about these aspects of relating to your children. How do you embrace your sons and your daughters? Do you praise your daughter's clothes and not your son's, or get upset if your daughter messes up her blouse and feel good that your son was rough enough to tear his pants even though you pretend to be angry?

Do you joke about your son's girlfriends and get a bit grim when you see your daughter flirting with someone? Do you make eyes at your daughter, wink at her, and act almost seductive while trying to look your son straight in the eyes and attempt to project an image of strength?

These questions are asked from my perspective, that of a father. They could be rephrased to embody some of the ways women can react differently toward daughters and sons.

Small, unspoken gestures and casual, unthinking contacts show children what aspects of their lives are valued by adults.

Young boys in need of praise almost without thought will act to reinforce the approval they get from being rough, competitive, domineering, and lecherous. Girls too will become sexy and learn to use gestures and their bodies in ways that get them praise. However, it is the adults who set the terms and conditions under which affection and attraction between people are turned into cultural phenomena. Affection is natural — infants and children need to like others and be liked. However, affection is structured by culture so that certain of its manifestations are encouraged and others discouraged. "Boys" and "girls" are made, not born. If you hope to see your children express their feelings without confusing affection with aggression or seduction, and have images of themselves as nurturing people, then you have to be nurturing yourself.

Racial Images and Racism

Adults in our society have at the very least vestiges of racism, and children first learn racism consciously or unconsciously from their parents. Race is not simply a matter of skin color or bone structure, and because it isn't, it takes a while for children to understand the meaning of race in their lives. My children, who are growing up in a multiracial and multicultural community, have learned the difference between race and color. In Berkeley there is no single dominant type of coloration or physique, and children try to describe each other as accurately as possible when they are talking about individuals rather than groups. For example, I've heard my children describing their friends as having light brown, brown, dark brown, blackish, whitish pink, reddish brown, pale white, brownish black, pale yellow, tan, yellow brown, and many other kinds of skin. They do not describe all white people as having white skin or all Black people as having black skin. They make individual descriptions and yet at the same time have come to understand how a light brown friend of theirs can be called black while someone with darker brown skin can be called white. It wasn't easy. They asked us many times why people with light skin were often called black while people with darker skin were called white. It was one of their first initiations into culture; into the world as constituted by social convention rather than physical appearance. Now they understand that black and white and yellow and brown and red are used in ways that go beyond simple descriptions of skin pigmentation.

Racism develops as children learn to perceive people as members of groups and not as individuals. When I grew up, for example, I never heard any overt racist talk, but there was constant talk of "us" and "them," "them" meaning in different instances Protestants, the Irish, Italians, and Blacks. Since all my friends and my parents' friends were Jewish, it was easy to think of "us" as a complex group of individuals and "them" as a mass of indistinguishable people.

Children are very sensitive to the way their parents describe other people and groups. They know which group their parents feel threatened by and which groups they feel superior to. Often without even being aware of doing so, they pick up their parents' fears and identifications. I remember one particular case where some six-year-old white boys manifested a fear and hatred of Black children that they must have picked up from home. It was at a school I visited periodically. I noticed that every time the children were on the playground this group of boys hid behind a tree. When every class had gone in from the yard, the boys would peek out to make sure no one was left, and then they ran like wild to their class. At first I thought they were just trying to cut class, but that didn't seem right, because they commented to me several times on how they were forced to be late. Once I asked who was forcing them, and one of these third-graders said, "Them," and another added, "You know, the Black kids." It seemed crazy — no one was paying attention to these boys, much less trying to "get" them. Somehow they had developed the idea that they were watched and would be attacked. Perhaps someone had threatened them a few months ago or their parents had warned them that Black children are violent. Whatever it was, their fear was turning into hatred that was generalized and racist. It was not directed to a particular Black child and so became directed at all of "them."

In the same school several of the Black students make fun of the way Asian students talk, call them yellow animals, and express racist attitudes of their own. It is almost as if they are taking out on Asian students what they get from white students.

Recently I encountered another revealing example of an early manifestation of racism. I was driving a group of children to the playground. The children in the back seat of the car decided to make a clubhouse. One of the girls suggested they put up a sign that said "No Blacks Allowed." The other children, including one who was half-Black, agreed. I was astonished and stopped the car. I asked the girl what she meant by putting up that sign. She said she didn't really mean "no Blacks," she just wanted to put up a sign. Another child agreed that it was a bad idea and suggested they put up a sign saying "No Yellows Allowed." I pushed the issue — that was as unfair and mean as the "No Blacks" sign. Besides, all the children knew Black and Asian children and admitted when pushed that they didn't intend to exclude those children from their clubhouse. Teri, the girl who suggested the original sign, didn't want, however, to let go of the idea and said to me, "You can't let everyone in a club because then it won't be a club."

I suggested that if the children needed to exclude some group from their club that they think of a group they wanted out that wouldn't really be hurt by the exclusion. The solution seemed to occur to them all at once, and they agreed on the sign "No Grownups."

Children are extremely sensitive to issues of inclusion and exclusion, to claims of inferiority and superiority, and to indications that certain groups threaten others. Racial attitudes can develop without any direct attempt to teach them, and sometimes manifestations of racism in children reveal more about their parents' attitudes than the parents themselves would be willing to acknowledge. Some of the parents of the white boys I mentioned above swore to me that there was no racism in their families and were genuinely puzzled by their children's behavior. When I pointed out the boys' use of "them" the parents admitted that at times they got frustrated with all the concern with race in the papers and at school and did talk angrily about "them." They weren't aware, though, that their children picked up their frustrations, fears, and prejudices.

The children I've been talking about so far are the ones who designate themselves as "us," the superior but threatened individuals. It's important when trying to understand the role of race in children's lives to understand the responses and sensibilities of "them." Implicit in any situation where racism functions is a fundamental human asymmetry. People who are victims of racism have as a matter of simple self-protection to mistrust people who might be racist. This applies to children as well as adults. Oppressed people need to understand as much as they can about the people who control and categorize them. It is functional in our society for Black people to withhold trust from whites, to be attuned to instances where racism might manifest itself, and to help their children develop the same sensitivity.

It is easy to misinterpret the self-protective behavior oppressed people develop. For example, I've seen many white teachers who assume that because their Black students at the beginning of the year are quiet and afraid to talk, they are nonverbal and therefore not too smart. What is actually happening is that the children are lying back, trying to figure out the teacher and discover whether he or she can be trusted. Teachers in this context don't usually realize that they are being observed. Even young children are aware of the images that whites are supposed to have of Blacks and look for clues to confirm these stereotypes. A teacher who is afraid to touch students, who talks in an unnaturally slow and concrete voice as if in the presence of mental defectives, or who assumes that the children hate learning and know nothing is understood as racist by the students even if he or she would vehemently deny it if anyone pointed it out.

Children from oppressed, poor, and minority communities have complex, often contradictory, images of themselves as members of a group that is singled out for prejudicial treatment. However, these images change as people struggle to overcome their oppression.

In our society, being black was initially defined by white society as having blood ties, no matter how remote, with a black African. There were two categories — Blacks and non-Blacks. If an Asian or a Jew or an Italian married a Black person, their children were Black. The oppressors defined the conditions of blackness just as Black people learned to develop and use the category of being white.

From being a negative definition, one that hinted of illegitimacy and closed off educational, economic, and social opportunities, blackness has changed to a positive identification with a proud past of achievement and resistance. The image of being black has been remade by Blacks of all complexions. When I began teaching seventeen years ago, my students, who were all black, hurt each other by making fun of each other's complexions. Words like *black* and *chocolate* were curses. This negative image of the self based on complexion was often reinforced by teachers who chose, almost without exception, the light-skinned students as their favorites.

However, that negative image was mixed with many strong, positive images about being black. The children all knew and admired strong black men and women, grandparents, neighborhood heroes. The students did not have wholly negative self-images as the psychological literature claimed. The children had many complex images of themselves that mixed strength and intelligence with a sense of being oppressed and powerless. When people began saying "Black Is Beautiful" during the sixties, it was not something completely new.

People who are poor and in a minority usually have very complex images of themselves, which their children also develop. Some of the images are of the strength of the community and the people which keeps life going under intolerable conditions. Others are images of hopelessness and resignation. Still others are of overthrowing the people who control their lives and having power. These images are complemented by images of assimilation into the majority community or of working for the people with power and developing a base for oneself. Images and fantasies of power and powerlessness are constantly present, and part of growing up in a poor community consists of sorting out these images and deciding how one will relate to other members of one's community and to people outside it who have control over it.

As some people struggle with their own liberation, those of us who are privileged to be neither poor nor oppressed have to struggle with our prejudices and deal directly with race and poverty with our own children.

The Elimination of Racism

Racism is deeply ingrained in our society. There is no one immune from the problem of "us" and "them." In order for white people to relate to nonwhite people in our society, we, the whites, have to face the vestiges of racism in ourselves and not be defensive or deceive ourselves into believing we are untouched by the culture around us. The elimination of racism in oneself means relating to other people as individuals — not denying similarities and differences, but over and beyond these being able to understand and relate to the uniqueness of each person. This implies working out a number of things in one's own mind and trying to get them clear for one's children. First off, none of us should or could have a single image of ourselves. Some of the images we have are general — I'm a Jew, an American, a New Yorker. My children are half-Jewish, not Jewish by religious definition, since a Jewish mother defines a Jew, but Jews by Hitler's definition. They are also part Scots and English and German. All of these images are accurate yet incomplete. Erica is Erica, Tonia is Tonia, Josh is Josh — there are images of their uniqueness as well as the lines they come from and the history they are part of, and the culture that is available to them. The same is true for all other people. They are unique and general; they see themselves as Black or Brown or Cree or Navajo or Italian or Japanese, and they also see themselves as individuals. When the individuality is forgotten or pushed away in the service of intolerance or hatred, racism or some form of bigotry results. What distressed me with many of the five- and six-year-olds I taught was that they learned before they even reached school to look at some other people and see types rather than individuals. For some of the white children it was so bad that after a month they didn't know the names of any of the Black children. I had to set up a situation where they were forced to learn the name of every child in the class. Interestingly enough, for some of the white children the simple act of learning the black children's names dissipated their fear and enabled them to relate with ease to children they had formerly avoided.

I've seen my own children occasionally picking up these feelings and also catch myself sometimes talking of having Black and Chicano friends while deliberately putting the emphasis on "Black" or "Chicano" as if that designation was what I valued rather than the friends themselves. There is no way we can avoid being caught up in racial conflict and confusion in this society. The best we can do is be aware of the traps and help our children become aware of them too. Here are some of the most common traps, as well as a few ways to avoid them.

The trap of talking about exceptions and making ethnic jokes. This comes up, for example, in these forms: "Herb, you're really tolerant. I thought Jews had problems with people who weren't Jewish" or "John is so hardworking and loving with his children. See, that shows that all Black men aren't like the people you read about in the papers" or

"José's really a fine person; he's not so macho as the others. . . ." Exceptions confirm the example. They provide people with ways of dealing with some people while refusing to confront stereotypes they have about groups. In the examples quoted above, it is not much different from saying, "Herb, you're not like other Jews," or "John isn't like other Black men," or "José's a good Chicano." Yet it is hard to convince people that they sometimes make racist statements inadvertently.

I remember once being at a multicultural conference that was dedicated to the development of understanding between peoples. I was one of the speakers and was introduced by a prominent citizen, a nice and open man who probably really believed in brotherhood. He got up and told the audience how interesting our conversation on the podium had been, how some of his best friends were Jewish. Then he launched into one of my favorite Jewish jokes, with a funny pseudo-Yiddish accent. The joke and the tone of his voice were insults. He was stealing my culture—in his mouth it was mockery. After the meeting I tried to explain to him why people shouldn't tell each other's jokes, why I could tell Jewish jokes and yet in his mouth they came out anti-Semitic and disrespectful from my perspective. He couldn't see what I was saying and I couldn't tell him a Protestant joke and pretend to use his accent. I couldn't think of any. Maybe Protestants don't make jokes about themselves, at least not in front of me. I contented myself with that putdown and worked my way out of the rage and violence and sense of disrespect I felt and yet knew wasn't intended.

One component of respect is honoring other people's culture, acknowledging what you learn or know from it, and not imitating or adopting it cheaply or for casual reasons or to meet your own psychological needs. Another is respecting all people and not singling out exceptions. Children pick up stereotypes of race and culture from the jokes adults tell and the accents they imitate. They also learn in a negative way that if someone is an exception, then all other people like him or her must be terrible in some way; that if Herb is a good Jew, then most Jews must be bad. When children hear their parents joking in a disrespectful way or putting down a whole group of people by picking out an exception, they'll feel free to be disrespectful themselves, and disrespect for another language, culture, color, or style is a main component of racism.

I've noticed that children don't like grown-ups to imitate them, either, and that they feel violated and react with anger or rejection. Often the imitation is done in a very generous spirit and the adults feel rejected and misunderstood. From the perspective of the adults the children's language is cute and colorful. From the perspective of the children their language is an attempt to describe and deal with the world. Their struggles to express what they mean or intend are serious, and it is easy to offend children by putting down their language by imitating it or joking about it.

This doesn't imply that there is no place for joking, imitation, mockery, or play. Rather there is a broader implication — if you want to joke in a way that will not offend or be disrespectful, joke about yourself. On an ethnic level, tell jokes about your people if you choose to. It will be clear what can and cannot be told in mixed company. If you tell jokes or imitate children, turn yourself into a child. It is no threat if you tell a joke on yourself, and it teaches the ability to accept self-criticism as well.

My children get outraged if I imitate them crying or talking babytalk or being stubborn or silly. If I become Herbie the baby, it is quite different. They can laugh at my silliness and, if there is some serious intent to my joke, deal with it privately in their own terms.

In many ways being a child and being a member of a powerless minority group have structural similarities. For children and adults it is often a matter of "us" and "them," and the danger of talking about exceptions and telling offensive jokes applies as much to children as it does to people who are culturally different.

The trap of confusing economics with race. Not all Black or Chicano or Puerto Rican people are poor, and not all white people are middle-class or rich. Poverty does terrible things to people — to children especially. They learn very early to struggle for food and resources, to be wary of people out to exploit them, to be distrustful of strangers, especially those representing government agencies. They learn that many middle-class people are uncomfortable in the presence of poverty and can be hustled out of a bit of money because of this discomfort. They also learn that most people don't care about other people being poor, and if pushed too far will call in police, social workers, welfare or probation officers to help them.

These aspects of being poor are understood across race. Poor white, black, brown, red, yellow children know of them, and also know that categories that have nothing to do with poverty are assimilated to aspects of being poor. To be Okie, Black, Chicano, Puerto Rican means to be poor, from the perspective of many white middle-class people. This is obvious even on such a supposedly sophisticated level as academic research in the social sciences. For years when Black and white people were studied in relationship to each other, there was no control for economic class. Almost thoughtlessly, poor Black children were compared with middle-class white children. Differences that emerged in these studies were usually attributed to race and not to poverty. Often race and poverty became so confused that "Black" meant "poor" in educational circles. This has begun to be straightened out by recent researchers.*

The confusion of race or ethnicity with economic situation is not merely an intellectual error. It is a self-protective strategy used by many individuals to keep from having to deal with the existence of poverty in such a rich nation. If to be Black means to be poor, and being Black is a permanent condition, then poverty is permanent too. In a confused way the attitude taken by many people is that certain types of people are condemned to poverty because of who they are. You know the old racist arguments — Blacks, Okies, Puerto Ricans, Indians are poor because they're lazy, drink too much, have too many children they don't care about. That's part of their culture. Therefore, there is no point in giving them jobs or helping them. They are bound to be poor, though, of course, there are a few exceptions. This argument is crude and illogical, but it has more subtle variations. The result of accepting this argument is to resign oneself to others' poverty. When a person is poor because of something beyond anyone's control, then one needn't feel too guilty about his condition.

Unfortunately many people believe that this callous attitude toward people victimized by poverty has to be passed on to their children. This isn't an easy task. Children tend to be very compassionate. They cry when they see other children hurt because they see how easily it could have been they. They are full of compassion for animals, mourn the death of pigeons, goldfish, and even insects. Even the most competitive five-year-olds I've known break down when they see movies of hungry children.

* For details of this, see *Inequality* by Christopher Jencks (Basic Books, New York 1972).

One way to root out compassion is to identify a type of person with poverty as if poverty were a biological feature. I've seen children who believe that being poor is part of being black or brown, and who also believe that poverty isn't so bad for black or brown or bronze Americans because they don't suffer from it.

These children are taught either directly or by listening to adult conversation that some people are more human than others and that with few exceptions poor people are that way because they couldn't be anything else. An implication of this is that those who are not poor deserve their position too, that they are somehow better.

The saddest experience I've had with children was in a poor white "Okie" community where the children and their parents were so resigned to being poor that they believed that it was a necessary part of their beings. They saw no way out, had no hope. This isn't true for people in poor Black, Chicano, and Puerto Rican communities I've worked in. There was much less confusion of culture with oppression, or identification of poverty as part of oneself. The children had a sense that they were being kept poor and struggled to make it. They chose many routes — politics, the streets, school — and many weren't allowed to make it. But they understood that doors were closed to them, that poverty was imposed and not natural.

It is essential if we are ever to achieve any coherent and compassionate society, that our children understand the horrors of poverty and the contingent nature of poverty. Everything we teach our children does not have to be pleasant. It is painful to see your children cry and hurt for others, but it is more painful to see other children hurt and hungry.

The trap of protecting your child from the issue of race. I've known a number of families where the parents have insisted that race is never an issue between people. Sometimes their children find themselves confronting racial issues in their own lives and are unable to discuss them with their parents. They have to deal with very difficult problems without help and not infrequently resent their parents. It is difficult to discuss race with children, to face highly emotional issues that cannot be resolved immediately and harmoniously. However, children are not so tender that they need to be protected from all pain. They want and, I believe, need to face the social and cultural issues that as adults they will have to struggle with.

Many children grow up in such a homogeneous environment that race exists for them on the level of fantasy. Differences between people are then easily invested with fantasies of strange customs and exotic powers.

Turning cultural and racial differences into moral differences, overlaying them with fear and a sense of competition between superior and inferior peoples, contaminates children's sense of their selves as well as distorts their sense of others. In terms of race and culture, the image people have of themselves becomes aggressive and overlaid with comparisons. I've seen little children fight over whether Jews are better than Black people, or whether Catholics are better than Protestants, before they knew what these categories meant. The understanding was on a level of them and us, them bad and us good. What the structure and content of "them" and "us" were never arose. If cultural differences do emerge in depth, a situation can develop in which everyone can learn. If racial differences and fears can be spoken of and dealt with, people can learn to deal with the worst in themselves, with the fears and hatred that they project onto race but that probably come from lack of self-respect and insecurity.

Children have to be told that grown-ups have some crazy

attitudes; that racism and cultural intolerance exist in our culture. They have to be prepared to encounter these attitudes in others and in themselves. This means specifically that they have to be helped over their fears of things that are different. Many peoples of the world are open to teach strangers about themselves. What they insist on, however, is respect. When treated respectfully as equals, people will accept you that way. However, when treated with scorn, mocked, used, or imitated in a thoughtless way, people become hostile and resentful. I've traveled a bit and am constantly appalled by many travelers who have no respect for the peoples whose lands they are visiting.

This doesn't mean that cultures shouldn't relate to each other, that interchange and influence shouldn't happen, or that cultural fusion is undesirable. On the contrary, respectful encounter of different peoples and modes of being leads to mutual enrichment and sometimes creative fusion. However, it is this respect that is crucial — respect and understanding of who you are and respect for the other, accompanied by a desire to understand the other not as an oddity or object, but as another human being with another perspective on being alive.

This means that as parents we have the responsibility of showing respect for differences and educating ourselves, of moving beyond isolated, homogeneous pockets of like people and trying to find out about others. It means being able to approach other people and cultures without the attitude that you already know everything or that you have to prove the superiority of your kind.

A gift that parents can give their children is diversity: a rich, varied and respectful community where their children will learn differences and be able to choose their own ways of living from a wide spectrum of cultures and styles.

Short of this there are small things one can do to help oneself and one's children. Look at yourself through other people's eyes. Look at the way you eat and dress, at the gestures you use, the way you fix your hair, the music you listen to — do this as if you were a strange being. Think of yourself as silly, be as mercilessly mocking toward yourself as you have ever been to other peoples. Tear your own culture apart, examine the notions of "better than" and "worse than" that work themselves into your culture. And then, if you can, put yourself back together, but without the judgments, simply as a person who has chosen to live and act in a certain way. If you haven't made the choice, would rather do other things, dress in other ways — you can, you know. Culture is made by people and unmade by them too.

I talk to my children a lot about cultural differences. We like to talk about the different ways people eat, about musical taste and ways of drawing and painting and dancing, about the structures of families and the kinds of houses people live in. My children haven't been told that one type of music is serious and one type isn't, or that some drawing is high art and other is more illustration, or that there is one best form of family structure.

Are forks better than chopsticks or fingers? Is eating sitting on a chair better than eating stooping down or sitting on a cushion? Is classical ballet better than the dancing in Broadway musicals? These seem like foolish social questions to me and translate to no more than "Is my culture better than yours?" That doesn't mean there is no room for judgment ever. There is good flamenco and bad flamenco; good ballet dancing and terrible dancing. Within a culture or within a form there is good practice and bad practice (though sometimes people mistake innovation for bad practice). It is just when one gets into developing hierarchies that conveniently place oneself on the top that racism and cultural intolerance creep in.

Many adults feel they have to restrict children's exposure to different cultural forms to insure that their children will appreciate "high" culture and not be seduced by "low" culture. I remember that my parents used to fight with my brother over his listening to so much rock-and-roll, as if rock-and-roll and Beethoven couldn't both be available or as if someone who liked only rock-and-roll was morally inferior to someone who liked only Beethoven. Music, dance, art, food are often used for social purposes beyond themselves. There is no need to close down children's ears or eyes or sensibilities. In a way, being a cultural snob is a form of racism — a putting down of one group of people in order to validate your own shaky claim of superiority. A service to our children and ourselves would be to stop such foolishness and listen to and look at things openly for what they can teach us, instead of as badges of social identity.

Good Work and Bad Work

In our culture there is "good" work and "bad" work and people go to great lengths to try to insure that their children will not be forced to do work that is not considered respectable. Unfortunately, these judgments have little to do with the intrinsic quality of the work. I remember my grandparents' commenting when I was a young child that my hands were surgeons' hands. It seemed a funny thing for them to say, since I was pretty clumsy and still have a hard time threading a needle or cutting along a straight line. Their meaning became clear only when I was twenty-five and engaged in a conversation with the father of one of my students. He had been a fisherman in Puerto Rico and was at that time a laborer in New York. We were talking about the beauties of Puerto Rico. I noticed that throughout the conversation he glanced, sometimes stared, at my hands. All of a sudden he lost his train of thought and said to me, "My son; I want him to have hands like yours." I looked at my hands and then his, which were callused and scarred, and were beautiful to me in the strength they expressed, compared to my hands that were best for holding a pen or pounding a typewriter. My hands were writers' hands, surgeons' hands, a prince's hands compared to those of Victor and of my grandfather.

Some time later Victor and I were talking about work. He told me that he could think of himself as a fisherman, in a way wouldn't mind if his sons could fish too, but that the commercial fishing ships were driving out his kind of fish. The problem, he said, was that he couldn't think of himself as a laborer at all, that he went to work and dreamed of Puerto Rico and the ocean while shoveling cement and knocking down walls. Then he got agitated — it wasn't that shoveling cement or knocking down walls was bad. Friends in Puerto Rico did it; they built things for their friends and community. It's just that he was doing work for someone he didn't know in New York to build a structure he couldn't use, to profit people who didn't care about him.

Many people in this country feel the same way about their work as Victor. And not all the alienating work is physical labor either. When the work you do provides no personal fulfillment, produces nothing of value to your community, is not part of a collective effort and is solely concerned with profit, then alienation follows. You can't think of yourself as a worker so much as someone who works to get money. Work is considered a sacrifice rather than fulfillment, and, of course, the sacrifice is usually justified in the name of one's children, who one hopes will get more and have to work less. Because of bitterness over work, children are often confused about what it is worth becoming. Their parents don't want children to have images of themselves as workers — as builders, or truckers, or bus drivers, or oil workers. Usually they want to instill in their children images of themselves as leaders, bosses, controllers, or images of themselves as independently wealthy professionals. For little children these images are strange — there is no reason from a child's perspective to believe that a doctor and a carpenter are of different value. One knows the body; the other knows wood. The same is true for cooks and teachers, taxicab drivers and lawyers, typists and welders.

Children find any activity that is out in the world, that involves working with people, or building or making things, admirable. I remember as a child admiring my uncle Rocky, who drives a taxi in New York, and my uncle Jim, who is a welder, and my grandfather, who was a framer. I still do — their attitude toward their work was loving and defensive at the time — they respected the work they did and yet felt guilty because there was so much pressure around for them to "better themselves." As a child I wanted to try doing everything but soon realized that my parents had different ideas for me. It was not good to work with one's hands (except as a surgeon). It was good to use one's mind, to be a professional, and not too bad to be an intellectual so long as you were a professor too. Despite all this I had all kinds of images of myself as a worker — myself as a philosopher, a teacher, a laborer like my grandfather. My brother still talks of having wanted to build bridges and highways. He also dreams of being a worker. Many women I know also have secret dreams of work that was closed to them.

It is important to let these secret dreams out, to allow and encourage children to think of themselves as being able to do any kind of work that they find fulfilling for itself and useful to others.

Think of it — what kind of work do you want your sons and daughters to do? What do you feel would be below them or destructive to them? Are you setting them up to be bored or to revolt against you? Many young people who grew up in the middle class over the last twenty years must have had secret dreams of being workers. Part of the commune phenomenon and the amazing number of craftspeople and printers and carpenters and mechanics who come from the middle-class suburbs must be attributed to secret dreams of being workers, of making, growing, or fixing things.

The so-called generation gap can partly be accounted for because parents who do not respect the work they do or the roles they play in the family are not respected by their children and are taken as negative models. They are examples of how not to use your time, intelligence, and body. Children form their own images of themselves as workers, as people rewarded for their efforts in intrinsic rather than extrinsic ways. Some of these images are romanticized, but they point to an image of self that is nurturing rather than resentful and hating.

Children need to be exposed to work of all sorts, to be encouraged to try things without worrying about class and social role. They need to see, as do we adults, that many different types of work can be fulfilling, can serve the needs of community. I don't believe carpentry, medicine, music, law, manufacturing, construction ought to be measured on a hierarchical scale.

Many parents want their children to be prepared for the marketplace and to make as much money as possible. I believe that's a mistake. We have to weigh the value of work to the person who works against the monetary value our society presently gives that work. Work without joy is debilitating, and often undermines self-respect to such a degree that family life is destroyed. I prefer that my children honor the work they do and live modestly than that they become obsessed with money and job status.

It is important not to scare children away from work they might eventually find fulfilling. On the contrary, it makes sense to encourage young people to try their hands at many things, to learn how to build models, fix cars and bikes, make clothes, build houses and forts, cook. As early as two and three, children begin to play at working in a grown-up way. And as early as two or three, children begin to realize that adults are trying to channel their play in certain directions. I know parents who go out of their way to encourage their girls to play doctor or pilot, but don't like them to play at planting a garden, cooking, or cleaning house. The same is true for boys — work and play get overloaded with adult judgments. Cooking, which can be a great pleasure, gets treated as a burden while playing at being a doctor, which can be casual fun, gets treated as serious business.

In our world, the more skills a person has and the greater variety of work he or she is willing to attempt, the more likely that person will survive on his or her own terms. There is nothing more occupationally restrictive than having a Ph.D. in English literature or being an engineer with detailed knowledge of only one special kind of valve. Many of the so-called high-status jobs in our society leave a person dependent and crippled by excessive specialization and the fear of trying work "beneath" one's qualifications.

Initially children know nothing of this — attitudes toward work are learned from how parents feel about their own work and the respect they have for the work of others. Children are curious about the work of adults. It is important that they see how things happen in the world, that they watch buildings go up, see printing presses, observe people preparing a field for planting, watch a doctor at work, visit the courts — come to believe in enormous possibilities for themselves and understand that they can experiment with work and try many things. And if possible have them work alongside of you — work together, share common work as well as play. There is nothing, as my father has told me many times, that builds greater respect between parent and child than working together and appreciating each other's efforts.

Private Images of the Self

We all have private dreams and fantasies that transcend family and culture and race; that take us beyond the limits of the real or possible and at the same time reach to the most personal parts of ourselves. It is these private images of the self that provide people the strength to act, to stay alive despite misery and defeat, to know themselves as unique, above and beyond all external definitions that are bound up with society and with history. They are the images that embody our freedom and ability to create new things, to make history and culture rather than be passive subjects of external forces. These *images of transformation* survive all our feelings of being manipulated and even occasionally invade the dreams or quiet moments of people who have made themselves hard and cold and powerful. Without these images there would be no hope in the world, but merely resignation and despair for most people, and unmixed and self-righteous power for a few.

I find watching young children play quietly and unselfconsciously a breathtaking experience. When they do not feel observed, they often seem to become involved so deeply in worlds they create that a trancelike state seems to exist. Whether they play with rocks and little bits of metal and wood or with elaborately crafted dolls and toys doesn't seem to matter much at that moment. Everything comes alive in the child's imagination — a rock can be a mountain or a monster, a doll a giant or a midget. It is as if in the course of play children run through all the possibilities for relationships they can imagine. They marry and love and destroy; control and subject themselves to others; animate the inanimate, talk to animals and trees and plants. Everything in a child's world can be infused with life during this intense private play. At first I thought perhaps the play merely involved a Freudian reenactment of children's testing themselves against their parents, or a rehearsal of roles the children saw around them. But there is so much more to private play than that. Animals become friends, families of people and animals live together and have children; Martians and monsters are created and often transformed into people; are sometimes defeated, sometimes befriended — the child, the player, is every one of the characters at once. Listen and often it will sound as if several children are playing or talking together because many voices can come from a child playing alone. It is almost as if the child playing was a dreamer moving through the dream with objects instead of internalized images; as if the child was the player as dreamer with more control than dreamers usually have.

The other day Joshua was playing in my study while I was writing. It was as if we were in two different rooms. The writing had totally possessed me, and I forgot he was in the room. After finishing a few pages, I turned around to see the floor of the study transformed into an elaborate world with rivers and cities, a cave and a mountain. The world was constructed out of scraps of wood, books, some blocks I have around, pencils and game pieces. It was peopled by chessmen, checkers, little animals, a Mr. Spock doll that dwarfed the other pieces, several toy cars, a moon rover toy car, and a number of small plastic monsters. Joshua was moving around the world talking to the creatures at times, at other times talking through them. One city was being destroyed, another one was being built. A group of animals and monsters were in a circle becoming friends. There was a war going on somewhere. Things were constantly changed as a scenario seemed to play itself out. One of the buildings was torn down and the blocks used for it were turned into boats for a group of checkers who were really kings and queens, so that they could take a trip to the mountain where Mr. Spock sat waiting. At one point Josh's eyes caught mine. He saw that he was observed and blushed, then got angry at me and reminded me that I promised not to look just as he promised not to ask questions while I was writing. He turned back to the world but couldn't play anymore; the trance seemed broken, the world was just a jumble of objects. He put things away.

I've seen other children playing in similar ways, though I have to suppress my voyeuristic tendencies in order not to drive children to secrecy. Private play is central to their development; it seems to be a time to sort out things they have been experiencing, as well as to experiment with doing new things. It is a gathering into themselves and becoming intimate with their own ways of doing and feeling things. It is the way images of the self as creator, capable of dealing with and possibly remaking the world, emerge. I know many adults whose images of themselves as creative people are tied up with images of childhood play, of worlds they made or secret friends they talked to, or stuffed animals who gave them advice.

This sense of one's self as unique is fundamentally a sense that one is an individual of worth and talent and feelings despite what the world does or says. It is a reserve of personal power that can lead to a longing for justice and a demand for respect. It is an image that can generate pride of self in the most difficult circumstances. It is what children show to adults when they feel they are being pushed around too much or not taken seriously enough or being treated without respect. It is that image of self that gives children the strength to say "Don't mess with me," to talk back to adults, to refuse to imitate adults blindly or become what others want them to be.

Heroes

Think of the people you respect. They do not have to be people you love or like, or even people you've ever met or are likely to meet. What qualities do these people have?

I've asked a number of people these questions and discovered that they are hard to answer. Everyone seems to be able to come up with a long list of people, some of whose qualities they respect. But there are usually reservations about respecting a person in all ways. For example, some people are respected for the way they use their money, others for their honesty toward their children, yet others for their generosity or self-discipline or brilliance. However, there are flaws and inconsistencies that immediately come to mind. Someone is generous toward family and a bastard toward employees; self-disciplined and capable of enormous dedication, yet not to be trusted as a friend; brilliant academically, yet picky and nasty toward other people's brilliance. It is obviously difficult in our society to be consistent. We all live so many lives, have so many demands made upon our time and affection, and have so many temptations to betray ourselves, our friends, and principles in order to be successful. Our images of our selves are contaminated with lack of self-respect, and our children see us, not as we wish to present ourselves, but much closer to the imperfect and partially formed beings most of us are. And children create or grab hold of heroes and superheroes, images of purity and strength and honesty, respected and admired fantasies that adults in the real world are measured by. It is not that grown-ups are expected to be Wonder Woman or Superman or Spider-Man or Falcon or members of the Justice League. Rather, children measure the actual against what they believe to be possible. They believe that adults have will and can make choices; that adults don't have to be mean or cruel; that bossing needn't exist. Of course, all these ways of behaving do exist. However, it is *the possible* that generates images of respect. Many college radicals of the sixties who were accused of having no respect showed the opposite in fact and developed their own images of respect, since ones given to them by the culture were so corrupt. Mao, Ché Guevara, Bob Dylan, Joan Baez, among others, were considered embodiments of the respect-worthy person, of the superheroes of a socially and politically sensitive group of people. More recently, many religious figures embody the purity and truthfulness and strength that create respect for the whole person. It is not so much that the yogis and saviors around are all the same, or that some might be serious and others sham. It is that the search for a hero, a figure worthy of admiration and respect, is part of the deep-felt need to believe that perfection and purity are possible. One component of this purity consists of honesty, a virtue that young children are particularly concerned with.

Honesty and Lying

Try to imagine what it must be like for a child to first understand what a lie is. I think children initially believe what they're told. When they discover that someone has deliberately tricked them, there must be a slight shaking of their world, the opening up of the possibility that everything they've been told may be deception; that whatever stability they perceive may be an illusion. Lying provides a philosophical crisis in children's lives: if lies are possible, how can I ever know when the truth is being told?

This might seem like an exaggeration, but I've seen too many children try to catch adults out on any little lie or evasion that comes up in conversation to underestimate the sensitivity children have toward understanding the ways adults lie. It sometimes even seems as if children have some extra sense that takes in everything adults say, while seeming to be fully preoccupied with play. Lying affects children not only when they are lied to, but when they witness grown-ups lying to each other, or talking about the lies they told in order to survive or get away with something.

If you are surrounded by people you know to be capable of lying, whether they lie to you or not, you have to be careful. Even children who are never lied to by their parents become wary and untrusting if they know that their parents lie to each other. They become unsure of how their behavior might be distorted or how their needs or actions might be lied about. If parents habitually lie to each other to the point where it becomes ritual, the whole grounding of life in actual events can become insecure.

There are different ways of lying. Some adults lie very crudely to children, as if they believe that children have no intelligence at all. They claim not to have money when the child knows where the money is; to be busy when it is clear they're sitting around drinking beer and watching TV; to say there's nothing interesting at the movies when there is a full-page ad for a children's movie in the paper. People have to check themselves for these single lies, which are ways of avoiding saying "no" to a child and dealing with the child's reaction. Lies of convenience like these are serious to children. They may avoid overt conflict, but they lead to resentment and disrespect. I've found it better to say "no" than to tell a lie that has the same effect, even if it means a little bit of overt disagreement and pain.

Feelings can also be lied about. Parents sometimes pretend not to be angry when they are; pretend to like people they don't; pretend their children's anger or defiance isn't serious when it is. Social lying is a major point of sensitivity with most children. They love to imitate adults expressing phony feelings, kissing each other and then going "Yuch" or embracing each other and making faces others can't see. The sad aspect of that play is that many children do grow up and give up their honesty about feelings and become the adults they were mocking.

Lies cause disappointment. I remember the pain I felt whenever my parents lied to their friends and relatives. As a child I was a purist — many children are. You want honesty and openness and learn that instead lies and secrets are part of what growing up is about. Losing respect for the adults around causes a dilemma. If they lie, should you lie too and give up a certain amount of respect in order to establish personal power? Or should you refuse to lie and take a stand against your parents? Or should you lie only in certain circumstances and be ruthlessly honest in the rest of your life? These adult dilemmas also exist for three-, four-, five-, and six-year-olds and often are never resolved.

Adults have to face the question: is lying a necessary part of functioning or not? It is possible to argue that it is; that, for example, under conditions of oppression it is important not to let your oppressors know too much about you or they might use the information to hurt you. It is also possible to carry that a step farther and say that truth is necessary within the family but that life with the rest of the world is a struggle, and lying is one of the weapons a person has to use. Taken a step short of chaos and madness, one can also argue that truth can be told only to the self. At this point there is no way to verify anything, which is a lonely and perilous way to live.

I believe that there are circumstances under which lying might be necessary and I am sure that I'd lie to protect someone from political persecution. However, my inclination is to say that beyond that, lies are not necessary and are damaging in personal relations. Still, it's not so easy to live with total honesty and it's also easy to abuse truth-telling. Sometimes children ask questions about feelings, and pure honesty can hurt and confuse them. For example, I know of a situation where a girl asked her father if he loved his mother and he answered that he didn't, that in fact he hated her. That answer caused the girl to wonder about his love for her and caused them both considerable grief. A more sensible answer could have been that he had problems with his mother and lots of times they had fights, but he still liked her in a way. That answer wouldn't have been totally truthful, but it would have been more sensitive to the nature of the question.

The girl wanted to know about her father's ability to love her as well as about his relationship with his mother. It was important to tell about his conflict and not pretend everything was smooth with his mother, but it was important not to be so cruel and unambiguous about being able to hate someone in the family.

Basically the truth in this and other similar situations shouldn't be avoided with children. Emphasis is what is crucial. One can be truthful and gentle at the same time. If you're asked by your children whether you love your wife or husband, whether you love all your children in the same way or have the same affection for all your brothers and sisters, it is important to tell the truth but not necessary to overdramatize and involve your children in your personal problems. You might, for example, prefer one of your children to your other children. How do you admit that to them without being cruel? I certainly don't know any best way, though I would be inclined in such a situation (which I hope never to get into) to admit that I had different feelings for different children but would treat everyone fairly and affectionately anyway. I know this is hedging a bit. However, when children raise painful personal questions they have usually anticipated answers and simply want to know whether adults will confirm or deny their perceptions. The child who asks about favoritism most likely feels it.

It's impossible sometimes to try to avoid hurting people if you're committed to being truthful, but it is possible to soften the way truth is told and make it clear that you don't enjoy seeing other people in pain.

The issue of lying is one I've agonized over and discussed I don't know how many times. Many people feel that I take too simplistic and purist an attitude toward lying. That may be, and a number of times I've felt that a bit more discretion would have been sensible. I know the truth can be unnecessarily cruel at times. I've had a number of disagreements with friends over what to do in the situation described above where there is a favorite child in a family. Many of them feel that it would be cruel to admit that favoritism in any way. I waver but tend to feel that in cases like this, children already know or have an inkling of the truth anyway, and it causes less damage ultimately to admit, in as caring a way as possible, unpleasant truths. However, with lying as with so many other important issues of child-rearing, there is no simple answer and the way one acts depends upon choices of values. I know I might change, but at present I believe that generally there is no place for lies in personal life though there are many temptations to lie, especially for children, who have to depend so much on adult approval and affection. Children are no more perfect than adults, and often they lie even in the most nurturing and wholesome of family situations. It's important to be as sensitive to the way children lie as to the way one deals with telling children unpleasant truths. Often children's lies result from the same conditions of fear and distrust that generate adult lies. Children are often afraid of what will happen to them if they admit to doing things adults don't approve of. They also sometimes lie because they want to protect part of their lives from adult scrutiny, because they feel adults are being unreasonable and putting too many limitations and restrictions on their activity.

Sometimes children lie simply because of immediate fear — a lamp is broken and they're afraid of making their parents angry. This kind of defensive lying can be overcome by adults' not overreacting but still expressing anger and making an end to the issue after that. Once children feel confident that adults won't destroy them, that single acts don't undermine parents' affection and opposition and an accident doesn't lead to the withdrawal of love, then lying will not be a habitual or particularly useful form of behavior. Every child I've known has lied at one time or another out of uncertainty about adult responses, or as a way of manipulating other people or avoiding responsibility for their own actions. Those children who have not been abused or neglected, and whose parents have been basically truthful have come to a regard for truth and gradually given up lying as they assumed more responsibility for their lives and became emotionally strong. There is no secret formula for eliminating children's lies. If you are basically truthful, if you are able to confront your children with their lies and yet not overreact to them or make your children feel rejected, and if you are patient and consistent, lying will not be of much use to your child and will not likely become a major problem.

Respect and the Image of Being a Parent

The images we have of ourselves as parents affect how we behave toward our children and how they respond to us. For example, many young parents resolve not to be like their own parents, but instead to be more kind, open, tolerant, understanding. They often fix on some adults they have admired and develop an image of themselves as perfect parents out of a combination of these adults and of the child they wished to be. Counter to this image is one of themselves being insecure, unnurtured, of being a lost child forced to become a parent. Security and insecurity, perfect love and thorough frustration exist side by side. These contrary images affect behavior in complex ways. Sometimes one is loving, strong, supportive toward one's children. At other times one is insecure, wants to be helped by the children, wants them to be perfect because one feels so messed up.

I have a friend who resolved never to be like his father, who had abandoned him as a child. Yet he found himself in a situation that reproduced his own father's life. He was poor, living with a woman he was not sure he loved. They were about to have a child, and he wanted to be a perfect father, to give the child the love and the economic security he didn't have. On the other hand, he didn't believe he could do it. There was no money, no decent job available; he wasn't sure he could love "her" child, didn't see himself as a father anyway, could only think to run away as his father had. His wife got sick and had a miscarriage, and they both realized how relieved they were not to have a child at that point in their lives. Now he is married again and has a child. He has been able to sort out the images he has of himself as a parent, to overcome fear of being like his father and at the same time give up the impossible dream of being a perfect parent of a perfect child. He is a nurturing parent who is steady and trusting, who does not overreact to the mistakes and fumbling ways children have as they grow. He not only loves his child, but enjoys her. Recently he told me that she seems part of him and completely herself at the same time, that he realizes that he loves her for herself and not as an embodiment of some image he had of himself or dream he had for her.

It is important for parents to ask themselves:

What are the images I have of myself as a parent?
What am I like as the good parent?
What am I like as the ogre parent?
Do I tie up my feelings about myself with expectations for my children?

When my child makes a mistake, do I feel it is my fault?
When my child does well, do I feel it is because of me?
Do I tie my child's life up with my own so that my child might be driven to lie?
Would I respect myself as a parent?

Children develop respect for adults on the basis of how they are treated and on how they see these adults treat others. Part of the trouble that exists within our society is that adults who act in cruel, selfish, and unreasonable ways want to command respect. You simply cannot command respect any more than you can buy or sell it.

The same is true with self-respect. No therapist can give it, no single achievement, no amount of money or fame or recognition can generate it. It grows out of consistent, committed, day-to-day activity, out of the images you develop of who you should be and how you try to live up to these images you have of your better self. Truly important aspects of existence, such as the development of self-respect and the acquiring of respect by others, cannot be taught, controlled, bought, or sold; they cannot be demanded, ordered, or, when once achieved, eliminated. There is a fundamental element of will in the lives of children and adults, of people. People are responsible for who they struggle to become or who they allow themselves to be. This is not to deny the reality of oppression. The American dream is a lie for many people. Hard work, strong will, and righteousness can just as easily lead to oppression as to success. Still, choice is involved over whether one will struggle or succumb, fight or murder, conform or remain oneself. And it is on these decisions about the life one will lead and the way it is lived that self-respect and respect are based. People can even learn to respect others when they don't respect themselves. To respect someone is to affirm the possible for oneself, to keep open the possibility of change that will lead to self-respect. That is why children develop images of their pure selves, have heroes and super-heroes, and, unless we crush it out of them, believe that it is possible to live in a just and compassionate world.

5

Being Fair and Believing in Justice

Be Fair to Me

Children are very sensitive to the way people treat each other. They understand kindness and sham affection; know the difference between brusqueness that masks kindness and genuine cruelty; can usually tell when people care about or despise each other; and can distinguish between the expression of emotion and theatre. There seems to be a part of children's minds that attends to the tone and intention behind adult acts as much as to their overt content. For example, recently one of my children's friends described an overnight stay at another friend's house in the following way: "Debby's parents smiled at each other at dinner, but as soon as they left the room the smiles went away. They talked all the time and seemed angry even with their stupid smiles. It made me so nervous I couldn't even listen." This nine-year-old girl was so absorbed in what lay beneath the surface that she couldn't take in the content of people's conversation.

This often happens when children feel very anxious in a

situation. They seem distracted, incapable of paying attention, when what is really happening is that they are trying to figure out what the adult is feeling or intends to do.

Recently I noticed two friends' children sitting and watching a political meeting in their living room. They were taking in the adults, examining them yet paying no attention to what the meeting was about. Afterward the children had formed an impression of every adult at the meeting and could tell me what they felt about each person. They didn't, however, have the slightest idea of what the meeting was about.

Children attend to tone and intent in order to make coherent sense out of the way people act, and use this information to decide how to act in the presence of others. Some adults are nice with their own children and mean with other people. Some treat one child well and are cruel to their other children. Some brothers and sisters get along well, others fight like anything. Some people are simply unpredictable — sweet and generous one day, grouchy and hostile the next. Children have to develop some coherent view of how people can be expected to act, especially toward them. As children observe the way people act, they notice differences, notice that some people are treated kindly, others indifferently, and others with no regard. Healthy children, as they develop a sense of their own place in the world, demand that they be treated no worse than anybody else in their family; that they be given the love, respect, affection, and possessions given other people. This negative demand for equity is precisely a demand to be treated fairly and precedes the development of a sense that one ought to treat others fairly too.

The self-referring sense of fairness manifests itself in children's demands for attention, in their accusations of not being listened to or taken seriously. To have a sense that one ought to be treated fairly is to take a position in the world as one among other people. It is not a small thing, and when it is belittled or disappointed, serious effects can take place in children's lives.

However, it's easy to confuse this insistence upon being treated fairly with selfishness. I remember a boy in my class, Sean, who was obsessed with fairness and policed all my actions to make sure he had his fair share of every small resource available. Sean insisted, for example, on getting the exact same snack as other children even to the point of absurdity. He'd measure the size of his slice of orange or apple against the size of other students' slices and occasionally went so far as to count the graham cracker crumbs on students' plates and insist that I share them out exactly. Despite all these demands Sean never asked for more than anyone else. Sean wasn't selfish and if he ended up with more than his share he would give it to another child.

However, a sense of fairness that extended to everyone was foreign to Sean's friend Fred. Fred was adamant about getting his fair share of everything but didn't care if anyone else was cheated or shortchanged. His sense of fairness applied to how he was treated and not to how everyone in a group treated everyone else. I pointed this out to him and asked him why he wouldn't share his things or worry about other children being treated fairly. He answered with something he must have heard an adult say: "Everyone has to take care of himself. You have to fight for your share and let other people take care of themselves."

Most children aren't as cynical as Fred, but learning to be fair can be a problem even for basically happy and generous children. The transition from wanting to be treated fairly to treating others fairly is a major step in the moral development of children.

Learning to Be Fair to Others

Being fair consists of treating other people with the same respect and consideration that you expect for yourself. It involves considering yourself as a member of a community of equals. The notion of a community or group of equal individuals is crucial since we all belong to many groups or communities, not all of which respect the principle of equality. For my grandparents, for example, the family did not consist of a group of equals. Adults had the authority to decide what children should do and how they should behave. My grandparents tried to treat all their children as equals in many ways but saw nothing wrong with giving more to my father than to his sisters. The oldest son was different — everyone had to understand that it was the family's responsibility to help him go through college and make something of himself. All children weren't equal — boys were more special than girls and the oldest son was the most special boy. This attitude was traditional, not peculiar to my grandparents. It wouldn't have done any good for my aunts to protest that giving boys special treatment wasn't fair. Things weren't supposed to be fair in that traditional family constellation.

I feel differently about the role of fairness within the family. Among the children there should be a community of equals — they should be treated as equals by adults and treat each other as equals. Fairness is a central value for me. However, there is a problem about whether young children and adults are or can be members of a community of equals. Adults have more responsibility, have more knowledge of the dangers of the world, have to nourish and protect children. The opposite isn't true — young children don't feed or support or protect their parents. The best compromise I can come up with is that adults and young children should behave as much as equals as is consistent with health and survival. There are times when we're forced to make decisions for our children — to put them to bed if they have a fever or are so exhausted that they're incoherent and out of control, to stop them from running impulsively across the street or showing off by setting a can of lighter fluid on fire. Fortunately these times are minimal. For the most part there is no need for any member of a family to be treated specially or have power to govern the lives of others.

Children watch for signs of unfairness, especially in the adult world. Do adults treat each other fairly? Do they treat some people as equals and with respect, and others with scorn? I imagine that the existence of unfairness is discovered by almost all children before they are six. They realize that there is a basic moral decision that they have to face: should I be fair with people or try to get as much as I can? Should fairness apply just to me? Or to my family? Friends? Where should it begin and where should it end? What are the boundaries of fairness, the limits of the community of equals that I belong to? These questions embody the central moral decision children, all people, face — what will the moral quality of my life be? They are serious and too complex to be answered once and for all. Children come to tentative answers for themselves, try out being selfish or being positively righteous in enforcing fairness in others. Other times they step back and observe. It is not only difficult to decide to be a fair person; it is as much a problem to know what fairness consists of in particular situations. Just the other day I went to a birthday party for an eight-year-old-friend of my children. One of the children at the party couldn't bear to see the presents opened and complained that it wasn't fair that just one child was getting all the presents. Nola, the girl whose birthday it was, became very distressed. She's a sensitive and generous child and was torn between wanting her presents and wondering whether indeed it was fair that she get all presents. She was about to cry. There was one more present to open and she couldn't bring herself to touch it. Fortunately she was rescued by another child who said, "It's fair. Nola has her birthday. We all have ours; why can't she have hers?" The strength of that argument convinced Nola, and she was released from the dilemma: she could have her presents and still be a fair person.

Children face situations where they have to make moral decisions all the time. They have to decide whether to think exclusively of themselves or to think of being members of a group of equals. It's hard to know what causes them to decide for one or another of these moral positions, but the quality of life within the family must surely have a strong effect. If you treat your children fairly, give them an equitable share of what you have, respect their feelings, and care for them, it is likely that they will treat others that way too. However, there is no guarantee — it is even possible to spoil a child through too much attention; to make him or her feel special, more important than others; and get the child to feel that fairness consists exclusively in giving him or her what they want. There are times when it makes sense to limit what you give to your child or do for him or her. Fairness also involves not being oppressed by the demands of your children. It is through understanding that adults and brothers and sisters and friends have needs and make demands that the sense of fairness generalizes. If being treated fairly oneself is contingent upon being considerate and respectful oneself, there is every reason to be fair.

A lot of testing occurs, however, before children learn

where they must give and where it is fair that they make demands on people. For example, children:

• want to be heard at the dinner table, but often pay no attention to other people's desire to be heard as well;

• want to see to it that if anyone gets a gift they do too;

• try to get people to pay exclusive attention to them and sometimes perform all kinds of cute and clever acts not for the pleasure of them, but for the attention and applause they generate.

One has to become attuned to these peformances, whether they are putting other children down or are played before an unwilling audience. There are times when adults have to intervene and let their children know that what they're doing isn't fair.

There are times when children have to be told that they are acting unfairly since often they don't realize it. When adults insincerely applaud children or give in all the time to outrageous demands, children lose sight of where the limits of people's tolerance and kindness are and how to function in a group of equals.

Children fumble a lot as they learn how much they have to give and what they should expect from others in order to be fair and be treated fairly. The other day a group of Tonia's friends was sitting around our living room playing cards. They wouldn't let Erica play, so she sat around watching the game, making nasty comments and calling out people's hands. Finally, Tonia exploded at Erica, and they started screaming at each other. They had both acted unfairly. Tonia wouldn't let Erica play, so she got even. They told each other that a dozen times in a half-dozen ways. Finally there was nothing to do but fight or settle the matter. Erica figured a way out. She said she'd be fair if Tonia would be fair, and all she really wanted to do was play cards with them anyway. They let her in the game and the issue was closed.

Negotiation, testing, discovering other people's responses and demands are the ways children learn to translate the idea of being fair to others into everyday activity. When all this takes place it is important as parents that we let our children work out their own problems with friends and if they are abused, support them and talk about what happened to the degree to which the children are interested. It is important that we be patient with being tested, refuse to allow our children to treat us or our friends unfairly even if it causes us pain or embarrassment to stop them, and never, never confuse helping a child develop an understanding of how to act fairly with the question of whether we love a child or not. One of the most unfair things a parent can do to children is threaten not to love them if they don't behave. *Enforcing limits and insisting that one's child be fair is an act of love, not an act that uses love.*

The Dilemma of Trying to Be Fair in an Unfair World

I promised Josh he could have a pet rat. We went to a pet store and he picked out a rat and paid for it out of his allowance. The rat hadn't been weaned yet, so we left it at the store and returned to get it three or four days later when it was old enough to be taken from its mother. When we returned and saw the baby rat, it was immediately clear that something was drastically wrong. One of the rat's back legs was swollen and flaming red. The clerk explained that there was a fight and whispered to me that the baby rat would soon die. I told that to Josh and convinced him to come with me to another store and try another rat. He was very quiet and nodded agreement. In the car he started crying softly, and explained to me that he wasn't sad because he didn't get his pet, it was the baby rat that he was crying for. He said it wasn't fair that things die and get hurt. He dissolved into sobs.

It isn't fair that living creatures get hurt and die. I let Josh cry — that was the only respectful thing to do. There is no comfort for such metaphysical grief, and children have to live through it, to face death and hurt as sorrowful facts of existence.

The unfairness of death and its inevitability is something we cannot control or overcome. Later that day our family was discussing the baby rat. The issue of fairness and unfairness came up again. Nurturing the rat was out of Josh's control; we all recognized that. But the girls agreed that whenever it was possible people should be fair, that fairness was important even if and possibly because death is unfair. The discussion reminded me of ones I had in college over existentialism. Children are philosophers in many ways. They have to struggle with basic issues as they decide who they will be in the world. Being fair, accepting the unfairness of death, deciding whether it is ever fair to kill another creature or whether they have a right to be unfair themselves because the world is unfair — these are all problems that children face and their concerns often force us as parents to define our positions, to make explicit how we feel about fairness. I believe in fairness as a fundamental value and have told that to my children, and also told them that other people don't and that they have to decide the issue for themselves.

For some children, deciding whether to be fair or not is a particularly difficult moral dilemma. Children who grow up in poor communities have to develop a very complex idea of what is and isn't fair to make sense out of their everyday experience. They see themselves getting less than children of privilege, are treated by some people as if they are inherently inferior, and are punished if they object to being treated this way. At the same time they are expected to be considerate and honest. The world is unfair; they have to tolerate this unfairness and learn to be fair themselves. That is the basic demand made on poor children — a demand that often results in the child's developing two sets of values, one kind and compassionate at home, and one cold and defiant with respect to the outside world. Most poor children learn to defy the unfair world in little ways, refuse to acknowledge that their unfair treatment should be accepted as a condition of life. This is puzzling to people who have not themselves been treated unfairly. I've seen many middle-class adults pleading with poor children to be honest and treat everybody fairly. And I've seen the wise smiles on the children's faces. They know that all this talk about treating others fairly is a trick to get them to act fairly while others cheat them.

Many of the dilemmas created by trying to be fair in an unfair world center around the treatment of objects. This is true to an extreme degree for poor people, but we are all faced with these problems. What is "mine" and what is "yours," the whole notion of ownership, is a central metaphor for emotional and personal equity, and is central to the way children's ideas about fairness develop. For that reason it makes sense to look at the development of economic understanding among three-, four-, five-, and six-year-olds. This is centered around the notion of "mine," one of the earliest words that many of our children learn.

Babies make demands — cry to be fed or changed — but

doing that is qualitatively different from staking a claim on something outside oneself that is embodied in the assertion "Mine!" or that is tested in the question "Mine?" Two- and three-year-olds wander around saying "mine" to everything and everybody, and it seems cute, a sign of growing up. However, by the time they are four or five the word *mine* often triggers battles within families and is charged with struggles over power and possessions. There are many times when I've wished that the word *mine* didn't exist in our language.

The movement from "me" to "mine" is one of the clearest instances of the early learning of culture. The notion of possessions, of owning people and things, is different from culture to culture. Some cultures such as ours divide the whole world up into parcels for ownership — there is my Mommy and Daddy, my toys, my house, my car, my business, my money. Contrasted to mine is "theirs" — their parents, their toys, their house. Somewhere in between *mine* and *theirs* falls *ours,* the idea that certain things or creatures belong to a unit beyond the individual such as the family or the government or the company.

In our society the notion of what belongs to the family and what belongs to the individual family member is a particularly complex one. For some communities family is a value above and beyond the individual. Resources are shared, adults take responsibility for their brothers' and sisters' children as well as their own, and there are businesses and homes and cars that are family-owned. I've seen family as a value operate in Black and Chicano and Puerto Rican communities. It was also a central value in my grandparents' life, though as my parents became more "Americanized," the size of family shrank down to include my mother, father, my grandmothers and grandfather, my brother, sister, and myself. Aunts, uncles, and cousins were no longer part of a coherent collectivity. In my generation it has shrunken farther to include a man, a woman, and their children. For some people I know there isn't even that minimal sense of family. I know an example where the mother, father, and two children each have their own rooms, eat their own meals at separate times, have different bedtimes and friends. It is as if their house is divided into four countries, each observing different rules.

This is an extreme instance of isolation within the family, but every family in our culture suffers from the problem of where and how to draw the line between "mine" and "ours," whether it is defined by blood ties, or reconstructed (as in the case of communes) on the basis of other forms of affinity.

Imagine being a two- or three-year-old trying to figure out what ownership means. Suppose you have a favorite doll. You play with it, keep it near your bed, but have no sense that you have a special claim on it. The doll is an object in the world to be explored, incorporated into fantasy, and eventually to be discarded like other objects that have served their function. Young children leave things around when they are finished with them, often to the chagrin of adults, who wish children could be born with a developed sense of possession and order. On this level a rock and an expensive doll may be valued no differently by a child. However, adults intervene at this point and introduce the notion of possession and the notion of value. In the case of the doll, adults usually say something like "Baby's doll" and often add "pretty Baby's doll," conveniently leaving out the rock or leaving it for the child to value the rock but to understand that the adults don't.

It would be possible for the adults to say that the doll was everybody's to play with, or that it belonged to the family, or to no one. But more usually in our society the doll belongs to someone, to Baby, who has to understand that he or she has a special privilege with respect to the doll, a command over its use. It is Baby's doll. A lot of young children master the idiom "Baby's doll," "Baby's bed," or "John's doll," or "Susan's bed" before learning how to use the word *mine.*

The possessive adds something to the quality of the relationship children have to things and people. A doll is no longer one among many, but special in that one has control over it. A bed belongs to one — cannot be used by anyone else.

A child's sense of possession is filled in by watching adults and brothers and sisters and by testing just about everything to see if it is a possession or not, and to see whose it is. Adults use the word *mine* and the possessive case more than they are aware of. People talk of "my kitchen," "my pipe," "my bed," "my car," "my radio," and even "my TV."*

There are a number of things children have to figure out when they encounter the possessive and realize as well that all things in the world are not invested with equal value. These learning problems consist of learning from other people:

how the world is divided;
how serious people are about owning things;
how flexible people are about giving up things or bending the boundaries of ownership;
the value of what they, the children, have;
how much they are entitled to.

It is out of personal resolutions of these issues that children's sense of what is due them and due others develops, and

* The TV is an interesting example of a problem object in our culture. Not every family can afford a TV for each person, so the TV becomes "ours," the whole family's. However, the programs do not — there are the children's programs, mother's programs, father's programs. Often battles arise over whose programs take precedence, and the whole struggle over power within the family can be centered on the TV.

this sense in turn leads to the development of a sense of what is fair: that is, a sense of how things *should* be divided.

Learning how the world is divided. Whom does the world belong to? Whom do the bedroom, kitchen, street belong to? Children ask these questions as soon as they understand the notion of possession: that is, as soon as they grasp that the world is divided into zones of privilege and influence. They want to discover the boundaries and know how they fit in. The most natural place to begin this exploration is at home. In our house, for example, I have a study, Judy has a workroom where she weaves, Tonia and Erica share a room, and Joshua has his own bedroom. The bathroom is common turf, as is the living room–dining room–kitchen complex.

There are many different ways of dividing up living space, and children become attuned to these variations. In some homes children are free to play only in their own rooms; in other places they rule the house, and their toys and clothes can be found in every corner. Sometimes children who have no place of their own at home or feel too confined in a rigidly divided space look for friends whose home is more open. At other times the opposite happens, and children from free-flowing homes hang out in very proper and strictly bounded spaces.

There are homes where children have no space at all; where it seems from the perspective of the child that everyone belongs but he or she. The attitude adults have toward the space in their home and toward their possessions impresses itself quite strongly on children, who may not like what they see but certainly understand it. If adults spend a lot of time defending or showing off their possessions, there is a good chance that children will be concerned about what is or isn't theirs and will also be defensive. On the other hand, if the adults are casual about possessions, indifferent to boundaries and territory, there is a good chance that their children will be relaxed too. However, one never knows how a particular child perceives the world, or interprets adult responses. There is no necessary relationship between how adults act or live and how their children will develop.

Still one's attitudes are not without influence. If one is obsessed with boundaries and possessions, concerned about property, thinks about the world in terms of ownership, then the possessive will likely be a problem for one's children. If property is a burden for adults, then one can expect children not to want property. If one is burdened by poverty, one can expect children to want possessions. Often children make choices in order to avoid what they consider their parents' biggest mistakes, or to compensate for and eliminate things that are sources of pain for their parents.

For example, if you are on the verge of bankruptcy, are constantly worried about having your house and car taken away, are nervous and cling tightly to everything you have, and constantly feel you are sacrificing your life to your family, it wouldn't be surprising to find your children wanting modest stability, simple living, and the security of not wanting much. From your perspective this might seem like your children rejecting your sacrifices. From the way they see the world, it might mean that they don't want to suffer the way you have, that they have learned from your pain.

Another quite different example would be a child who sees his or her parents suffering from poverty yet retaining a kindness and patience that seem saintly. I have known children growing up in such circumstances who developed a rage and aggression toward the world because of how much they saw their parents suffer. As early as four or five these children were ready to do anything to help their parents, even to the point of becoming unkind, impatient, deceitful, violent toward the world outside the family. They simply couldn't bear their parents' pain and defined their lives as a struggle to negate it or avoid it themselves.

It is important for adults to be aware of how they divide up the world or feel it should be divided up. This holds for small, immediate matters like who has use of what space and objects in the home, as well as for larger questions of property ownership and division of the resources of the earth. It is interesting to listen to four-year-olds imitating adults talk about property as if it were a metaphysical value. Recently I heard one four-year-old chase another away from the street in front of his house by yelling, "Get off of my property."

There was no such thing as property where I grew up. Most of the people rented apartments. The streets, backyards, and alleys belonged to everyone. You could chase someone out of your apartment, or maybe off the stoop in front of your house, but that was as far as it went. If anything, there was a strong sense of the commonness of the streets and sidewalks, of the fact that they did not belong to anybody and could be used by everybody. "Property" is a notion that fixes itself in the mind of a young child. It is a signal of privilege, a license to chase people away, to make a unique claim over a part of the earth. Our society says that it is fair to chase people off one's property, and also fair to have property. For many children the notion of fairness is tied to the notion of privilege from the beginning of their lives. It is the opposite of living in a community of equals.

The quality of one's concern for the lives of other people is bound up with the way children understand the concept "mine" and develop a sense of how the world should be divided or used. As parents it is very important for us to be attuned to the ways we introduce children to objects and people. I've found it necessary to eliminate the possessive as much as possible to make it clear that though some things are mine or Judy's or the children's, a great amount of our possessions and space is *ours*.

For example, in every household there are tools and instruments and utensils. Except in special instances these needn't belong to anybody, but they need simply to be available for people who can and want or have to use them. In my study there are many markers and pencils and crayons that are available to be used by whoever cares to, including neighborhood children, who occasionally ask me if they can go to my study and play or draw or write. However, on my desk there is one special pen that I write my books with, and that is only mine to use. Ownership is special, an exception, not the total way in which all things are divided.

The same thing can be true of toys — some privately owned and some for all the children (or in my case, children and adults who care to play with them). This is a problem, especially if, as we did, you start out buying things for individual children and realize only after a while that it would have been wiser to have more things that could be shared and fewer personal possessions. Recently Judy and I have taken to buying individual and collective presents. For example, on Christmas we'll buy a gift for each child and games or books or art supplies for everyone to share. We have to make a conscious effort to do this and deal with the problems sharing generates.

There are times when our children fight over things that they share. For example, if there's a two-person game, all three of them might want to play at the same time; or two of them might want to read a book at the same time. This calls for negotiation, for flipping coins to make decisions impersonal, for discussion and occasional conflict. It seems easier to break down and buy each child in the house one of everything. This is deceptive, because out of negotiating and bargaining over how to share resources children become closer to each other, learn how to live in the world together. One of the most important consequences of sharing, especially if there is no bullying involved, is that children learn to help each other and begin to develop a sense that there has to be a balance between what is their fair share and what is fair for others to have too.

It is difficult for young children who have no experience with sharing and are accustomed to personal ownership to understand how to make use of limited resources. There were times when I was teaching that the classroom material was limited. We had one microscope, no full set of textbooks, not enough crayons. Some children had no problems sharing what was there. Other children simply couldn't bear the idea of sharing. They insisted on having their books, their boxes of crayons, and the use of the microscope whenever they wanted. In one case, one of the children, who was six, offered to buy a box of crayons and a book from me and informed me that he would ask his parents to buy him a microscope to bring to school the next day for his use. I spoke to his parents that night, and they certainly would have bought him the microscope. I told them that though it was outrageous that we had such meager supplies, it was also an excellent learning opportunity for their son. After all, there are limited resources on earth, and it's good to learn early how to share them rather than fight over them.

Most children are not so self-absorbed, however, and there are a number of things that one can do to show children how sharing and collective activity can lead to strength and actually increase the resources available to every individual. Some of the ways children can be helped to experience the rewards of collective action in their lives are:

• by showing children how they can build more interesting and complex structures by pooling their blocks and construction sets;
• by having them work on building projects (such as making a swing or ladder or secret hideout or tree house) that individual children can't do, but that can be done by the group;
• by suggesting that children (if you have more than one) help each other clean their rooms and see whether it takes less time and effort to do it together than it takes to do it alone;
• by cooking and cleaning and setting the table together and letting children know that by helping you the work you have to do is easier;
• by playing group games;
• by sharing resources with other adults and letting your child know how your life and power are extended through such things as service cooperatives, collective food buying, pooling resources to set up a business or make and repair things.

Finally it is important to remember that when you think about your child's fair share, it is necessary to consider the other children on earth and to face the consequences in their lives of the choices you make. We should never forget that most children and most people on earth do not have their fair share.

The seriousness of being an owner. It is not always easy to act on one's beliefs or ideas. Feelings sometimes get in the way, as do old patterns of behaving. Some people seem casual about possessions until they lose them or are asked to share them. Others seem to be able to give away things they treasure with apparent joy. Children are aware of the feelings with which things are done and sense the truth about adults' responses to possessions, whatever the adults might say about them. Not only do they sense it, they need to know it. One of the main jobs of childhood is figuring out what triggers adult responses — what makes adults happy, sad, angry, violent, indifferent, amused. Children need to find out adults' sore points, weak points, breaking points, soft points. They use this knowledge to navigate the world; to assert themselves without being destroyed; to please when they want to please someone; and sometimes to exploit and manipulate adults in order to get what they want. Therefore, they watch and they test. The world for children is charged with emotion and value. It is very hard for children in our culture to relate casually to objects when almost everything has an owner and has been assigned a value. Think of the things most children hear all the time that fill up the world with value and emotion:

"You can't touch that, it can break and we can't afford another one."

"Do whatever you want with this; it isn't worth much."

"What do you want with that raggedy doll? This new one is worth so much more."

"That's a cheap car the Robertses bought."

"Harold's bike isn't as good as yours."

And think of a young child going throughout the house touching everything, saying "mine" or looking at you to see how you'll react — what makes you scream or say "Don't touch," what amuses you, what seems to leave you indifferent. Little children want to know how serious adults are about ownership, and as children get older they try to discover the joys and problems ownership visits on people. They are trying to figure out how serious they should be about things, how they should divide the world or believe it should be divided.

This exploration is taxing for adults, but healthy and sensible. I would be more worried by a child who shows no interest in things of the world than one who seems to tear the world apart.

Children push adults to reveal themselves, and it is possible to learn a great deal about how one feels by studying one's reactions to being tested by children. For example, I like to believe that possessions are not very crucial in my life and have learned that I take ownership much more seriously than my rhetoric would have it. There are a number of toys and metal figures in my study. It was fine with me if my children played with them — until one got broken, that is; then I found myself angry and tense, shouted at the children, chased them out of the study. I didn't even know those toys were that important to me.

There are more serious problems than toys, however. What about jewels, statues, property — how important are they in your life? Are there times when they are more important than people, where you would rather hurt someone than lose an object? Children need to know how far they can trust grown-ups and whether measures of the values of things also apply to people.

This leads to the third learning problem children face as they try to figure out how to deal with possessions.

How flexible are people about giving up things or bending the boundaries of ownership? Generosity is an important phenomenon in the lives of children. The tension between wanting to help people in need and feeling a need to protect oneself from need is very common. I experienced that tension very early and knew that somehow that generosity could cause problems. My mother's mother, Rose, was both admired and ridiculed for her generosity — if she had something, she would give half of it away. If people in need came to her, she would help them to the point of becoming needy herself. Her generosity made it impossible for her to accumulate money or things, and she was periodically on the verge of needing help herself. My mother both admired and resented her. Such thoroughgoing and disinterested generosity, which asks for nothing in return, almost certainly guarantees a marginal existence in our society. As much as Rose's children admired her compassion, they also suffered from it. They never felt financially secure, had to work themselves to survive, and had to deal with the guilt they felt for not being as generous as their mother. My mother told me a number of times about how at a very early age she felt the need to create a stable financial base for her sisters and mother. She told me how hard it is to be too generous, warned of the difficulties that can arise if you don't care for yourself first and then be generous with what's left over.

Generosity is a problem we have to face with our children. How strongly do we want our children to feel about people and property? Is there some balance between self-protection and compassion that is worth striking? Are there times when objects and goods are more important than people? Are there times when there seems to be no choice but to turn away from people in need?

Many adults feel that they can hide problems in their lives from their children. That is only partially true. Children may guess at the specifics of what bothers their parents, and only experience or hear about some of what their parents do away from home. But they sense the emotional strain adults live with, pick up on stories and tales, exasperated comments, confessions of guilt that slip out. They try to piece together a portrait of the quality of relations their parents have within the world, and no amount of isolation or deception will keep children from picking up hints and speculating on the moral lives of their parents.

For that reason parents' actions frequently create moral dilemmas for their children. If parents are selfish, can turn away from poverty, can say "no" to friends in need, and at the same time profess to give their children everything, the children can come to understand that what they receive is taken from what other people are denied.

Children can certainly be selfish and foolishly want everything for themselves. They can also be generous and want to help everyone. The way they come to terms with the opposition between self-protection and generosity often has a great effect on their lives as adults and possibly accounts for many political choices adults make. One of the central determinants in the resolution of that opposition is the value children learn to place on things.

The values of what children own. The notion of ownership is tied up with the notion of value. Adults not only give things to children, they also try to teach children to value things the way adults do. Some dolls are expensive, others are cheap; some clothes are worth more than others; some toys are precious and to be treated with care, others can be roughed up and broken. Often children do not see the world as adults do and value things that adults consider worthless. Conflicts develop over what seem to adults to be unimportant issues, though they may be central to the way children place value in their worlds. For example, an old diaper or beat-up doll or stuffed animal may be a treasure for a child and junk for an adult. Just throw out the wrong toy or doll, and you'll quickly experience what a child values.

I remember once trying to throw out a beaten-up stuffed bear of Josh's. He never played with it or talked about it, so I assumed he wouldn't miss it. However, as soon as he walked into his room, he noticed it was gone. It was almost as if he felt the empty space and experienced direct loss. He turned to me with anger. There was no way he could know that I'd done anything with the bear. I didn't want to get into the issue either, since I realized that there was something disrespectful about what I'd done. The bear had to be retrieved and Josh's values respected.

Conflicts of this sort are probably inevitable. Children are not born with innate sense of what is valued by their parents. This statement is obvious, but not at all trivial. Sometimes it is very hard for adults to realize that value is learned and that learning inevitably involves reaching out, testing for responses, and making mistakes. Children are often thought of as naughty and defiant when actually they are testing to find out what their parents value and what their parents feel about the object they value. It's as difficult for a child to understand why grown-ups value a particular rug or statue as it is for adults to understand the value of an old doll or pacifier or diaper in a child's world.

Part of understanding children consists of putting adult values aside and trying to perceive the world through new eyes. Take the value out of things, eliminate hierarchies and judgments, and you'll get closer to a child's view of reality. Place a group of objects on a table — say a fork, a pen, a pair of scissors, and a pack of matches. Stare at them and try to eliminate from your mind any sense of their functions. See them if you can as things to discover and understand for the first time. It's almost impossible for us adults to do this. We are cultured — that is, we know things through the uses they have and the values our culture gives them. Children learn these uses and after a while figure out what adults value. But they also develop values of their own that relate to their interests and perceptions. I remember once being visited by several former students. While we were reminiscing about the time when they were in my class, they mentioned an incident I had completely forgotten. It seems that one of the students brought a small piece of blanket to school and used to sniff it whenever she became nervous. The other children made fun of her for being so babyish. One day I found the blanket in the wastebasket. Someone had stolen it and thrown it away. I evidently picked it out of the basket and put it in my briefcase. The next day the girl came to school distraught and told me what had happened. When I showed her the scrap in my briefcase she kissed me impulsively in front of the class. The students concluded their story by saying that they learned then how important the blanket was to Shana and they also learned that they could trust me. One of them said that what was best about that class and all of the good classes he's ever been in is that the students' values were respected.

Understanding what someone else values requires respect. Children should be respected as individuals who make choices, who weigh and balance things, and who have a right to choose their own values as long as the values don't involve hurting other people. It's very important for adults to respect their children's values and along with that let children know what they as adults value and why they value it. Values can no more be imposed than respect can be demanded or purchased. The most we can do is tell our children, "I value this and hope you will too." They will decide for themselves whether our values have meaning in their lives. In practical terms, this means, "Be careful with what you throw out." That nondescript rock might be a dinosaur in disguise. If you have any doubts about whether an object is valued, ask your children about how important it is and respect their answers.

Teaching children what they are entitled to, or economics in the nursery. Generally speaking, adults in our society are encouraged to teach their children three basic economic principles: (1) people deserve what they have because they worked for it; (2) you deserve whatever you can get; and (3) intelligence and hard work are usually rewarded, but hustling on the boundaries of legality helps too.

These three principles are not understood in the same way by all people, and the way adults try to get their children to accept these principles is strongly influenced by social and economic class. Children of the rich are generally taught that they deserve what they have, that they can afford to be generous within limits, and that in order to be a respectable member of their family they must learn to care for what they have: that is, make sure the fortune remains stable or grows.

In the middle class these economic principles function often differently. There isn't an assumption of wealth and security so much as an attitude of defending what one has and scratching for a bit more. There is no basic security in middle-class life in the United States, and the anxiety this insecurity involves is frequently conveyed to very young children.

For poor people things are as complex and more painful. Poor people have to prepare their children to survive under conditions of poverty at the same time as trying to prepare them to escape poverty. Sometimes these skills contradict each other — the toughness needed to survive in poverty can often create the barrier to the social and economic mobility that allows one to escape it.

A consequence of these differences is to extend children's notion of fairness beyond the self, the family, and the local community. At some time between the ages of five and ten, children begin to get an idea that their parents and neighbors are not the only people who have major effects upon their lives. The welfare man, the teacher, the looters, the bad element, the boss, the workers all enter children's worlds and have an effect upon how they decide whether or not they are being treated fairly in terms of what everyone else in the society has. Poor children, for example, *learn* that they are poor by discovering that other people don't suffer the same deprivations. As a sense of the whole of the society begins to develop, children place themselves and try to figure out why they were born into the historical situations they live in. There is nothing necessary about being poor or moderately comfortable or very well off in the children's world. The question of fairness is central for all children. I've known poor and rich children raise the question "Why am I here instead of in the opposite situation?" with equal concern and intensity. Children discover politics that way, discover that the world is not uniform, that things don't have to be the way they are. Many adults feel that these discoveries should be glossed over, that children's concerns about why things are the way they are should be explained away without giving serious thought to the questions raised. I can't put those questions aside — when Josh or Erica or Tonia or my pupils ask me why some children are poor or rich, why there is hunger, why grown-ups let hunger happen, I have no easy answers. The children's questions are not abstract. They are the same questions I ask myself and try to find ways to answer through small acts that might help to undo the unfairness we experience every day.

Political action is one way to answer the children's questions. However, that is not significant without personal action that affects the lives of our children as well. Child-rearing is not one thing in our society. What you offer to and expect of your child depends upon your class and race, upon the resources you have and those you feel you need. But it depends upon something else too. Not every rich, middle-class, or poor parent treats his or her child alike; there are differences in the way children are treated that transcend class and race, and often these differences have to do with dreams about how the world should be rather than an acceptance of how it is. Children can be prepared to accept things as they are (which is no guarantee that they will accept them), or they can be welcomed to be part of the struggle to create a new world based on the value of people instead of possessions. Some ways this can be done in everyday life are:

• helping children learn to share work and responsibility with people who care about them. Learning to treat people with respect happens in little ways and has to do with how one treats waiters and waitresses, cab drivers and bus drivers, people who clean up others' homes, who teach, build, perform. Children pick up their parents' attitudes and can easily fall into being snobs if their parents are snobs. It is important to rethink one's attitudes toward people and their work.

Children admire work and devalue certain forms of work only if their parents do. It is contradictory to try to help your children become open and caring and at the same time try to convince them that the only work good enough for them is intellectual. A way to do this is have everyone in the house do many different kinds of work so that children see that it is possible to be a doctor and a chef and a dishwasher all in the same life. Cooperative work is possible in every household. It is the spirit with which it is done that determines whether work becomes odious or part of common effort that simply happens. If adults assign work to children and then sit back and watch, children feel like servants. If everyone works together, the feeling of being bossed around disappears.

• sharing resources. Children can learn that what resources exist within the family are to be shared; that if there is only one loaf of bread, it will be divided among everyone. This idea, which is the opposite of people learning that they must fight to get their share, is nicely embodied in the West African saying: "Every family has many hands and heads but only one stomach."

Children have to learn that there might be hard times, and that hard times are borne best by pulling together rather than panicking. This seems a healthier way to deal with insecurity than trying to hide things from one's children. Sometimes it is hard to resist bitterness when things begin to go bad. It is best to focus one's anger and frustration on the source of the trouble — the boss or corporation or public bureaucracy — rather than to turn it into guilt, take it on oneself, and let it tear the family apart.

• not having too much. It makes sense to give children toys and tools. But there is no need to do it on a competitive basis, to buy with or better than one's neighbors. Of course, there will be pressures from one's children to buy everything on TV, to get everything anyone else has. One simply has to resist, though every once in a while it makes sense to let children buy a toy advertised on TV. Make sure the toy has not been misrepresented — doesn't work, breaks easily. There is no surer way to educate children about how ads are often ripoffs than by letting them be cheated by the media and then talking about it.

• treating your children as if they weren't that special. This is the hardest thing to explain. Parents have a special love for their children and make very sharp distinctions between the way they act toward their children and the way they act toward other people's children. One's own child is not merely special, but superior. That is the dream that many parents harbor and try to make happen. Yet in a loving world we would think of all the children as ours and fight to see that they all developed as fully and richly as possible. A graffito painted on a wall said, "And there shall be no people of privilege but all of our children." The gift we can give to our children beyond our special private love is to show them not how they are better than other children, but how they are just like the other children with whom they must share the world.

From Fairness to Justice

I play package games with my children in toy stores. Most games and toys are packed in boxes that are from a third to three quarters empty in order to make the toys seem grander than they are. One should never buy a toy by looking at the box only — it is necessary to look inside, and quite an adventure to do it with children. Sometimes the contents of the box will be so skimpy that the children will be sure that either something is missing or somebody is being cheated. I remember Tonia once exclaiming in a truly indignant voice, "It isn't fair" — and it isn't.

Only the issue didn't end there, for Tonia also said to me that the clerk was cheating us. The woman overheard Tonia and got upset. She said, "Honey, I'm not cheating you; I only work here and do what they tell me."

Tonia was sad for the clerk and puzzled — how could you be cheated by someone you never see? I tried to explain that the people who made the toy were the ones. Tonia then asked if it were the people who painted it or put it together or put it in boxes. No, it was the owners, the people who hired the workers and made the profit. I groped to explain what profit was, and by that time Tonia was tired of my explanations and angry at the owners, whoever they were. Something in the idea of being cheated by people you never will see or know infuriated her.

This sense of impersonal unfairness, or being tricked by people who make and sell things, goes beyond the early egocentric sense of fairness as being equated with getting one's share or being treated well. It goes beyond the self and refers to how people act, regardless of whether their actions affect you. It is a movement from a personal sense of fairness to a sense of justice — of the way all people ought to be treated and ought to treat each other.

Many children never develop a sense of justice and carry a totally ego-centered sense of fairness into their adult lives. At most they grudgingly acknowledge that it makes sense to treat others fairly if you want to be treated fairly. However, there is no need to treat others fairly if you can get away with cheating them.

I've seen children steal from each other, from stores, from their parents, and the only worry they have is about getting caught. They have been taught to expect many things from the world, have been told by their parents that they are special and that it is only fair that they get the best. Children are encouraged to compete as individuals, driven to excel. They are reinforced in thousands of ways for selfish behavior, for worrying about themselves first and others later. At the same time they can't rest or have any inner peace while driving themselves to get more and more.

It takes inner security, strength, and self-discipline to look at others in terms of their own lives with no concern for what you can get or what others feel about you. Some children seem to be able to forget worries about themselves, to look at the world, and to observe the way people treat each other. They can identify the needs they feel for being loved and secure, for having things, with feelings others have, and take a stand for the other without worrying about themselves.

My children know every teacher at their school and are

angry at the way some of them treat their students. I've overheard other kindergarteners and first-graders talk about mean teachers and have observed several five-year-olds run up and hit a playground supervisor because he was abusing another child. Children sometimes turn on their parents in the same way and hit or curse them because of the way they acted toward another child or adult.

I'm not sure how this sense of feeling that other people ought to be treated fairly develops. Some children never seem to care about others and remain centered about how they are treated. Others believe in fairness for their friends as well as for themselves. Still others generalize fairness to every person and show early compassion. As I mentioned before, I believe it has something to do with inner security, with a sense some children have that they aren't always being judged, that they are loved for themselves simply and unambiguously, no matter what they might do. It has to do with being strong and self-disciplined and therefore not needing to be violent with others. There is a self-respecting attitude and a respectful attitude toward others that make it possible to look outside and to wish everyone were loved and loving.

The Development of a Sense of Justice

A sense of what justice is, of what is fair and unfair for all the people in the world, develops slowly and is exciting to watch. I have seen some of that process with my children, who are struggling to understand why the world is the way it is, and wondering whether it is possible to change. A few years ago a group of people I work with were invited to give a training session for parents and teachers in a farm workers' cooperative nursery school in Los Banos in the San Joaquin

Valley in California. The sessions were held at the school, which was located in a Quonset hut on the county fairgrounds. In order to make my work coherent to my own children and because I thought it might be fun, I took Tonia, Erica, and Josh with me. Of course, the children wanted to know where we were going and why. I tried to explain in the car on the way down through the valley. I pointed out the big farms we were passing and explained that in most large farms the land was owned by some people and worked by others. The owners were usually rich and the workers poor. Tonia wanted to know why the owners didn't give the workers more. The solution seemed simple to her, and I could only reply that the owners didn't want to share what they had with the workers. Then Erica said that the farm workers should get together and make the owners give them more. I then told the children about the United Farmworkers, explained how many of them were Chicano and Filipino, and told something of the struggle to organize unions and improve working conditions. Then I mentioned that some Chicanos were trying a solution other than organizing. They were putting the little money they had together, buying land, and farming it together. The school we were visiting in Los Banos was for the children of members of one such Chicano farm workers' cooperative.

The two days we spent in Los Banos were fine. We slept in the hut on top of bales of hay. Tonia and Erica helped me demonstrate the learning materials I brought with me. They and Josh hooked up with some of the children at the school and picked up a bit of Spanish. We were treated as honored guests, and the children loved being in such a family context with old and young people, with parents, children, and grandparents. We don't have relatives on the West Coast, and an extended family was a new experience for my children.

A few weeks later I was going to the supermarket in Berkeley. Erica suggested we go to Safeway instead of the Coop since one of her close friends got some special candy at Safeway. I told Erica I wouldn't go to Safeway since they did things that helped keep farm workers poor. Then I explained as best I could about union and nonunion grapes, lettuce, and wine. We drove by a Safeway that was being picketed. I pointed out the UFWA flag, and we got out and talked to the pickets. Finally we went to the Coop and looked for lettuce and grapes with the union label.

A few days later Erica started to organize a boycott of Safeway in her nursery school class. She discovered that one of her teachers bought the class snacks at Safeway and told the teacher to buy snacks somewhere else because Safeway hurt the farm workers. The teacher wasn't too happy and probably thought some adult put her up to it. However, Safeway shopping bags disappeared from the class.

Erica wasn't content with that. She started propagandizing her classmates. She explained that Safeway wouldn't pay money to farm workers and kept them poor. She didn't understand any of the intermediate steps that connected the farm workers with retail food outlets. For her the relationship between Safeway and the farm workers was direct despite my attempts to explain the steps that led from field work to food sales. She and a group of friends went to Tonia, who at that time was a first-grader in my class, and asked for help writing signs to put up over the school reading, "Keep Away From Safeway" and "Safeway is Badway — Help the Farmworkers." I kept out of the affair as Tonia joined in on Erica's crusade. Tonia understood more of the relationship between Safeway and the growers, and explained the issues she saw to her friends. The movement picked up momentum for a while. The posters went up — some teachers thought it was cute, others believed no matter what I said that it was all part of my plot to radicalize the school and brainwash the children. But no one raised too strong an objection to the posters, and after a few days the children got bored with making posters.

Trouble, however, came from some of the parents of Tonia and Erica's friends who had been confronted by their children about shopping at Safeway. Some of the parents responded sensibly, asked their children what their argument was, and engaged in serious discussion, and in a few cases joined the boycott. However, some parents got very angry at their children and claimed there were more important things to worry about than farm workers, and also that Safeway had a right to do whatever they wanted. I overheard Erica and Tonia talking with some friends about their parents' responses. The children were distressed. They hadn't changed their minds about Safeway, since their parents had made no effort to persuade them. Rather they were upset about their parents and wouldn't forget the problem Safeway posed — the refusal to take the children's sense of justice seriously began to create cracks in their families.

Many young children first question the authority and virtue of their parents by observing them perform or tolerate injustices. Children want their parents to be good and expect their parents to act to correct obvious wrongs. They watch their parents react to panhandlers, to fights, to pleas for help, to war and the military. It is a difficult business to sort out what is right and wrong, to understand why grown-ups can stand other people being hungry, why some wars are good to fight and some bad, why some people hurt others. It is possible to refer answers to this dilemma simply back to oneself, to whether events affect what you own or believe is due you. Some children are encouraged to do this and come to believe that all morality ultimately has to do with one's self. However, many children don't accept that, try to puzzle out more universal principles of how things should be between people. These compassionate dreams of children don't fit very well with the events in the world — badness and cruelty are problems children have to face. As adults we have to be prepared to talk about what we feel the world should be like and make clear to our children what we do to deal with cruelty. This holds on a personal level — on the level of being cruel to someone else or tolerating cruelty that one encounters every day; it also holds on a larger level with respect to attitudes and actions we take dealing with political and social questions.

When my children questioned me about the farm workers, and their friends questioned their parents, at least two major issues were involved. The children were trying to figure out how they should feel about people exploiting other people. They were also, and as importantly, trying to figure out who their parents were, what kind of people gave birth to them.

For one of the children, Lily, the Safeway boycott game turned into a particularly painful dilemma. Lily is a very sensitive child — quiet, polite, shy-seeming, but really very bold and observant, willing to try anything, accept any challenge. She doesn't scare and doesn't back off from difficult work. But she also never shows off or makes much of a fuss over doing something other children can't do. She is earnest, almost too adult in her way of going about living.

She told her parents that they shouldn't go to Safeway because Safeway was unfair to the farm workers. Her mother told her that she was silly, and her father added that the farm workers were none of their business anyway, that people had to work out their own problems, that school was no place for politics and that children can't understand such complicated issues anyway.

She refused to back down and asked him if Safeway was unfair to the farm workers. That's all she wanted to know, she said. Her father answered in a technically correct way: "Safeway does not have any farm workers in its stores and therefore doesn't do anything directly to farm workers." Finally he told Lily that they shop at Safeway because it is cheap and that it was important to get the best deal for yourself.

The next day Lily came to me and asked about the Farmworkers and told me what her parents had said. She was five at the time and wanted to know if farmers worked at Safeway. She and Erica were arguing over the issue and Erica trapped herself into insisting that there were farm workers at the Berkeley Safeway (an impression also supported by the fact that Erica saw a few members of UFWA on the picket line at Safeway).

I had to find a way to get at the truth without humiliating either child, but also had to face the problem of contradicting Lily's father and making her and Erica parties to our political differences. This happens all the time — children are exposed to a variety of moral and social and political attitudes, and though they may usually begin by taking their parents' ideas for truth, they often change position as they analyze for themselves all the different views they hear.

I had no intention of avoiding Lily's question or of smoothing over my political differences with her father. On the other hand, I wanted to let her figure out who was correct, on the basis of an understanding of what actually happened, and wanted her to know that my feelings about her had nothing to do with the fact that her father and I disagreed on this issue. In fact, I told her, her father and I were friends and agreed on most issues and would talk this issue out in the near future. Then I got back to the question of Safeway's relation to farm workers. I began indirectly and approached the problem in steps and through questions of my own (this is usually a sensible way to deal with a charged problem where information is needed and ideas have to be sorted out). First, I asked the girls what Safeway sells.

Erica answered juice, candy, toothbrushes, and Lily added apples, lettuce, and meat.

I told the girls to think specifically about lettuce and asked them if the lettuce was grown in the Safeway store.

They thought that was a funny and silly idea. Obviously it was grown on a farm.

Then how did Safeway get it?

Bought it.

From whom?

A farm worker who grew the lettuce.

At that point I realized that the girls didn't know what farm workers were — that they thought that farm workers and farmers were the same, and that Erica thought that all the farm workers were like the people we met in Los Banos who were running their own collective farms. It was important to make the distinction between the owner of a farm and the people who worked in the fields, so I asked how much lettuce Safeway sold.

Lily said there was so much lettuce that you probably couldn't count it, that once she saw boxes and boxes of lettuce being taken off a truck and piled up behind Safeway.

Could one farmer grow and pick all that lettuce?

Erica suggested that lots of little farmers could, or if there was a big farm, the farmer could hire people to help him.

I told her that the farms Safeway buys lettuce from are very, very big, and that the people farmers hire to help them are farm workers, adding that the farm workers don't work for Safeway and that they aren't farmers.

At that point Erica seemed a little exasperated — so what's the problem with the farm workers; are the farmers mean or something?

At that point I explained that many farmers were mean in a special way. They cared more about making a lot of money from their crops than about the fact that their workers lived under terrible conditions. Many farmers didn't pay their workers enough money to take care of their families.

At that point I showed the girls some pictures of farm labor camps, which upset and angered them. I could have taken out the pictures before all of our talk, but though that would have upset the girls and put them emotionally on the farm workers' side, they wouldn't have known what they were supporting. The analysis, the dialogue, and the consequent understanding were crucial if their comparison were to turn into commitment and intelligent action.

After looking at those pictures, Erica and Lily blurted out, "Safeway shouldn't buy from those mean farmers," which I then explained was exactly the point of the boycott. If we didn't buy at Safeway, maybe we could convince Safeway not to buy from farmers who treated farm workers badly or persuade the farmers to treat the farm workers decently.

Lily's father wasn't particularly pleased with the effects of our conversation. Though he was impressed with her ability to describe the situation, he felt that she had been propagandized by me and that some struggle between his authority and my authority was at issue. Safeway and the farm workers were secondary in his mind. This is often the case with parents whose children express views that are different from their own. They translate issues of political and social understanding into a struggle for personal power. They talk about bad influences when they should be talking about the issues with their children, answering questions to the degree that their children are interested, and they should trust that if they are sincere and honest, their children will understand why they believe as they do and possibly come to hold similar beliefs.

A few days later Lily's father, Tom, and I talked about Lily and about the farm workers. He told me that upon reflection he was proud to see her thinking for herself and wondered if it made sense to open the issue up again and tell her that he was rethinking his own ideas. I urged him to do that, and explained my reasons for supporting the boycott. He explained his opposition, which was based on a general feeling that unions had abused many of their powers. I agreed that there were instances where union leadership hadn't acted in the interest of its members or of the general public but suggested he look into the particulars of this struggle. It was even possible that some investigation could be done with Lily. Tom agreed to open the issue again, do some investigation, admit to Lily he might have been wrong, and then, after thinking about what he had learned, decide what to do. The most difficult part of the problem, he explained, was admitting to his child that he might have been wrong. He said he hadn't been prepared for that loss of face, that his father never admitted he was wrong under any circumstances, and besides what could Lily think of a father who changed his mind or was wrong. As Tom talked he began to see how his maintaining a particular political stance was bound up with his feelings about the proper authority of a parent. He added that he had never thought of how much he acted like his father and laughed at how as a child he had wished his father wouldn't be so rigid. A few days later he told me that Lily and he were beginning to investigate the farm worker situation and that to his surprise the result of his admission had been for Lily and him to become closer. Not only had he not lost her respect but he felt that in some unarticulated way she respected him more.

The Safeway story didn't end there in our house. Josh, who was four, then also took up the farm workers' cause and went around telling his friends' parents not to go to Mudway (his name for Safeway) because they hurt our friends, the farm workers, and made them poor. Josh's understanding and Erica's and Tonia's are on different levels. For Josh it is a personal and immediate thing — a combination of not liking people who hurt your friends and feeling that it is not fair to make people poor. For Erica it is a bit more complicated. She understands that Farmworkers is trying to get supermarkets to buy products of farms that treat the farm workers well. For Tonia, who reads and, therefore, has access to much more information, it is beginning to be a matter of economic exploitation, racism, complicity between large retail business and large farms, and so on. It would be unreasonable to expect four- and eight-year-olds to understand the same things about the world, but at the base of their different understanding is a common sense of wanting things in the world to be fair for everybody.

Justice and Competition

Deciding on how to feel about the rights of others is a problem for many children. On the one hand, they hear that justice must be upheld, that it is a sacred value, one upon which our nation is founded. On the other hand, they are told to think of themselves and their families first and encouraged to learn how to beat others out. The desire for justice and the need to put justice aside in the service of competition exist side-by-side in many children. The tension this creates can lead to pain and confusion. The winners of games and contests cry, feel empty, feel for the losers, and at the same time look down on the losers and exult. The losers feel inferior and jealous, and admire the winners at the same time that they hate the competition itself. Children feel the same way about grades, about what they own and want to own, about clothes and friends. Everyone wants equality and justice and wants to be a winner too. There is no way — one has to choose between subordinating competition to a sense of justice and vice versa. Something has to be given up.

When I was teaching in Harlem, a number of my students had a hero. He was about twenty, loving, friendly, and generous towards children. He was in an informal way a marvelous teacher and psychologist. He spent hours with young people, playing with them, buying games and athletic equipment, talking to the kids about the world. He was the only one in the neighborhood whom the kids wanted to referee their basketball games. No matter how much they might not like his calls, they knew he was fair and respected his decisions.

He also was what the kids called a booker. There was always a book under his arm and he used to love to sit on the stoop in front of his house and read stories to whoever would listen. It amazed me how carefully chosen and appropriate his stories were. They were short, dramatic, sometimes funny but always with a point that related to his message to the kids, which was play the system, get out of the ghetto and get a profession, and come back home and help the people on the streets. He couldn't live what he preached. He had dropped out of high school though he wanted to be a lawyer, gotten into trouble, done some time, and was a successful numbers runner. Instead of being overwhelmed by the circumstances of his life and abandoning himself to cynicism and despair, he chose to do what he could, to struggle with his own moral ambiguities, to be as just as survival on the streets would allow. The children admired him, and some of them who are now adults have tried to live what he taught.

Many people face the same contradiction he faced — how to survive and be just at the same time. There is no simple answer. We have to struggle with the issue as he did and do as much as we can to build a just society. Our children will watch us and, we hope, join in the struggle too.

6

Joy

IT IS WONDERFUL to have children and watch them grow and learn and teach one through their unique and new perceptions of the world. It is also difficult, since growth means testing the limits of personal strength, exercising will, learning how to come to terms with the world, and understanding how other people think and feel. A strong and healthy child has to be stubborn and defiant occasionally and be mischievous as well as loving, sensitive, and fun. The most sensible way to experience the joy of having children is to give up the idea of a life free of conflict and learn to celebrate the joy as it comes and minimize the grief, disappointment, and trouble. I remember overhearing a conversation between my grandmother and one of her friends. The friend was complaining about her children, going on about how they didn't appreciate what their parents did for them, how they had the wrong friends, didn't do well enough in school, wouldn't eat, or ate too much. My grandmother listened for a while, then ended the conversation by saying, "Expect trouble and then learn to enjoy."

Expecting Trouble

Expecting trouble is not the same thing as being grim or pessimistic. It is a way of acknowledging that conflict and disagreement are inevitable and, in a nurturing context, can lead to growth. It is also a way of putting the problems that arise between parents and children in a balanced perspective so that they don't overwhelm life and push joy out.

There are a number of impediments to joy, ways of creating problems for ourselves and our children that we as parents should be sensitive to and could avoid or minimize. These are:

(1) *Wanting perfection and believing that your child is the most intelligent, or strongest, or most beautiful child on earth.* Imagine what a child who is expected to be perfect has to live with. He or she must conceal mistakes and can never experience the joy of showing off newly acquired strengths. And his or her parents forfeit the joy of surprise, of witnessing unexpected growth. Any accomplishment in such a context is taken for granted and any failing can be cause for major disappointment and serious conflict.

It may even be possible for a child to be "perfect" at home. However, once a child moves out of that fantasy world, he or she has to face the fact that everyone is not as deceived or impressed as his or her parents. It is better not to want a perfect child and to love and support the child you have.

(2) *Worrying too much.* If you expect trouble and know that children are strong enough to survive minor falls, skirmishes, occasional fights with friends, a D or two in school, you won't have to expend energy worrying about all the little problems that can befall your child. Worrying too much

undermines a child's strength and self-discipline. A parent's worry is often taken as a lack of trust. I have a tendency to worry and have seen my children hesitate to climb a tree or stretch out in the water or on a walk if I seem very worried about their hurting themselves. It's been important for me to learn how to worry about important things and trust my children's strength and judgment in most areas of their daily life.

(3) *Wanting your child to stay a cute baby forever.* Many parents are afraid of the growth of independence and mistake their children's efforts to manage their own lives for disobedience and defiance. Terms like "the terrible twos" embody that attitude. A two-year-old's attempts to act grown up, to test the limits of his or her strength, can certainly be trying for parents. But they can also be a source of pleasure if they're perceived as manifestations of the emergence of power and personality.

(4) *Wanting your children to be better than you and constantly pushing activities and manners on them to "better" them.* You may succeed in "bettering" your child but at the cost of respect. Wanting someone to be better than you is a sign of lack of self-respect which children pick up on immediately. This doesn't mean that if you're poor it's damaging to try to give your child skills so he or she won't be poor. It refers instead to the quality of life, to the feeling you have for yourself despite external conditions. A family where mutual respect and self-respect exist has an intrinsic joy that cannot be manufactured or destroyed. It's as if your child could say with joy and pride "I belong here" no matter what the external conditions happen to be. Part of being a parent consists of taking stock of one's own life and offering the best of oneself to children as much as possible.

(5) *Romanticizing the burdens of the parent role.* There

are times when children take over too much of one's life and seem like nothing but trouble. If you feel at all vulnerable, it's easy at those times to feel that children are a joyless burden, an affliction. This is especially true, since most of us don't live in extended families where there are many adults who share responsibility for each child. I've found that every time depression seems to be developing it helps to do something unexpected and fun with my children. We do things like skipping school to go to an amusement park or ball game or movie, drive to the beach, or camp out. All these things break the usual rhythm of life and give us all a chance to forget that we were getting on each other's nerves. They are randomizing opportunities for us to have fun together.

(6) *Not being able to play or playing too hard.* A well-played game, one that takes place in a spirit of fun rather than competition, creates a bond between the players that transcends the game itself. Playing with children, sharing in an activity that has fun as its only goal, generates warmth and love as well as a sense of companionship and affection. When play is turned to competition or when an adult is too serious to play, an impoverishment of the affection children develop toward their parents can develop. One reason why people like each other is that they have fun together. Even if everything goes along smoothly and without conflict, there is something basically missing from a life without joy.

(7) *Feeling guilty for having problems with your child.* We all have problems, and it makes more sense to try to solve or minimize them than to seek solutions or systems that promise carefree child-rearing. Healthy children are active and challenging. Greater problems arise from trying to manipulate children in order to have a stress-free relationship rather than simply expecting trouble and doing your best to handle it rather than to hide it. There is no need to feel

guilty—we all have problems with our children, because though they come from us, they have to create their own identities.

Learning to Enjoy

I've been puzzling over my grandmother's phrase "learn to enjoy." It implies that beyond the spontaneous and natural joy we can have being with our children it is possible to learn how to enjoy being a parent even in the most difficult of times. I'm confident that she meant precisely that. Her life in Europe was terrible and her early days in the United States were difficult. Yet she and my grandfather and their friends knew how to improvise joy in the most unlikely circumstances. They joked and sang to their children, knew how to forget a fight or argument two minutes after it was over, and managed to steal a little time to play, no matter how hard they worked. They learned how to manage sorrow and fatigue so that there was always a little time for joy and celebration. And in the most difficult situations they always saw strengths, not failure. I think that is the key to sustaining joy: perceiving and enjoying strength rather than being overcome by powerlessness and failure. It is the most important thing I learned from my grandparents and the one that has made being a teacher and a parent a joyful and fulfilling part of my life.

I remember my first class in 1962. I had just graduated from Teachers College, Columbia, and had got my first job in February, the middle of the school year. The class had had ten or twelve substitutes since September and had become a dumping ground for students no other teachers wanted. I was overjoyed at having a job, at finally being able to have my own class and to teach. Despite all my enthusiasm, the first few weeks were hell. The students were testing me out, and were sure I'd abandon them as all the other substitutes had. I took to coming earlier every morning and staying after school every afternoon. Some of the most difficult students came to talk to me and hang around the classroom before school. They also stayed after school. Those times, they were a delight to be with, intelligent, curious, full of stories and ideas. However, from 9 to 3 they were impossible, falling off chairs, throwing things around the room, screaming and fighting. The contradiction between their school behavior and the strength they showed before and after school obsessed me. It was the first time I came to see that something was wrong with the school, not the children. I suffered my students' behavior and tried to set up a classroom that was congenial to them. But through that terrible six months, I enjoyed being with them, learned to enjoy their strengths and expect trouble from them at the same time.

Recently I witnessed another example of the importance of perceiving strengths in the most unlikely situations. A friend was preparing her daughter to take an individual I.Q. test in order to get into a special program. One of the parts of the test consisted of repeating a series of numbers. The tester says, for example, 1, 7, 2, 4, 9, 7, 6, and then the person tested is supposed to repeat as many of the digits he or she remembers. Nancy was repeating strings of digits to her daughter Willow, who always got the sequence wrong. For example, Nancy would say, 5, 6, 1, 7, 2, 5, and Willow would say, 1, 2, 5, 5, 6. When I came into the room, there was obviously a lot of tension between them. Nancy kept telling Willow she was wrong and wouldn't get into the program if she didn't concentrate harder on repeating the numbers. After listening a while, I suggested that we copy down Willow's answers and look at what was right about them instead of getting upset about what was obviously wrong. After a few times of comparing Willow's responses to the original sequences it became clear what Willow was doing. On a sequence like 4, 7, 2, 1, 2, 6, 9, her answer was 1, 2, 2, 4, 6, 7, 9. She had got all the numbers in the sequence correct and had reorganized them according to size. She was not merely wrong, but instead was doing more than was expected of her.

I've seen thinking like Willow's many times. Children often create unexpected and ingenious solutions to problems we adults believe have simple and unique solutions. Children also frequently see problems in their own way, and take unexpected twists and turns in their thinking. It is not at all uncommon for adults to misinterpret children's modes of creative thinking as errors or stupidity. To avoid doing this it helps to be curious instead of judgmental, to look for strengths instead of assuming errors. It can be delightful to follow a child's train of thought, to see *how* he or she is thinking, and to try to reconstruct his or her perceptions of a problem.

Looking for strengths is an act of love that can often lead to joy. I have a friend whose son plays the saxophone extremely well and dreams of being a professional musician. The son practices six or seven hours a day and has managed to become a straight D student in school in the process. For several years the two of them battled wildly — the father threatening to end the saxophone lessons if school grades weren't improved, the son threatening to run away to a rock band. Finally in despair my friend told his son that their caring for each other was more important than school grades and even acknowledged that his son had some skill as a musician. At that point the son, who was fourteen, asked for help.

He wanted to learn to play the piano, to read notes, to find out about the history of music. He wanted to build from his strengths, and he welcomed the support of his father with joy that was mutual. His father told me that for the first time in years he could listen to his son's playing and simply enjoy it.

Joy, the pleasure people have in each other's company, is based on the respect people have for each other's strengths, the comfort that comes from being with people who don't judge you, and the possibility that you might care for each other indefinitely. As parents we have too much to lose by not learning how to enjoy being with our children. There are many ways we can do this:

- by doing things and going places with our children;
- by sharing our work and histories with them, telling them stories of our lives and of their grandparents and relatives;
- by introducing them to our own special friends and letting them get to know people we care about;
- by watching them grow strong and loving with their friends and helping them through the inevitable crises of growth;
- by playing together;
- by answering questions and teaching them skills, and through doing that feeling useful ourselves;
- by trying something we've never done before with our children, like building a radio or going ice-skating, and blundering through it together;
- by sharing trouble and experiencing the joy of coming through it;
- by having the children around and not being lonely;
- by savoring the newness they offer; the possibility of renewal, of justice, of a decent life with a minimum of pain;
- by enjoying seeing them happy;

- by watching and nurturing the growth of self-discipline, strength, respect, and a sense of justice and ourselves learning in the process;
- by learning to see the world anew through our children's eyes, to understand their freshness of vision, and through doing that becoming refreshed ourselves;
- and finally, by coming to like each other and realize that lifelong bonds of affection are possible.

Inevitably we will play a modest role in our children's lives; we'll grow apart as they make friends, fall in love, become parents, and make the same or different mistakes with their children. No matter how painful a moment or a month of our lives together might be, it will pass and our children will have more important things to do in their lives than spend so much time with us. We should take what joy we can together, given the brevity of our lives and the amount of grief there is in the world.